# F4

## Corporate and Business Law (ENG)

## Study Manual

ACCA

British Library Cataloguing-in-Publication Data
A catalogue record for this book is available from the British Library

Published by InterActive World Wide Limited
Westgate House, 8-9 Holborn
London EC1N 2LL

**www.iaww.com**
**www.studyinteractive.org**

ISBN-978-1-907217-51-7
First Edition 2010
Printed in Romania

We are grateful to the Association of Chartered Certified Accountants (ACCA), the Chartered Institute of Management Accountants (CIMA) and the Institute of Chartered Accountants of England and Wales (ICAEW) for their permission to reproduce past examination questions.  All the solutions to these questions have been prepared by InteractiveWorld Wide Limited.

London
School of Business
& Finance

shaping success in business and finance

# Foreword

Thank you for choosing to study with the London School of Business and Finance.

A dynamic, quality-oriented and innovative educational institution, the London School of Business and Finance offers specialised programmes, designed with students and employers in mind. We are always at the frontline, driving the latest professional developments and trends.

LSBF attracts the highest-quality candidates from over 140 countries worldwide. We work in partnership with leading accountancy firms, banks and best-practice organisations – enabling thousands of students to realise their full potential in accountancy, finance and the business world.

With an international perspective, LSBF has developed a rich portfolio of professional qualifications and executive education programmes. To complement our face-to-face and cutting-edge online learning products, LSBF is now pleased to offer tailored study materials to support students in their preparation for exams.

The exam-focused content in this manual will provide you with a comprehensive and up-to-date understanding of the ACCA syllabus. We have an award-winning team of tutors, who are highly experienced in helping students through their professional exams and have received consistently excellent feedback.

I hope that you will find this manual helpful and wish you the best of luck in your studies.

**Aaron Etingen**

ACCA, MSI, Founder and CEO

# Contents

*29* *30* *31*

London
School of Business
& Finance

shaping success in business and finance

# F4
## (ENG)

About ACCA
Paper F4
Corporate and
Business Law
(ENG)

# Aim of the Paper

The aim of the paper is to develop knowledge and skills in the understanding of the general legal framework, and of specific legal areas relating to business recognising the need to seek further specialist legal advice where necessary.

# Outline of the Syllabus

### Business Law

1. English Legal System

2. Law of Contract

3. Law of Tort

4. Law of Employment

### Corporate Law

5. Law of Agency

6. Partnership Law

7. Company Law

8. Corporate Governance

9. Fraudulent Behaviour

# Format of the Exam Paper

The syllabus is assessed by a three hour paper-based examination. The examination consists of:

- seven 10-mark questions assessing knowledge of the law; and

- three 10-mark scenario questions assessing application of the law.

# F4
# (ENG)

## Syllabus and
## Study Guide

# Corporate and Business Law (ENG) (F4) June & December 2010

This syllabus and study guide is designed to help with planning study and to provide detailed information on what could be assessed in any examination session.

## THE STRUCTURE OF THE SYLLABUS AND STUDY GUIDE

### Relational diagram of paper with other papers

This diagram shows direct and indirect links between this paper and other papers preceding or following it. Some papers are directly underpinned by other papers such as Advanced Performance Management by Performance Management. These links are shown as solid line arrows. Other papers only have indirect relationships with each other such as links existing between the accounting and auditing papers. The links between these are shown as dotted line arrows. This diagram indicates where you are expected to have underpinning knowledge and where it would be useful to review previous learning before undertaking study.

### Overall aim of the syllabus

This explains briefly the overall objective of the paper and indicates in the broadest sense the capabilities to be developed within the paper.

### Main capabilities

This paper's aim is broken down into several main capabilities which divide the syllabus and study guide into discrete sections.

### Relational diagram of the main capabilities

This diagram illustrates the flows and links between the main capabilities (sections) of the syllabus and should be used as an aid to planning teaching and learning in a structured way.

### Syllabus rationale

This is a narrative explaining how the syllabus is structured and how the main capabilities are linked. The rationale also explains in further detail what the examination intends to assess and why.

### Detailed syllabus

This shows the breakdown of the main capabilities (sections) of the syllabus into subject areas. This is the blueprint for the detailed study guide.

### Approach to examining the syllabus

This section briefly explains the structure of the examination and how it is assessed.

### Study Guide

This is the main document that students, tuition providers and publishers should use as the basis of their studies, instruction and materials. Examinations will be based on the detail of the study guide which comprehensively identifies what could be assessed in any examination session. The study guide is a precise reflection and breakdown of the syllabus. It is divided into sections based on the main capabilities identified in the syllabus. These sections are divided into subject areas which relate to the sub-capabilities included in the detailed syllabus. Subject areas are broken down into sub-headings which describe the detailed outcomes that could be assessed in examinations. These outcomes are described using verbs indicating what exams may require students to demonstrate, and the broad intellectual level at which these may need to be demonstrated (*see intellectual levels below).

### Reading lists

ACCA has two official publishers: BPP Learning Media and Kaplan Publishing. Both these publishers base their study texts on the detailed contents of the study guides as published by ACCA. ACCA takes no editorial responsibility for the detailed content of these study texts although ACCA examiners will annually review their content for general appropriateness and relevance in supporting effective study towards ACCA examinations. In addition ACCA examiners will recommend other

text books where appropriate, which students may read in order to widen their reading beyond the approved study texts. Relevant articles will also be published in *student accountant.*

## INTELLECTUAL LEVELS

The syllabus is designed to progressively broaden and deepen the knowledge, skills and professional values demonstrated by the student on their way through the qualification.

The specific capabilities within the detailed syllabuses and study guides are assessed at one of three intellectual or cognitive levels:

Level 1: Knowledge and comprehension
Level 2: Application and analysis
Level 3: Synthesis and evaluation

Very broadly, these intellectual levels relate to the three cognitive levels at which the Knowledge module, the Skills module and the Professional level are assessed.

Each subject area in the detailed study guide included in this document is given a 1, 2, or 3 superscript, denoting intellectual level, marked at the end of each relevant line. This gives an indication of the intellectual depth at which an area could be assessed within the examination. However, while level 1 broadly equates with the Knowledge module, level 2 equates to the Skills module and level 3 to the Professional level, some lower level skills can continue to be assessed as the student progresses through each module and level. This reflects that at each stage of study there will be a requirement to broaden, as well as deepen capabilities. It is also possible that occasionally some higher level capabilities may be assessed at lower levels.

## LEARNING HOURS

The ACCA qualification does not prescribe or recommend any particular number of learning hours for examinations because study and learning patterns and styles vary greatly between people and organisations. This also recognises the wide diversity of personal, professional and educational circumstances in which ACCA students find themselves.

Each syllabus contains between 23 and 35 main subject area headings depending on the nature of the subject and how these areas have been broken down.

## GUIDE TO EXAM STRUCTURE

The structure of examinations varies within and between modules and levels.

The Fundamentals level examinations contain 100% compulsory questions to encourage candidates to study across the breadth of each syllabus.

The Knowledge module is assessed by equivalent two-hour paper based and computer based examinations.

The Skills module examinations are all paper based three-hour papers. The structure of papers varies from ten questions in the *Corporate and Business Law* (F4) paper to four 25 mark questions in *Financial Management* (F9). Individual questions within all Skills module papers will attract between 10 and 30 marks.

The Professional level papers are all three-hour paper based examinations, all containing two sections. Section A is compulsory, but there will be some choice offered in Section B.

For all three hour examination papers, ACCA has introduced 15 minutes reading and planning time.

This additional time is allowed at the beginning of each three-hour examination to allow candidates to read the questions and to begin planning their answers before they start writing in their answer books. This time should be used to ensure that all the information and exam requirements are properly read and understood.

During reading and planning time candidates may only annotate their question paper. They may not write anything in their answer booklets until told to do so by the invigilator.

The Essentials module papers all have a Section A containing a major case study question with all requirements totalling 50 marks relating to this case. Section B gives students a choice of two from three 25 mark questions.

Section A of each of the Options papers contains 50-70 compulsory marks from two questions, each attracting between 25 and 40 marks. Section B will offer a choice of two from three questions totalling 30-50 marks, with each question attracting between 15 and 25 marks.

The pass mark for all ACCA Qualification examination papers is 50%.

## GUIDE TO EXAMINATION ASSESSMENT

ACCA reserves the right to examine anything contained within the study guide at any examination session. This includes knowledge, techniques, principles, theories, and concepts as specified.

For the financial accounting, audit and assurance, law and tax papers except where indicated otherwise, ACCA will publish *examinable documents* once a year to indicate exactly what regulations and legislation could potentially be assessed within identified examination sessions..

For paper based examinations regulation *issued* or legislation *passed* on or before 30th September annually, will be assessed from June 1st of the following year to May 31st of the year after. . Please refer to the examinable documents for the paper (where relevant) for further information.

Regulation issued or legislation passed in accordance with the above dates may be examinable even if the *effective* date is in the future.

The term issued or passed relates to when regulation or legislation has been formally approved.

The term effective relates to when regulation or legislation must be applied to an entity transactions and business practices.

The study guide offers more detailed guidance on the depth and level at which the examinable documents will be examined. The study guide should therefore be read in conjunction with the examinable documents list.

## NOTE ON CASE LAW

Candidates should support their answers with analysis referring to cases or examples. There is no need to detail the facts of the case. Remember, it is the point of law that the case establishes that is important, although knowing the facts of cases can be helpful as sometimes questions include scenarios based on well-known cases. Further it is not necessary to quote section numbers of Acts.

# Syllabus

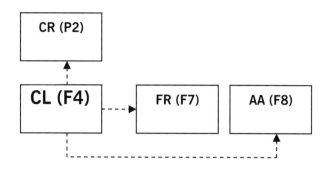

## AIM

To develop knowledge and skills in the understanding of the general legal framework, and of specific legal areas relating to business, recognising the need to seek further specialist legal advice where necessary.

## MAIN CAPABILITIES

On successful completion of this paper candidates should be able to:

**A** Identify the essential elements of the legal system, including the main sources of law

**B** Recognise and apply the appropriate legal rules relating to the law of obligations

**C** Explain and apply the law relating to employment relationships

**D** Distinguish between alternative forms and constitutions of business organisations

**E** Recognise and compare types of capital and the financing of companies

**F** Describe and explain how companies are managed, administered and regulated

**G** Recognise the legal implications relating to companies in difficulty or in crisis

**H** Demonstrate an understanding of governance and ethical issues relating to business.

## RELATIONAL DIAGRAM OF MAIN CAPABILITIES

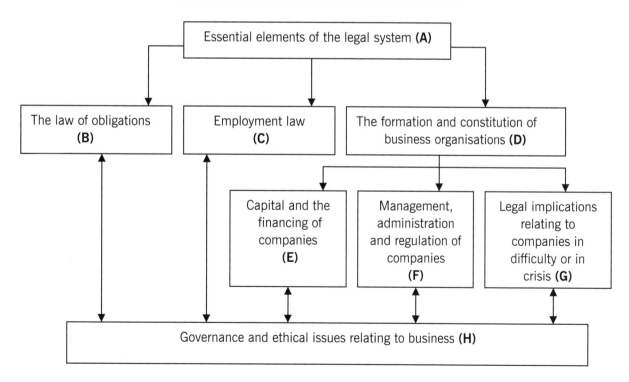

## RATIONALE

*Corporate and Business Law* is divided into eight areas. The syllabus starts with an introduction to the overall English legal system such as the court system and sources of law – including – human rights legislation. It then leads into the area of the law of obligations including contract and tort, which underpin business transactions generally.

The syllabus then covers a range of specific legal areas relating to various aspects of business of most concern to finance professionals. These are the law relating to employment and the law relating to companies. These laws include the formation and constitution of companies, the financing of companies and types of capital, and the day-to-day management, the administration and regulation of companies and legal aspects of companies facing difficulty or in crisis.

The final section links back to all the previous areas. This section deals with corporate governance, ethics and ethical behaviour relating to business including criminal law.

## DETAILED SYLLABUS

### A    Essential elements of the legal system

1.   Court structure

2.   Sources of law

3.   Human rights

### B    The law of obligations

1.   Formation of contract

2.   Content of contracts

3.   Breach of contract and remedies

4.   The law of torts

5.   Professional negligence

### C    Employment law

1.   Contract of employment

2.   Dismissal and redundancy

### D    The formation and constitution of business organisations

1.   Agency law

2.   Partnerships

3.   Corporations and legal personality

4.   Company formations

### E    Capital and the financing of companies

1.   Share capital

2.   Loan capital

3.   Capital maintenance and dividend law

### F    Management, administration and regulation of companies

1.   Company directors

2.   Other company officers

3.   Company meetings and resolutions

### G    Legal implications relating to companies in difficulty or in crisis

1.   Insolvency

### H    Governance and ethical issues relating to business

1.   Corporate governance

2.   Fraudulent behaviour

## APPROACH TO EXAMINING THE SYLLABUS

The syllabus is assessed by a three hour paper-based examination.

The examination consists of seven 10 mark questions assessing knowledge of the law, and three 10 mark application questions.

London
School of Business
& Finance

shaping success in business and finance

# Study Guide

## A ESSENTIAL ELEMENTS OF THE LEGAL SYSTEM

### 1. Court structure

a) Define law and distinguish types of law.[1]

b) Explain the structure and operation of the courts and tribunals systems.[1]

### 2. Sources of law

a) Explain what is meant by case law and precedent within the context of the hierarchy of the courts.[2]

b) Explain legislation and evaluate delegated legislation.[2]

c) Illustrate the rules and presumptions used by the courts in interpreting statutes.[1]

### 3. Human rights

a) Identify the concept of human rights as expressed in the Human Rights Act 1998.[2]

b) Explain the impact of human rights law on statutory interpretation.[2]

c) Explain the impact of human rights law on the common law.[2]

## B THE LAW OF OBLIGATIONS

### 1. Formation of contract

a) Analyse the nature of a simple contract.[2]

b) Explain the meaning of offer and distinguish it from invitations to treat.[2]

c) Explain the meaning and consequence of acceptance.[2]

d) Explain the need for consideration.[2]

e) Analyse the doctrine of privity.[2]

f) Distinguish the presumptions relating to intention to create legal relations.[2]

### 2. Content of contracts

a) Distinguish terms from mere representations.[2]

b) Define the various contractual terms.[1]

c) Explain the effect of exclusion clauses and evaluate their control.[2]

### 3. Breach of contract and remedies

a) Explain the meaning and effect of breach of contract.[2]

b) Explain the rules relating to the award of damages.[2]

c) Analyse the equitable remedies for breach of contract.[2]

### 4. The law of torts

a) Explain the meaning of tort.[2]

b) Identify examples of torts including 'passing off' and negligence.[2]

c) Explain the duty of care and its breach.[2]

d) Explain the meaning of causality and remoteness of damage.[2]

e) Discuss defences to actions in negligence.[2]

### 5. Professional negligence

a) Explain and analyse the duty of care of accountants and auditors.[2]

## C EMPLOYMENT LAW

### 1. Contract of employment

a) Distinguish between employees and the self-employed.[2]

b) Explain the nature of the contract of employment and give examples of the main duties placed on the parties to such a contract.[2]

**2. Dismissal and redundancy**

a) Distinguish between wrongful and unfair dismissal including constructive dismissal.[2]

b) Explain what is meant by redundancy.[2]

c) Discuss the remedies available to those who have been subject to unfair dismissal or redundancy.[2]

**D THE FORMATION AND CONSTITUTION OF BUSINESS ORGANISATIONS**

**1. Agency law**

a) Define the role of the agent and give examples of such relationships paying particular regard to partners and company directors.[2]

b) Explain how the agency relationship is established.[2]

c) Define the authority of the agent.[2]

d) Explain the potential liability of both principal and agent.[2]

**2. Partnerships**

a) Demonstrate a knowledge of the legislation governing the partnership, both unlimited and limited.[1]

b) Discuss how partnerships are established.[2]

c) Explain the authority of partners in relation to partnership activity.[2]

d) Analyse the liability of various partners for partnership debts.[2]

e) Explain the way in which partnerships can be brought to an end.[2]

**3. Corporations and legal personality**

a) Distinguish between sole traders, partnerships and companies.[2]

b) Explain the meaning and effect of limited liability.[2]

c) Analyse different types of companies, especially private and public companies.[2]

d) Illustrate the effect of separate personality.[2]

e) Recognise instances where separate personality will be ignored.[2]

**4. Company formations**

a) Explain the role and duties of company promoters.[2]

b) Describe the procedure for registering companies, both public and private.[2]

c) Describe the statutory books, records and returns that companies must keep or make.[1]

d) Describe the contents of model articles of association.[1]

e) Analyse the effect of a company's constitutional documents.[2]

f) Explain how articles of association can be changed.[2]

g) Explain the controls over the names that companies may or may not use.[2]

**E CAPITAL AND THE FINANCING OF COMPANIES**

**1. Share capital**

a) Examine the different meanings of capital.[2]

b) Illustrate the difference between various classes of shares.[2]

c) Explain the procedure for altering class rights.[2]

**2. Loan capital**

a) Define companies' borrowing powers.[1]

b) Explain the meaning of debenture.[2]

c) Distinguish loan capital from share capital.[2]

d) Explain the concept of a company charge and distinguish between fixed and floating charges.[2]

e) Describe the need and the procedure for registering company charges.[2]

### 3. Capital maintenance and dividend law

a) Explain the doctrine of capital maintenance and capital reduction.[2]

b) Examine the effect of issuing shares at either a discount, or at a premium.[2]

c) Explain the rules governing the distribution of dividends in both private and public companies.[2]

### F MANAGEMENT, ADMINISTRATION AND REGULATION OF COMPANIES

### 1. Company directors

a) Explain the role of directors in the operation of a company.[2]

b) Discuss the ways in which directors are appointed, can lose their office or be subject to a disqualification order.[2]

c) Distinguish between the powers of the board of directors, the managing director and individual directors to bind their company.[2]

d) Explain the duties that directors owe to their companies.[2]

e) Demonstrate an understanding of the way in which statute law has attempted to control directors.[2]

### 2. Other company officers

a) Discuss the appointment procedure relating to, and the duties and powers of, a company secretary.[2]

b) Discuss the appointment procedure relating to, and the duties and powers of company auditors.[2]

### 3. Company meetings and resolutions

a) Distinguish between types of meetings: ordinary general meetings and annual general meetings.[1]

b) Explain the procedure for calling such meetings.[2]

c) Detail the procedure for conducting company meetings.[1]

d) Distinguish between types of resolutions: ordinary, special, and written.[2]

### G LEGAL IMPLICATIONS RELATING TO COMPANIES IN DIFFICULTY OR IN CRISIS

### 1. Insolvency

a) Explain the meaning of and procedure involved in voluntary liquidation.[2]

b) Explain the meaning of and procedure involved in compulsory liquidation.[2]

c) Explain administration as an alternative to winding up.[2]

### H GOVERNANCE AND ETHICAL ISSUES RELATING TO BUSINESS

### 1. Corporate governance

a) Explain the idea of corporate governance.[2]

b) Recognise the extra-legal codes of corporate governance.[2]

c) Identify and explain the legal regulation of corporate governance.[2]

### 2. Fraudulent behaviour

a) Recognise the nature and legal control over insider dealing.[2]

b) Recognise the nature and legal control over money laundering.[2]

c) Discuss potential criminal activity in the operation, management and winding up of companies.[2]

d) Distinguish between fraudulent and wrongful trading.[2]

# F4
# (ENG)

## Examinable
## Documents

# Examinable Documents June 2010 And December 2010

## Paper F4 Corporate And Business Law

Knowledge of new examinable regulations and legislation issued by 30th September will be examinable in examination sessions being held in the following calendar year. Documents may be examinable even if the effective date is in the future. This means that all regulations and legislation issued by 30th September 2009 will be examinable in the June and December 2010 examinations.

The study guide offers more detailed guidance on the depth and level at which the examinable documents will be examined. The study guide should be read in conjunction with the examinable documents list.

### Note on Case Law

Candidates should support their answers with analysis referring to cases or examples. There is no need to detail the facts of the case. Remember, it is the point of law that the case establishes that is important, although knowing the facts of cases can be helpful as sometimes questions include scenarios based on well-known cases.

London
School of Business
& Finance

shaping success in business and finance

# Paper F4 (ENG)

## English Legal System

Knowledge of the Human Rights Act 1998 and the Constitutional Reform Act 2005 is required.

## The Law of Obligations

Knowledge of the Unfair Contract Terms Act 1977, the Unfair Terms in Consumer Contracts Regulations Act 1999, and the Contracts (Rights of Third Parties) Act 1999 is required.

## Employment Law

Knowledge of the Employment Rights Act 1996 and the Employment Tribunals (Constitution and Rules of Procedure) Regulations 2004 is required.

## Partnership Law

Knowledge will be required of the Partnership Act 1890, the Limited Partnerships Act 1907, the Limited Liability Partnerships Act 2000, and the Civil Liability Act 1978.

## Company Law

Knowledge of the Companies Act 2006 is required. Knowledge is also required of the Business Names Act 1985, the Company Directors Disqualification Act 1986, the Insolvency Act 1986, and the Financial Services and Markets Act 2000.

## Governance and Ethical Issues

Knowledge of the Combined Code on Corporate Governance is required.

Knowledge of the Criminal Justice Act 1993 in relation to insider dealing, and the Proceeds of Crime Act 2002, the Prevention of Terrorism Act 2005 and the Money Laundering Regulations 2007 in relation to money laundering, is required.

London
School of Business
& Finance

shaping success in business and finance

# F4
## (ENG)

## Pilot Paper F4
## (ENG)

Please note that the Pilot Paper is the original ACCA document and is for guidance only. It has not been updated for any subsequent changes in laws and regulations, so some technical details may have changed since the original Pilot Paper was issued. For up-to-date exam questions and answers, please see the relevant Revision Kit.

London
School of Business
& Finance

shaping success in business and finance

# Corporate and Business Law (English)

**Time allowed**
Reading and planning:     15 minutes
Writing:                  3 hours

ALL TEN questions are compulsory and MUST be attempted.

**Do NOT open this paper until instructed by the supervisor.**

**During reading and planning time only the question paper may be annotated. You must NOT write in your answer booklet until instructed by the supervisor.**

**This question paper must not be removed from the examination hall.**

**The Association of Chartered Certified Accountants**

Paper F4 (ENG)

ACCA

This is a blank page

ALL TEN questions are compulsory and MUST be attempted

1   Explain the meaning and effect of delegated legislation, and evaluate its advantages and disadvantages, and how it is controlled by both Parliament and the courts.

(10 marks)

2   In relation to the contents of a contract explain the following:

(a)  terms;                                                                                                                            (2 marks)

(b)  conditions;                                                                                                                      (3 marks)

(c)  warranties;                                                                                                                     (3 marks)

(d)  innominate terms.                                                                                                         (2 marks)

(10 marks)

3   In relation to the tort of negligence explain the meaning of 'duty of care'.

(10 marks)

4   State the documents necessary and the procedure to be followed in registering a public limited company and enabling it to start trading.

(10 marks)

5   In relation to company law explain and distinguish between the following:

(a)  annual general meeting;                                                                                           (5 marks)

(b)  extraordinary general meeting;                                                                              (2 marks)

(c)  class meeting.                                                                                                            (3 marks)

(10 marks)

6   (a)  Explain briefly what is meant by 'corporate governance'.                              (4 marks)

(b)  Within the context of corporate governance examine the role of, and relationship between executive directors and non-executive directors.                                                                               (6 marks)

(10 marks)

7   In relation to employment law, explain the operation of the rules relating to redundancy.

(10 marks)

**8**   Al operates a small business manufacturing specialist engine filters. In January he placed an advertisement in a car trade magazine stating that he would supply filters at £60 per filter, but would consider a reduction in the price for substantial orders. He received a letter from Bash Cars plc requesting his terms of supply for 1,000 filters. Al replied, offering to supply the filters at a cost of £50 each. Bash Cars plc responded to Al's letter stating that they accepted his offer but that they would only pay £45 per filter. Al wrote back to Bash Cars plc stating that he would supply the filters but only at the original price of £50. When Al's letter arrived, the purchasing director of Bash Cars plc did not notice the alteration of the price and ordered the 1,000 filters from Al, which he supplied.

**Required:**

**Analyse the situation from the perspective of contract law and in particular advise  Al what price he is entitled to claim from Bash Cars plc.**

**(10 marks)**

**9**   Flop Ltd was in financial difficulties. In January, in order to raise capital it issued 10,000 £1 shares to Gus, but only asked him to pay 75 pence per share at the time of issue. The directors of Flop Ltd intended asking Gus for the other 25 pence per share at a later date. However, in June it realised that it needed even more than the £2,500 it could raise from Gus's existing shareholding. So in order to persuade Gus to provide the needed money Flop Ltd told him that if he bought a further 10,000 shares he would only have to pay a total of 50 pence for each £1 share, and it would write off the money owed on the original share purchase.

Gus agreed to this, but the injection of cash did not save Flop and in December it went into insolvent liquidation, owing a considerable amount of money.

**Required:**

**Explain any potential liability that Gus might have on the shares he holds in Flop Ltd.**

**(10 marks)**

**10**   In January the board of directors of Huge plc decided to make a take over bid for Large plc. After the decision was taken, but before it is announced the following chain of events occurs:

(i)   Slye a director of Huge plc buys shares in Large plc;

(ii)   Slye tells his friend Mate about the likelihood of the take-over and Mate buys shares in Large plc;

(iii)   at a dinner party Slye, without actually telling him about the take-over proposal, advises his brother Tim to buy shares in Large plc and Tim does so.

**Required:**

**Consider the legal position of Slye, Mate and Tim under the law relating to insider dealing.**

**(10 marks)**

**End of Question Paper**

London
School of Business
& Finance

shaping success in business and finance

# English legal system

## Syllabus Content

1.  Court structure

    a)  Define law and distinguish types of law.

    b)  Explain the structure and operation of the courts and tribunals systems.

2.  Sources of law

    a)  Explain what is meant by case law and precedent within the context of the hierarchy of the courts.

    b)  Explain legislation and evaluate delegated legislation.

    c)  Illustrate the rules and presumptions used by the courts in interpreting statutes.

3.  Human rights

    a)  Identify the concept of human rights as expressed in the Human Rights Act 1998.

    b)  Explain the impact of human rights law on statutory interpretation.

    c)  Explain the impact of human rights law on the common law.

## Chapter Content Diagram

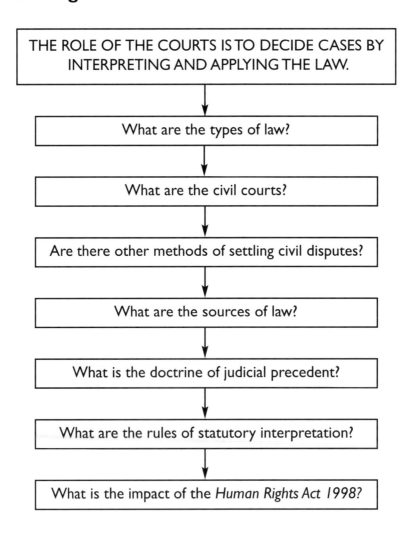

THE ROLE OF THE COURTS IS TO DECIDE CASES BY INTERPRETING AND APPLYING THE LAW.

What are the types of law?

What are the civil courts?

Are there other methods of settling civil disputes?

What are the sources of law?

What is the doctrine of judicial precedent?

What are the rules of statutory interpretation?

What is the impact of the *Human Rights Act 1998*?

# Chapter Contents

# WHAT IS LAW?

Law can be simply defined as a system of rules. These rules create rights and obligations, regulate disputes and control behaviour. This manual deals with English law which applies to England and Wales. Scotland has a different legal system.

Three main sources of English law are:

1. Legislation
2. Case law
3. European Community law

The sources of law will be dealt with in detail later in this chapter.

# DISTINGUISH TYPES OF LAW

### 1. Statute law and common law

Statute law originates from Parliament (Acts of Parliament) whereas common law originates from decisions by judges in previous court cases. The two sources of law co-exist and where the common law adequately deals with an area of law there may be no need for Parliament to create any legislation. Parliament may on occasions pass a codifying statute to bring together all the existing common law into one statute.

Parliament is supreme in its law making powers. The courts cannot question the validity of an Act of Parliament and must apply any new statute which conflicts with the existing common law rules, except if the legislation conflicts with either EC law or the European Convention on Human Rights.

### 2. Common law and Equity

There are two distinct types of case law. These are common law and equity.

Common law and equity were both developed by judges deciding legal principles in court cases, but the difference lies in the way each was developed.

Common law originally developed from deciding cases according to local customs which eventually became common to the whole country. This is how the doctrine of precedent originally began. Common law was extremely restrictive and inflexible. Historically in order to bring an action a writ had to be obtained. If no writ was available for a particular action no claim could be brought.

Equity was initially developed by the Court of Chancery in a response to a need and demand for equitable remedies and to supplement the restrictive common law system. The court based its decisions on what would be a fair and equitable outcome in a case rather than the more rigid decisions and remedies originating from the common law courts. Equity, in developing piecemeal to remedy injustices of the common law, is an incomplete system of law whereas common law is a complete system.

Prior to the Judicature Acts of 1873-1975 equity and common law were two very distinct systems of law. A claimant could either go to the common law courts for common law remedies or the Court of Chancery for equitable remedies. The Judicature Acts brought together the two systems and therefore allowed a claimant to seek both common law and equitable remedies in one court. The civil remedy available at common law is damages. Equity provides other remedies such as rescission, injunction and specific performance.

Common law rights and remedies are available as of right. Whereas equity is based on fairness & justice, and so its rights and remedies are given at the discretion of the court. The court exercises its discretion according to well-known principles (maxims), for example:

- "Delay defeats the Equities", which means that anyone who wishes to bring an equitable action must do so as soon as practicable. If a claimant delays he will lose his right to equitable remedies.

- "He who comes to Equity must come with clean hands". This means that only those who have been fair in their own actions will be able to claim equitable remedies.

Whereas common law is principally concerned with rights and obligations over property, equity is concerned with personal rights and obligations. For example, the common law remedy of damages for breach of contract compensates the innocent party for his financial loss, whereas the equitable remedy of specific performance compels a person to carry out a contractual obligation.

Both common law and equity are subject to the doctrine of judicial precedent.

If there is a conflict, Equity prevails over Common Law.

### 3. Civil Law and Criminal Law

| CIVIL | CRIMINAL |
|-------|----------|
| *Civil law* sets out the rights and duties of persons as between themselves. The person whose rights have been infringed can claim a **remedy** from the wrongdoer. The aim, therefore, of the civil law is to provide a means whereby an injured party can obtain compensation. | *Criminal law* is concerned with conduct that is considered so undesirable that the State **punishes** persons who transgress. The aim, therefore, of the criminal law is to regulate society by the threat of punishment. |
| The **claimant** **sues** the **defendant**. | The **State** **prosecutes** the **accused/defendant**. |
| If the claimant can prove the **wrong** on the **balance of probabilities** his litigation is successful and the defendant is held **liable**. | If the **State** can prove the **offence beyond reasonable doubt** the prosecution is successful and the defendant is found **guilty** of the offence and **convicted**. |
| The civil court will order the defendant to pay **damages** or it might order some other remedy such as **specific performance** or **injunction**. | The criminal court will **sentence** the defendant to a **fine** or it might impose some other punishment such as **imprisonment**. |
| The major civil courts are dealt with in the next section. | The major criminal courts are: |

Examples of civil actions are the law of tort, the law of contract, the law of employment, the law of agency, the law of partnership, and company law although many breaches of company law are covered by the criminal law as well.

1. **The Magistrates Courts**, where magistrates conduct trials of minor crimes and either way offences.
2. **The Crown Courts**, where a judge sitting with a jury conducts trials of serious crimes or either way offences.

# THE CIVIL COURTS

### Overview

**THE MAIN COURTS**
- Supreme Court
- Court of Appeal (Civil Division)
- High Court of Justice
- County Courts

**OTHER COURTS**
- Magistrates Courts
- Employment Appeal Tribunal
- European Court of Justice
- European Court of Human Rights

```
EUROPEAN          EUROPEAN
COURT             COURT
OF                OF
JUSTICE           HUMAN RIGHTS


HOUSE
OF
LORDS


COURT
OF
APPEAL


COUNTY    HIGH COURT        MAGISTRATES    EMPLOYMENT
COURT     OF                COURT          APPEAL
          JUSTICE                          TRIBUNAL


                                           EMPLOYMENT
                                           TRIBUNALS
```

## The Civil Courts in Detail

### County Courts

The county courts hear first instance (ie the first time the claim is heard in a court) civil claims in for example contract, tort, divorce and ancillary relief (division of financial assets) proceedings landlord & tenant, probate, and insolvency. The High court will also deal with these matters. The claimant will usually issue lesser value and less complex cases in the county court rather than the Queen's Bench division of the High court.

Court Composition:

- a single District judge sitting alone deals with small track claims.
- a single Circuit judge sitting alone hears fast track and multi-track claims.

Appeals from the county court can be either to the High Court or the Court of Appeal. Probate and insolvency appeals lie to the Chancery Division of the High Court of Justice and family appeals lie to the Family Division of the High Court of Justice.

## High Court of Justice

The High Court is divided into three divisions: the Queen's Bench Division, the Chancery Division and the Family Division. Each division has a divisional court, which deals with appeals.

- **The Queen's Bench Division**: mainly hears first instance contract and tort multi-track claims.

  **The Queen's Bench Divisional Court** hears judicial review cases. An important function of the court is to supervise the quality of decisions in the lower courts.

- **The Chancery Division**: its first instance civil jurisdiction includes disputes arising from wills and probate matters, company law, partnership law, intellectual property disputes and corporate and personal insolvency disputes.

  **The Chancery Divisional Court** hears appeals from the County Courts on probate and insolvency matters.

  **The Companies Court** is part of the chancery division. Its main role is to deal with the compulsory liquidation of companies and matters arising from the Insolvency Act and the Companies Act (see company law and insolvency chapters).

- **The Family Division**: it has first instance civil jurisdiction in all matrimonial matters.

  **The Family Divisional Court** hears appeals from the Magistrates Court on family matters.

At first instance a single High Court judge sits alone; but as a Divisional (appellate) Court two or sometimes three High Court judges sit.

Appeal from the High Court's first instance jurisdiction lies to the Court of Appeal; although exceptionally a leap-frog appeal may be made direct to the Supreme Court if the appeal is on a point of law of importance on which there is already in existence a binding Court of Appeal precedent. Appeals from the Divisional Courts lie to the Supreme Court.

The **three-track system** is of particular relevance to contract and tort claims in both the County Court and the High Court.

On receipt of a claim, the court in which the claim has been issued will allocate the case to one of three case management tracks. Allocation will be determined by the financial value of the claim, the issues of law and the likely duration of the final hearing.

The County Court will hear all cases allocated to the small claims track, the majority of fast track cases and some multi-track cases. The High Court hears some fast track cases and most multi-track cases.

- The **small claims track** is for simple claims valued at no more than £5,000. The final hearings tend to be less formal and litigants are encouraged to represent themselves, as costs of legal representation are not generally awarded for the successful party. There are limited grounds for appeal against the judge's decision in the case.

- The **fast track** provides a streamlined procedure for moderately-valued claims (£5,000 to £25,000).

- The **multi-track** provides a flexible procedure for high value (over £25,000) and/or complex claims.

## Court of Appeal (Civil Division)

The Civil Division of the Court of Appeal hears appeals from the County Courts and the High Court of Justice.

Normally, three Lord Justices of Appeal will sit to hear a case.

Appeal from a decision of the Court of Appeal lies to the Supreme Court.

### Supreme Court (House of Lords)

The Court hears appeals from the Court of Appeal and the High Court of Justice.

The Court is usually made up of five Lords of Appeal in Ordinary who sit to hear a case.

Prior to October 2009 the Supreme Court was called the Appellate Committee of the House of Lords (for short, the House of Lords).

### Magistrates Courts

The main function of the Magistrates courts are to deal with criminal matters. However, the court can also sit as a 'family proceedings court' and it has a small but important civil first instance jurisdiction dealing with matters under the Children Act 1989, such as council care orders.

It also has jurisdiction to deal with recovery of council tax arrears.

### Employment Appeal Tribunal

The tribunal hears appeals on a point of law from the local Employment Tribunals. The Employment Tribunals deal with actions by employees against employers, for example, claims for unfair dismissal.

The tribunal is composed of one High Court judge plus two or four expert laymen.

The right of Appeal is to the Court of Appeal.

# TRIBUNALS

### Introduction

Tribunals are a different type of body that exist independently of the courts. There are two types of tribunal.

1.  Domestic tribunals. These are so-called because they are set up by a particular body to regulate the conduct of their members.

2.  Administrative tribunals. These are established by an Act of Parliament as a means of settling certain specialised civil disputes as an alternative to the court system. The most important are the Employment Tribunals.

### Employment Tribunals

There are numerous Employment Tribunals around the country.

The Employment Tribunals deal with actions by employees against their employers, for example, claims for unfair dismissal and redundancy.

Cases will be heard by one legally qualified chairman plus two expert laymen drawn from panels representing both sides of the industry, one representing employers and one representing employees.

Any appeal of a decision of the tribunal lies with the Employment Appeal Tribunal.

There are advantages and disadvantages of the employment tribunal system for hearing employment cases over the civil court system:

### Advantages

1.  Accessibility

    Tribunals are designed to be accessible for employees wishing to bring a claim. The employee may seek legal representation if desired, but can usually act in person.

2.  Less intimidating

    Tribunals are designed to be less intimidating that the courtroom for claimants.

3. Speed

Proceedings are generally quicker and therefore the claim can be settled quicker in the tribunal than the court system.

4. Cost

The cost of proceedings in a tribunal is generally less than in the court system.

5. Input of expert laymen leads to practicality of result.

The purpose of the laymen is to provide relevant experience to assist the chairman. This can be contrasted with the situation in court where a court judge may have no practical experience of the case he is hearing.

### Disadvantages

1. Legal Aid not available to claimants.

If the claimant does require legal representation this will have to be self-funded (unless their lawyer takes on the claim on a no win no fee basis), which may cause hardship particularly at a time when the claimant may have lost his job and may discourage potential claimants from bringing a claim.

2. Claim procedures

Despite the intention that proceedings should be less formal the claimant must complete a form to initiate proceedings (form ET1), may have to attend several hearings and may have to produce written evidence, which may prove to be a significant obstacle for a claimant without legal representation.

## SOURCES OF LAW

### Identification

| Legislation |
| :---: |

| Case Law |
| :---: |

| European Community Law |
| :---: |

## I.  Legislation

Legislation is created by Parliament in the form of Acts of Parliament.

Legislation may be used to develop law by:

- Enacting new law, for example the Limited Liability Partnerships Act 2000 created a new form of business entity (see chapter 8);
- Repealing and amending existing legislation;
- Reversing (or overruling) judicial precedent;
- Consolidating existing statute (ie, bringing together a number of different items of legislation on the same topic);
- Codifying existing law of all sources (which means bringing together all sources of law on the same topic in one statute).  For example, the Partnership Act 1890.
- Implementing European Community directives.  For example, much of the Equal Pay Act 1970 was made in response to the Equal Treatment directive.

Sometimes an Act may be used for a number of the purposes given above. For example, the Companies Act 2006.

There are two sub-types of legislation:

| 1. Act of Parliament | 2. Delegated legislation |
| --- | --- |

## 1. Act of Parliament

An Act of Parliament is made by Parliament itself, and not any other institution.

An Act originates as a Bill, which must go through the following stages in both the House of Commons and House of Lords to become an Act of Parliament.

### (i)    First reading

This is purely formal. The title of the Bill and the name of the member introducing it are read out by an official and the Bill is then ordered to be printed.

### (ii)    Second reading

This is a debate on the general principles of the Bill.

### (iii)    Committee stage

At this stage the Bill is examined in detail by a committee.

### (iv)    Report stage

At the report stage the committee which has considered the Bill will report back to the House on its discussion and proposed amendments. The House votes on each clause.

### (v)    Third reading

This constitutes the final debate on the general principles of the Bill, and a vote is taken.

After the Bill has passed through both Houses of Parliament, it receives the Royal Assent. As soon as the Royal Assent is granted the Bill becomes an Act.

Although the Bill becomes an Act (ie law) at the date of Royal Assent, it does not necessarily become operative immediately. Most Acts come into force piecemeal either on dates specified in the Act or by way of a separate Commencement Order.

### Doctrine of Sovereignty of Parliament

Parliament is sovereign, which means that it has supreme law-making authority. In particular:

- In theory Parliament can make any law, and in any way, it sees fit.
- In theory it is only Parliament that can make new law.
- Each Parliament is sovereign.

Due to the legislative sovereignty of Parliament, the courts cannot question the validity of an Act of Parliament and must apply the law contained in it. There are two exceptions:

- The courts must declare void and refuse to apply any Act that contravenes European Community law;

- If an Act contravenes the European Convention on Human Rights (see later), the Human Rights Act 1998 states that the High Court and courts above the High Court in the court hierarchy may make a declaration of incompatibility (though they, and all other courts and tribunals, must still apply the incompatible Act).

## 2. Delegated Legislation

Delegated legislation arises where Parliament delegates its law making powers to others. Powers are given to create delegated legislation to other bodies or individuals in the enabling Act or the parent Act. The parent Act will actually delegate the power to others to create legislation required by the Act and specifically state which matters are delegated.

There are many types of delegated legislation. For example:

1. STATUTORY INSTRUMENTS

   The most common and important form of delegated legislation are Statutory Instruments. These are drafted by government ministers and civil servants. The parent Act of Parliament might only contain the general purpose and aims of the Act. The statutory instrument then deals with the detailed regulations required to make the Legislation workable and provides much greater technical detail.

2. ORDERS IN COUNCIL

   Orders in Council are created where legislation is made through the Privy Council. This avoids the need to go through the full parliamentary process and can therefore be used where there is a need for emergency measures or constitutional matters where a statutory instrument would be inappropriate.

3. BYE LAWS

   Bye laws are laws made by local authorities dealing with local issues.

### Advantages and disadvantages of the use of delegated legislation as compared with statute.

ADVANTAGES:

1. Statutory instruments save Parliamentary time. Parliament can spend time debating the main principles of the Act and the day to day detail can be then dealt with by the relevant government ministry. Parliament would not have sufficient time to deal with all the detailed drafting dealt with by statutory instruments.

2. Legislation may need or benefit from expertise provided from the appropriate government ministry or by professional groups and industry experts. The legislation may be technical in nature and MPs would not have sufficient knowledge to deal with this. In the case of bye laws local knowledge may be needed.

3. Delegated legislation can be very flexible. Changes to statutory instruments can be used to change perhaps one detail in previous legislation without having to introduce a new Act. For example, where only the level of a fine needs to be changed.

4. Delegated legislation can enable legislation to be made when a quick legislative response is required, for example, in an emergency situation.

DISADVANTAGES:

1. The main disadvantage of statutory instruments in particular is that they create a number of different sources of law. It is not possible to just go to one statute to ascertain what the law is in relation to a particular situation or problem and it may be necessary to refer to a statute and then a series of different statutory instruments to piece together all the relevant legislation. This can, therefore, make it difficult to keep up with legislation for the public or anyone using the legislation and can cause confusion.

2. Delegated legislation can be seen as undemocratic as the law is effectively not being made by the MPs who are the elected for this purpose.

3. Parliament may lose control of its law making function.

**Controls on Delegated Legislation**

Delegated legislation is controlled by both Parliament and the courts.

1. PARLIAMENTARY CONTROLS

   Parliament can create control through the parent Act by only delegating very specific details to be dealt with through delegated legislation. If the parent Act states that the person or body to whom powers are delegated can make such regulations as they see fit, inevitably this may lead to less control.

   Within Parliament there is a Joint Select Committee on Statutory Instruments with the function of scrutinising the drafting of statutory instruments, although not their technical content.

   Delegated legislation must go through the correct parliamentary procedures before it becomes law.

   (a) Some statutory instruments must be approved by an affirmative resolution of Parliament.

   (b) The majority of statutory instruments can be challenged within 40 days of being laid before Parliament.

2. CONTROLS BY THE COURTS

   There are the following controls imposed by the courts:

   (a) As with all legislation, the Courts have to interpret legislation using the general rules of interpretation. Delegated legislation which creates absurd results in practice may be reined in by the courts.

   (b) Delegated legislation can be the subject of judicial review in the courts. It can be challenged on the grounds that the delegated person or body exceeded the powers given to them in creating the legislation and thus acted ultra vires.

   (c) Under the provisions of the **Human Rights Act 1998**, the courts can refuse to apply delegated legislation (except Orders-in-Council) to the extent that it contravenes human rights. Courts can strike out such delegated legislation that is found to be contrary to the *Human Rights Act 1998*.

# Statutory Interpretation

When a judge hears a case in court it will be necessary for the judge to consider and apply all the relevant legislation to that particular case.

In applying the statutes to the case in front of the judge he has to ascertain the intention of Parliament when the legislation was drafted. It is not always a straightforward process to interpret legislation, as the meaning of the words contained in the legislation may be unclear or give rise to a number of different possible interpretations. The case in question may not be what Parliament had in mind when drafting the legislation and therefore specific words contained in the statute may be difficult to apply to the particular case.

It is for this reason that judges use a number of rules which assist them in interpreting legislation and mean that the courts will have a consistent approach to this process. The main rules of interpretation are the literal rule, the golden rule and the mischief rule.

# The major rules of interpretation

### 1. The Literal Rule

The principal rationale behind the use of the literal rule is that the words contained in the statute will represent what Parliament has actually said so a judge should look at the words used by Parliament and not what he thinks Parliament might mean. Therefore, the literal rule requires judges to give the words contained in the statute their most obvious, ordinary, dictionary or grammatical meaning, even in cases where this leads to a result that may seem unjust or one which was probably unintended by Parliament.

Example:

An example of the use of the literal rule is the case of **Fisher v Bell** [1961]. In this case the relevant legislation stated that the "offer for sale" of an offensive weapon was prohibited. The court decided that using the ordinary grammatical meaning of offer for sale the defendant had not offered the flick knife for sale that had been part of his window display. His window display was merely an invitation to treat not an offer for sale. The defendant could therefore not be guilty of the offence.

## 2. The Golden Rule

The golden rule will only be used by the courts in the event that the literal rule fails and either provides more than one meaning of a word, leads to inconsistency with the rest of the statute or leads to absurdity. The golden rule is therefore an extension of the literal rule.

Example:

The golden rule was used in the case of **Re Sigsworth** 1935. The court interpreted the word "heir" contained in the Administration of Estates Act 1925 so as not to mean the deceased's son, who had murdered the deceased. In applying the literal rule the word "heir" could have meant the son, but this would have been absurd, as the son would be profiting from his crime. The court held that by application of the golden rule the word heir should mean "rightful heir".

## 3. The Mischief Rule (or Purposive Rule)

In using the mischief rule the courts need to consider what mischief Parliament intended to remedy when creating the legislation. In order to determine this a judge will need to consider the common law rules in existence before the statute came into force and what was the defect or mischief in the common law, which Parliament sought to redress by passing the statute.

Example:

In the case of **Gorris v Scott** [1874] the court considered an Act, which had been created to stop the spread of contagious diseases. The legislation required animals to be kept in pens whilst being transported on a ferry. The claimant's claim to recover damages for loss of his sheep (washed overboard) that were not contained in pens failed, as the purpose of the act was to stop infectious diseases and because the sheep were not lost due to disease no claim could be made under this legislation.

# The secondary rules of interpretation

### Interpreting lists of words

The following rules are used by the courts when interpreting lists of words contained in a statute:

## 1. Euisdem generis rule

The euisdem generis rule applies where a list of specific items contained in legislation ends with general words.

Example:

**Powell v Kempton Park Racecourse** [1889]. s1 Betting Act 1853 prohibited betting in a "house, office, room or other place". The general words at the end of the list should have the same meaning as those specifically listed. In this case the list of items created a class of indoor places so the meaning of the words "any other place" had to be limited to the same class and therefore could not mean an outdoor place.

## 2. Expressio unius est exclusio alterius

This means that if a list contained in a statute expressly includes an item, all other things are expressly excluded. For example, if a statute referred to cows, sheep, pigs and horses only, goats should be excluded from the provisions.

## 3. Noscitur a sociis ('a thing is known by its companions')

This rule means that an item contained in a list is affected by the surrounding words and should be interpreted accordingly.

# Presumptions

Where parts of the statute before the judge are not clear the court may be assisted by certain rebuttable presumptions. The main presumptions are as follows:

1. A presumption against legislation extending beyond the territorial jurisdiction of the UK.
2. A presumption that legislation does not have retrospective effect.
3. A presumption that legislation does not put the UK in breach of its international obligations.
4. A presumption that legislation does not result in the exclusion of the jurisdiction of the court.
5. A presumption that legislation does not bind the Crown.
6. A presumption that statutes do not alter the common law.

### Human Rights

See following section.

## 2. Case law

The second principal source of English law is case law. Case law refers to both common law and equity.

Case law has developed through the previous decisions of judges in court cases. The system that has developed is known as the doctrine of judicial precedent.

# Doctrine of Judicial Precedent

### What is the doctrine?

The doctrine refers to the system, which has been adopted by judges, of following previous precedents.

Some precedents are **binding** whereas others are merely **persuasive**.

There are three factors to consider when determining whether or not a previous decision of a court in a case will be binding.

### 1. The hierarchy of the courts

The first factor to consider is the hierarchy of the courts. The doctrine of stare decisis (to stand by a decision) means that courts are bound by previous decisions of courts which stand equal to or above them in the court system.

In general precedents of the higher courts bind the lower ones but not vice versa.

SUPREME COURT

COURT OF APPEAL

HIGH COURT OF JUSTICE                    COUNTY COURT

The specific rules are as follows:

- Precedents of the Supreme Court bind all the lower courts.
  The Supreme Court is not bound by its own previous precedents.

- Precedents of Court of Appeal bind all the lower courts.
  The Court of Appeal is usually bound by its previous precedents.

- The High Court is not bound by its own previous precedents.
  Note: County Court decisions are not reported.

Further:

- Precedents of the European Court of Human Rights (ECtHR) are not binding but they are highly persuasive.
- Precedents of the European Court of Justice bind all UK courts.
- Precedents of foreign courts are not binding but they may be persuasive.

**2. Ratio decidendi** (binding) **and obiter dicta** (not binding)

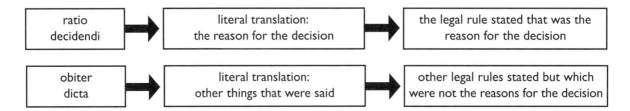

| ratio decidendi | → | literal translation: the reason for the decision | → | the legal rule stated that was the reason for the decision |
| obiter dicta | → | literal translation: other things that were said | → | other legal rules stated but which were not the reasons for the decision |

The second factor is whether the legal principle stated in the previous case by the judge was either the ratio decidendi of the case or was obiter dicta of the judge.

In deciding a case before the court a judge will consider the applicable law. The ratio decidendi of a particular case is the legal rule that led the judge to decide the case in the way he did. This is the element of the decision which will bind future judges and courts.

Obiter dicta are other statements of law cited by a judge which are mentioned as part of the judgement, but do not form the basis on which the decision was reached. For example, in the case of *Hedley Byrne v Heller* (see chapter on Tort) the defendant was not liable due to successful reliance on an exclusion clause, but the judge went on to consider whether a duty of care could ever be relevant in the circumstances, even though this could not apply in this case. Judges may often make general comments regarding the area of law, which are not specific to the case, these are obiter dicta.

Obiter dicta do not form part of the ratio decidendi of the case and therefore do not form a binding precedent to be followed by other courts or judges, but may be persuasive in the future.

**3. The material facts of the cases**

The third factor to consider is the material facts of the case. Where the facts of a previous case are significantly different to the case before the court the judge can distinguish the case from the previous case and therefore will not be obliged to follow the decision in the previous case. For example, the court was able to distinguish the facts of *Balfour v Balfour* in deciding *Merritt v Merritt* and the court was able to distinguish *Stilk v Myrick* in deciding the case of *Hartley v Ponsonby* (see chapter 2).

If the material facts of the previous case are on all fours (the same) with the current case the previous decision of the court will be binding. If the material facts are similar the previous decision will be persuasive.

# Advantages and disadvantages of judicial precedent

### Advantages

There are several main advantages of the doctrine:

1. The way in which cases with identical or similar facts cases are decided in the same way promotes consistency and certainty. This means that if anyone is considering bringing a case to court they should be able to predict the likely outcome, which in some cases may prevent needless litigation and wasted legal costs.

2. The doctrine promotes fairness with all cases which are the same being decided in the same way.

3. The doctrine allows for flexibility. The law can adapt and change with society. Judges are able to develop the law in areas where it is needed depending on the cases before the court and responding to real life situations, which makes the law practical in contrast to statute law which may be very difficult to interpret in real situations.

### Disadvantages

There are several main disadvantages of the doctrine:

1. The vast number of cases that appear before the courts means that the law can become complex and inconsistent. To research some areas of the law may be extremely time consuming due to the number of cases it is necessary to review.

2. Judges themselves may find it hard to follow precedents, as previous court decisions may seem unfair and illogical.

3. The only way to change the law may be by appeal to a higher court which increases legal costs for the litigant. The doctrine can therefore make the law rigid as it is only really the higher courts who are apply to develop the law where they are not bound by previous decisions of the lower courts. This may lead to a lack of development and judges in some cases will follow precedents from very old cases.

4. Judges may not be able to exercise any discretion. The law may finally become reactive rather than proactive.

## 3.    European Community law

The third source of English law is European Community Law.  Since entry to the European Union English law has been subject to European Community law, for example European regulations and some directives, which is superior to English law.  The Treaty of Rome provides that English law is to be brought in line with the treaty.

No further knowledge of European community law is required for the F4 syllabus.

## HUMAN RIGHTS

### Background

Prior to the coming into force of the Human Rights Act 1998 in October 2000, any person who wished to sue the State for breaching his human rights could only bring his action in the European Court of Human Rights (in Strasbourg).  Since the Convention rights were not part of English law, the State could ignore any judgement of the ECtHR if it wanted to.

The Human Rights Act 1998 incorporates many of the Convention rights into English law and the overall effect is that persons can now sue the State in the English courts for breach of the incorporated rights.

Since the Act came into force public bodies must now act in accordance with the convention and the convention rights. The main convention rights are:

- The right to life.
- Prohibition of torture.
- Right to liberty
- No punishment without law
- Right to a fair trial.
- Right to respect for private life.
- Right to freedom of thought, conscience and religion.
- Right to freedom of expression.
- Right to freedom of peaceful assembly.

The Act directly applies in respect of actions of individuals against the state or public bodies (not private disputes between two individuals).  Public bodies that are subject to the Act will include the government, local authorities, courts and tribunals, police and the prison service.

A case can still be taken to the ECtHR, but only after proceedings in the English courts have been exhausted.

# Impacts of the *HRA 1998* on the English Legal System

### Impact on the doctrine of judicial precedent

1. Judges must take into account precedents of the European Court of Human Rights when analysing previous precedents of the UK courts. Precedents of the ECtHR are therefore strongly persuasive.

   Example:

   **R v Secretary of State for the Home Department [2002]** UK legislation allowed the Secretary of State to fix the minimum time in prison for persons convicted of murder. The HL followed the ECtHR's decision in **Stafford v UK [2002]** and held that the UK legislation (allowing the Secretary of State to fix the tariff for convicted murderers) was incompatible with Article 6 of the Convention rights (the right to a fair trial by an impartial and independent tribunal).

   **Note** that the ECtHR does not apply to itself the doctrine of binding precedent: it is free to depart from its previous precedents since the Convention rights are regarded as a 'living instrument'.

   For example in **Stafford v UK [2002]** it did not follow its own previous precedent in **Wynne v UK**.

   **Wynne v UK [1994]** ECtHR UK legislation allowed the Secretary of State to fix the minimum time in prison for persons convicted of murder. The ECtHR held that the UK legislation was not incompatible with Article 6 of the Convention rights (the right to a fair trial by an impartial and independent tribunal).

2. Judges must refuse to follow any pre-2000 UK precedent that is in conflict with the HRA 1998 – this means that a court is not bound to follow such a previous precedent which would otherwise be binding.

   Example:

   **Mendoza v Ghaidan [2003] CA**. The Rent Act 1977 allowed a person to inherit a statutory tenancy from his "wife or husband". The court was asked to decide whether a person could inherit a statutory tenancy from a same-sex partner with whom he was living. The Court of Appeal interpreted the words "wife or husband" in the Act to include people living together "as if they were wife or husband" so as to accord with Art 14 (prohibition of discrimination). In doing so the Court refused to be bound by a previous precedent of the HL (predating the HRA 1998) holding exactly the opposite. (In 2004 the HL upheld this approach of the CA).

### Impact on the interpretation of legislation

1. Judges must take into account precedents of the European Court of Human Rights when interpreting legislation.

   For example in **R v Secretary of State for the Home Department [2002]** the HL followed the ECtHR's decision in **Stafford v UK [2002]**.

2. s3 HRA 1998 provides that Judges must interpret legislation in a way that is compatible with the Convention rights so far as is possible.

   For example **Mendoza v Ghaidan [2003]** (the CA interpreted the words "wife or husband" in the Rent Act 1977 to include people living together "as if they were wife or husband" so as to accord with Art 14 (prohibition of discrimination): and thus allowed a same sex partner to inherit a statutory tenancy under the Act).

3. If this is not possible, then High Court judges and above may make a declaration of incompatibility.

   In **R v Secretary of State for the Home Department [2002]**, for example, the HL issued a declaration of incompatibility.

4. But the courts must still apply incompatible primary legislation (for human rights purposes this means Acts of Parliament plus Orders-in-Council). It is then for Parliament to decide whether or not to alter incompatible legislation.

**Impact on the doctrine of sovereignty and on the process of making legislation**

1. When Parliament is making new legislation, the Minister (or other person responsible for the Bill) must make a written declaration either to the effect that the Bill is thought to be compatible with the HRA 1998 or that it is incompatible but it is wished to proceed with the Bill anyway. In this way the doctrine of sovereignty of Parliament is preserved in that Parliament can still make any law it wishes. However, the declaration will bring the matter to the attention of MPs, political commentators and thus the public.

2. If the courts have declared a piece of primary legislation incompatible, it will then be up to Parliament to decide whether or not to change it. Thus the aspect of the doctrine of sovereignty, that the courts cannot strike down an Act of Parliament and must apply it, is preserved.

3. The HRA 1998 provides for a fast-track procedure where the legislature wishes to remedy incompatible legislation. The procedure empowers Ministers of the Crown to issue statutory instruments altering incompatible primary legislation.

# 2

## Law of contract – Formation

# Syllabus content

FORMATION OF CONTRACT

a) The nature of a simple contract.

b) Explain the meaning of offer and distinguish it from invitations to treat.

c) Explain the meaning and consequence of acceptance.

d) Explain the need for consideration.

e) Distinguish the presumptions relating to intention to create legal relations.

# Chapter contents

NATURE OF A CONTRACT

AGREEMENT – OFFER AND ACCEPTANCE

Offer

Acceptance

CONSIDERATION

The Part Payment Problem – rule in *Pinnel's* case

INTENTION TO CREATE LEGAL RELATIONS

# NATURE OF A CONTRACT

A contract is a legally enforceable agreement between two or more parties.

With a few notable exceptions, for example a contract for the sale of land, there is no legal requirement for a contract to be in writing. Many contracts are made orally. Written contracts provide the advantage that the contract will provide documentary evidence of the agreement entered into by the parties in case of a dispute or if the terms of the contract are breached.

A legally binding contract will only come into existence once **all** three essential elements are present.

### 1. AGREEMENT

There must be an agreement between the parties. This is generally occurs when one party makes an offer which is accepted by another party.

### 2. CONSIDERATION

There must be some sort of value or detriment passing between the parties.

### 3. INTENTION TO CREATE LEGAL RELATIONS.

The parties must intend their agreement to be legal in nature and therefore capable of legal enforcement in the event of breach of contract.

Each element will be considered in detail in the following sections.

# AGREEMENT – OFFER AND ACCEPTANCE

The existence of a contract requires there to be an agreement between the parties.

**THE BASIC RULE IS:**

In order for a binding contract to exist there must be both offer and acceptance.

The party who makes the offer is known as the offeror and the party to whom the offer is made is known as the offeree.

## 1.1 Offer

Definition of an offer: a definite and unequivocal statement of willingness to be bound by contract on specified terms without further negotiations.

An offer does not have to be made to a specific person for it to be valid. An offer can be made to an individual, a group of people or even can be made to the whole world (**Carlill v Carbolic Smoke Ball Company** [1893] see below).

1.2 An offer is not:

**A. An invitation to treat**

An invitation to treat is usually a statement of a party's willingness to receive offers or enter into negotiations and is therefore an invitation to the other party to make an offer. An invitation to treat is not an offer so is not capable of acceptance.

**Gibson v Manchester City Council** [1979] HL. The Council sent a letter to Gibson stating \"We may be prepared to sell the house to you at the purchase price of £2,725\". Held. This was not an offer capable of acceptance by Gibson because the Council did not definitely state that they would sell the house. It was an invitation to treat.

The following are generally considered by the courts to be invitations to treat and **not** offers

(i)    Advertisements.

In the case of **Partridge v Crittenden** [1968] a newspaper advert advertising the sale of 'Bramblefinch cocks and hens for 25 shillings each' was held to be an invitation to treat and not an offer.

Note that it may be unfair to the advertiser if advertisements were regarded as offers. The advertiser may wish to reject responses to the advert either in a situation where too many responses are received (and he therefore would not be able to fulfil all his contractual obligations) or in a situation where he may not wish to sell to certain people for moral or practical reasons.

**Exception:**

Take it or leave it adverts.

In exceptional cases newspaper advertisements can be capable of being an offer but this is only where it is made clear by the wording of the advert that the advertiser does not intend there to be any further negotiations.

For example, **Carlill v Carbolic Smoke Ball Company** [1893]. The defendant company invented a smoke ball which it believed to be a cure for influenza and other similar illnesses. It ran an advertising campaign. The advertisements (on posters) promised to pay £100 to any person who used the smoke ball in accordance with the instructions and subsequently caught flu. Mrs Carlill read the poster, acquired a smoke ball, used it as directed, and caught flu. The defendant refused to pay Mrs Carlill arguing that there was no contract obliging it to do so. The House of Lords found the advert to be an offer, as the wording of the advert made it clear that it was a take it or leave situation where there was no chance of further negotiations on the part of the claimant and therefore could not be an invitation to treat.

(ii)    Shop Displays either:

**Window displays**

Most shop window displays will be an invitation to treat, as it cannot be certain that the shop owner will always be prepared to actually sell the goods to every customer that expresses an interest in buying the goods.

For example, **Fisher v Bell** [1960]. A shopkeeper displayed a flick knife with a price tag in his shop window. The Court held that the display of goods in a window is not an offer to sell to anyone who offered the price on the price tag, but an invitation to others to make offers.

**Goods displayed on shelves**

In the same way the display of goods on shop shelves will also be an invitation to treat. It is the customer who makes the offer to buy at the checkout and the shop can accept the offer by selling the goods to the customer.

For example, **Pharmaceutical Society of GB v Boots Cash Chemists** [1953], where the court held that the display of goods was not an offer but an invitation to treat. The contract was made when the customers offered to pay for the goods at the cash desk. The pharmacist could then accept or reject the offer.

**Pharmaceutical Society of Great Britain v Boots Cash Chemists** [1953] HL

The defendants operated a self-service shop in which the customers selected their purchases from shelves displaying the goods, and paid at a cash desk. The Pharmacy and Poisons Act 1933 requires that the sale of drugs must be supervised by a pharmacist. A pharmacist was present at the cash desk but not at the shelves. The claimants claimed that Boots were infringing the law by offering poisonous drugs for sale to the public. **Held.** The display of goods was not an offer but an invitation to treat. The contract was made when the customers offered to pay for the goods at the cash desk. The pharmacist could then accept or reject the offer

Note that there may always be exceptional circumstances as with advertisements and the **Carlill** case which may mean that a court may decide that shop display could be an offer. This will depend on the facts.

### B. A mere statement of selling price in response to a request for information

In order for there to be an offer the offeror must confirm that he is actually willing to sell to the offeree rather than simply confirm a price at which he may be prepared to sell.

For example, **Harvey v Facey** [1893]. In response to an enquiry from the claimant the defendant stated the lowest price which would be acceptable, but he did not state whether or not he would sell. The court held that there was no contract. The statement of the minimum selling price was not an offer.

### Harvey v Facey [1893]

The following communications were exchanged between the parties. Claimant: "Will you sell us Bumper Hall Pen, telegram lowest price". Defendant: "Lowest price for Bumper Hall Pen £900". Claimant: "We agree to buy Bumper Hall Pen for £900 as asked by you". To this last telegram there was no reply and the claimant claimed there was a contract between himself and the defendant. Held. There was no contract. The second telegram was not an offer but a mere statement of selling price, ie, the lowest price if it were to be sold."

### C. A mere statement of intention

A statement that a party intends to hold an auction to sell various items does not amount to an offer.

For example the case of **Harris v Nickerson [1968]**. The defendant advertised that he would sell certain furniture on a specified date. The claimant arrived at the sale but the goods had been withdrawn. The claimant claimed expenses and damages saying he had accepted by attending the sale. The court held that the advertisement was a mere statement of intention, not an offer. The claim failed.

When a bidder makes a bid at an auction this is an offer which can be accepted by the auctioneer.

1.3 An offer is not effective unless and until it has been communicated to the offeree

The offer must be communicated to the offeree in order to be accepted. Therefore, if a finder of an article returns a lost article to its owner he has no contractual right to any reward offered unless he knew of the reward before he returned the article.

1.4 Termination of an offer

Once an offer has been terminated by the offeror it cannot then be accepted by the offeree.

There are three ways in which an offer can be terminated:

### (1) revocation by the offeror

Revocation can be by way of an express statement made to the offeree or by way of an act or conduct.

Before an offer is accepted by the offeree it can be revoked at any time. The offer can **even** be withdrawn in circumstances where there was an agreement to keep it open for a certain length of time.

For example, in the case of **Routledge v Grant** [1828], Grant offered to buy Routledge's horse and gave him six weeks to decide whether to accept or not. Before the six weeks had elapsed and at a time when Routledge had not accepted, Grant withdrew his offer. The Court held that the defendant could withdraw his offer.

### Option Agreements

If there is an option agreement in place, which is a separate contract between the parties requiring the offeror to keep the offer open for acceptance by the offeree for a certain length of time, if the offer is revoked during the option period there will be a breach of this collateral option agreement. The offeror can then claim damages for loss of opportunity under the option contract.

Revocation is only effective if it is communicated to the offeree.

London
School of Business
& Finance

shaping success in business and finance

In the case of **Byrne v Van Tienhoven** [1880] the offeror attempted to revoke the offer after the offeree had accepted. The Court held that this was ineffective.

Note the postal rule (see below) does not apply to revocation of offers. It is therefore not sufficient to post a letter to effect revocation. The letter must actually be received.

Communication of the fact that the offer has been revoked can be effected by either the offeror or a reliable third party as in the case of **Dickinson v Dodds** [1876]. In this case the Court held that communication of the revocation was effective if effected by a third party. The crucial point is that the offeree was fully aware of the revocation.

## Unilateral Contracts

A unilateral contract exists where one party to the contract accepts the offeror's offer by performing an act. For example if X offers a reward for finding his missing cat, if Y finds and returns the cat he is accepting X's offer.

If a unilateral contract exists, the offer cannot be revoked once the process of acceptance has started. When the act of acceptance has commenced or once the offeree has begun to perform the act which if completed would amount to acceptance the offer cannot be withdrawn at this stage.

For example, **Errington v Errington** [1952]

A man offered to transfer his house to this son and daughter-in-law if they cleared the mortgage debt by paying all instalments when due. The couple began paying the instalments but when the man died his personal representatives attempted to withdraw the offer. The court held that the man's offer could not now be revoked because the couple had, by paying some instalments, commenced the act of acceptance

## (2) Rejection by the offeree

If the offeree rejects the offer this terminates the offeror's offer. The offeree may either reject the offer outright or may seek to change some of the terms, to make the offer more favourable.

## Counter offers

A counter-offer is a response to an offer which introduces new terms to the offer. It is effectively an offer made in response to an offer. If a counter-offer is made this can never be a valid acceptance of the original offer and has the effect of terminating that offer.

In the case of **Hyde v Wrench** [1840] when the counter-offer was rejected by the defendant the court deemed this to be implied rejection of the original offer to sell at the stated price. The original offer was no longer capable of acceptance.

**Hyde v Wrench** [1840]. Wrench offered to sell his farm for £1,000. Hyde offered £950, which Wrench refused. Hyde then purported to accept the offer of £1,000. **Held.** There was no contract because the counter offer was an implied rejection of the original offer to sell at £1,000.

## (3) Lapse

In certain cases offers will come to an end or lapse. This will occur:

- On the death of the offeree.

- On the death of offeror (but not if offeree accepts in ignorance of the death).

- If there has been failure to satisfy a condition subject to which the offer was made. If the original offer was a conditional offer and the condition is not satisfied it will not be possible to accept the offer.

- by the passage of time either:

  - on expiry of a fixed period of time set out in the contract;

  or, if no period of time is specified,

  - on expiry of a reasonable period of time from the date of the offer.

# 2. Acceptance

2.1 Definition of acceptance

The unqualified and unconditional assent to all the terms of the offer.

Acceptance may be effected orally, in writing or by conduct. In *Carlill v Carbolic Smoke Ball* (see above) acceptance was effected by conduct which was Mrs Carlill using the smoke ball in the prescribed manner & catching flu.

2.2 Communication of acceptance

## THE BASIC RULE:

ACCEPTANCE IS NOT EFFECTIVE UNTIL AND UNLESS IT HAS BEEN COMMUNICATED TO THE OFFEROR.

In the case of **Entores v Miles Far Eastern Corporation** [1955], the claimants made an offer by telex to the defendants in Amsterdam. The defendants accepted the offer by telex. The Court held that acceptance is **not** effective until and unless it is communicated. Therefore the contract was made in London where the acceptance was received.

### The postal rule exception

An exception to the communication of acceptance rule is the postal rule exception.

In the cases of **Adams v Lindsell** [1818] and **Household Fire Insurance v Grant** [1879] it was held that there will be valid acceptance of an offer as soon as the letter confirming acceptance is posted.

### Household Fire Insurance v Grant [1879].

Grant applied for shares in a company (ie he made an offer). The company posted an acceptance letter of allotment to Grant but he never received it. The company went into liquidation and Grant was sued for the balance outstanding on his shares. **Held.** Acceptance was complete when the letter of allotment was posted and Grant was therefore liable to pay the outstanding balance.

The contract is formed at the time the letter is posted.

*Provided that* the letter is correctly **addressed and stamped and posted**

*Even though* the letter may never reach the offeror.

For this rule to apply, however, the offeror must specify or imply that acceptance by post is acceptable. The rule can be excluded if the offeror states that he must receive notice of the acceptance.

2.3 Method of communication

The offeror may choose to specify a particular method of acceptance, but this must be very clearly specified in the offer if this is to be binding on the offeree. Any other equally expeditious method of acceptance can generally be used, for example, hand delivering a letter rather than posting it.

Silence cannot constitute acceptance of an offer, which follows the basic rule that acceptance must be communicated to the offeror.

For example, **Felthouse v Bindley** [1862].

The claimant wrote to his nephew offering to buy the nephew's horse and stating "if I hear no more about him I consider it mine for £30 15s". The nephew did not reply. The court held that the nephew's silence did not amount to acceptance.

Note that an offer can only be validly accepted by the offeree if the offeror is actually authorised to accept the offer.

# CONSIDERATION

## 2.1  Basic rule

Each party to the contract must give consideration for the contract to be legally enforceable.

An exception to this rule is agreements made in the form of a deed.

## 2.2  Definitions

There are two **basic definitions of consideration:**

### (i)  Currie v Misa [1875] definition

'some right, interest, profit or benefit accruing to one party, or some forbearance, detriment, loss or responsibility given, suffered or undertaken by the other'.

### (ii)  Dunlop v Selfridge [1915] definition

'one party's act or forbearance (promised or actual) is the price of the other party's act or forbearance (promised or actual)'.

**Further definitions:**

### (i)  Executory consideration

Executory consideration occurs where there is a promise to do something at a point in the future by both parties not at the time that the contract is formed. For example a promise to deliver goods by ship in three week's time and a reciprocal promise to pay for these goods on delivery. Each party is making a promise to do something in the future, not performing an act at the time the contract is made.

### (ii)  Executed consideration

Executory consideration can be contrasted with executed consideration. In the case of executed consideration the contract will be formed at the time that the parties actually perform an act rather than make a promise to perform an act in the future.

For example, in the case of **Carlill v Carbolic Smoke Ball Co** [1893], the contract was formed by the acts of Carlill i.e. the use of the smoke ball in response to the offer of the Defendant.

## 2.3  Rules Relating to Consideration

1. CONSIDERATION MUST NOT BE PAST

Past consideration

Past consideration is no consideration.

An act will be past consideration when it has been wholly performed before a promise has been made by the other party.

**McArdle, Re** [1951].

X made improvements to her mother-in-law's house. The rest of the family then promised to reimburse her. The payment was not made. **Held.** The improvements had been carried out before the promise was made. Therefore the consideration was past and accordingly the promise unenforceable.

**Exceptions:**

There are exceptions to the rule that past consideration is not good consideration, for example, with the provision of services. Where one party has been asked to provide a service there is a presumption that reasonable payment will be made in return. A promise to pay a sum after the service has been performed is simply fixing the correct level of remuneration.

### Re Casey's Patents [1892]

Casey spent two years promoting a patent jointly owned by two persons who requested him so to act. Later, Casey was promised that he would receive a one-third share of the patent in payment for his work. The court held that the promise was binding, as an implication existed when Casey began to work for the owners of the patent that he would ultimately be paid for his services.

## 2. CONSIDERATION MUST BE SUFFICIENT BUT NEED NOT BE ADEQUATE

There is a general rule that consideration must be sufficient but need not be adequate.

*SUFFICIENT* consideration means 2 things:

(i)     The consideration given must be **valuable**. This means that it must have some monetary value to the other party to the contract.

For example, in the case of **Chappell and Co. v Nestle Co**. [1960] a sweet wrapper was found to be sufficient consideration, as it did have a value to the party involved.

By way of contrast in *White v Bluett [1853]*, the alleged consideration was a son's promise to his father that he would cease complaining to him. **Held.** Such a promise could not be measured in terms of money and was therefore not capable of amounting to valuable consideration.

### Consideration *NEED NOT BE ADEQUATE*

Consideration need not be adequate means that a party to an agreement does not have to provide equal consideration to that received in return. If one of the parties reaches a bad deal with the other party this does not invalidate the contract.

### Thomas v Thomas [1842]

The executors of a will agreed to allow the deceased's widow to occupy his house in return for her promise to pay rent of £1 per year. The court held that the rent of £1 amounted to adequate condsideration despite the fact that this was clearly not a market rent for such a property.

(ii)    The consideration given must be **capable in law** of amounting to consideration

The following are not valid legal consideration:

A   Performance of an illegal act.

For example, agreeing to take stolen goods in exchange for payment.

B   Performance of an existing statutory duty.

For example in the case of **Collins v Godefroy** [1831], the claimant was under subpoena to attend court to give evidence was not able to enforce promise a promise from the defendant to pay him for attending, as he was already under a statutory duty to attend.

### Exception

**If the one party actually performs more than an existing duty this can amount to sufficient consideration.**

For example, in the case of **Glasbrook Bros v Glamorgan CC** [1925], Glasbrook Bros asked the Glamorgan police to provide extra police officers to protect its property against striking miners. Glasbrook Bros signed an agreement promising to pay the officers' expenses. Glasbrook Bros refused to pay the bill on the grounds that the police were doing no more than their legal duty and therefore there was no consideration. The court held that Glasbrook Bros were bound by the promise. The police had exceeded their legal duty by providing more officers than they thought necessary and therefore had given consideration.

C   Performance of an existing contractual duty

**A common question is whether a party to a contract can obtain additional payment in excess of that agreed under the terms of the contract, and whether they are able to enforce any promise of additional payment?**

This situation arises if there is already a contract in existence between the parties and one party (the promisor) promises additional payment to the other (the promisee) in excess of the original contractual price for the promisee to fulfil their contractual obligations. **The general rule is that performance of the existing contractual duty is not sufficient consideration for the promise of the additional reward and the promisee will not be able to enforce this promise.**

The leading case in this area is **Stilk v Myrick** [1809] HL.

The terms of a crew's contract of employment obliged them "to exert themselves to the utmost". During the voyage two sailors deserted and the captain promised to divide the wages of those two among the remaining crew if they worked the ship home. The court held that the captain's promise was not enforceable, as the crew had done no more than they were already contractually bound to do and therefore had given no consideration for the promise of additonal payment.

**Exceptions**

1   **If the promisee goes beyond his existing contractual duties this will be sufficient consideration.**

Contrast the case of **Stilk v Myrick** with the case of Hartley v Ponsonby [1857], which was a shipping case with similar facts. Again, during a voyage sailors deserted a ship but there were so many deserters in this instance that the ship was rendered unseaworthy. Additonal payment was offered to those remaining to continue the voyage. The court held that in agreeing to sail an unseaworthy ship the remaining sailors went beyond their existing contractual duty and so had given consideration for the captain's promise. Accordingly, they succeeded in their claim for the extra wages.

2   **Performance of existing contractual duty may be sufficient if this confers some benefit of a practical nature on the promisor**

In the case of **Williams v Roffey** [1990] the defendants offered the claimants additional payment in respect of their existing contractual duties in order to ensure that the contract was performed on time. It was essential that the job was completed on time as the defendants were bound by a time penalty clause in another contract. The court decided that this promise was legally enforceable, as the defendants had received a practical benefit (i.e. they avoided penalty in their other contract) and it had been the defendant who had made the offer voluntarily without any approach by the claimant.

**It is essential to note that if there is any pressure on the part of the promisee to obtain the additional promise this will make the promise unenforceable.**

3   **Performance of an existing contractual duty is sufficient to support a promise from a third party for payment, where the promisor derives a benefit from the performance of the contractual obligation.**

For example, in the case of **Shadwell v Shadwell** [1860]

N was engaged to be married to E, which at the time amounted to a binding contract. U promised N an allowance if he would carry out his contractual obligation and marry E. The court held that N's act of marrying E was sufficient consideration to support the promise from U.

## 2.4 Part Payment and the Rule in *Pinnel's case*

Note that this is the opposite situation to the Stilk v Myrick scenario. Here one of the parties is attempting to avoid his contractual duties and to pay less than he is required to do under the terms of the contract rather than attempting to obtain additional payment.

The question here is if X owes Y a debt of £1,000 and promises to pay £500 in return for a promise from Y to forgo the balance of £500, has X provided sufficient consideration to legally hold Y to this promise?

**As a general rule payment of a smaller sum in settlement of a debt does not discharge a debt of a greater amount.**

Therefore, Y is still able to claim the full amount.

This was the rule established by **Pinnel's case [1602]**. If one party promises to waive his rights to payment in an existing contract there is therefore forbearance or loss on his part. The other party to whom this promise is made must also suffer loss or provide a benefit to the party making the promise in order to provide consideration. If no consideration is provided the promise to waive the existing contractual rights will not be a legally binding contract and will therefore not be capable of enforcement.

A more modern case example of the rule used by the courts is **Foakes v Beer** [1884]. The defendant obtained a judgement for debt against the claimant in the sum of £2,090. The parties agreed that if Dr F paid £500 at once and the balance by instalments Mrs B would not take "any proceedings whatever on the judgement". Dr F paid the £2,090, but Mrs B then claimed interest on the judgement debt. The court held that Dr F had to pay the interest. The agreement between the parties did not help him because it was unsupported by consideration.

FOUR EXCEPTIONS:

**There are four exceptions to the rule in Pinnel's case.**

I   **Where there is accord and satisfaction between the debtor and the creditor, the debt is discharged.**

Accord means that the creditor agrees to discharge the existing contractual obligations. Satisfaction means that consideration has been provided by the debtor to hold the creditor to his promise.

(i) Accord

The agreement must be freely entered into by the promisor for there to be sufficient accord. For example in the case of D & C Builders v Rees the claimant was able to sue for the balance of the amount owing as there was no acccord between the parties.

**D & C Builders v Rees** [1966]

The defendant owed £482 to the claimant (a building company) for work carried out. The defendant, knowing the claimant was in desperate need of money to stave off bankruptcy, offered £300 by cheque in settlement of the debt saying that if the claimant refused it would get nothing. The claimant accepted the £300 reluctantly in settlement but then sued for the balance. The claimant was successful in suing for the balance. Several reasons contributed to the court's decision. (1) In view of the pressure put on the claimant and the claimant's reluctance there was no true accord. (2) Payment by cheque and cash are, in these circumstances, no different. Therefore the payment by cheque did not amount to consideration: it conferred no benefit over and above payment in cash. (3) The equitable doctrine of promissory estoppel (see below) did not apply because the defendant had acted inequitably

London
School of Business
& Finance

shaping success in business and finance

(ii) Satisfaction

For there to be satisfaction, some consideration has to be given.

In Pinnel's case itself it was established that consideration could be given for the promise to accept a smaller sum by either:

- **making part payment if this was at an earlier time; or**

- **by providing different consideration perhaps in the form of a chattel or benefit in kind.**

2.  Where **payment of smaller sum** is by a third party this discharges the debt from all concerned.

    **Hirachand Punamchand v Temple** [1911]

    The creditor accepted a smaller sum from the debtor's father in full settlement. The court held that the creditor could not sue the debtor for the balance as it would be a fraud on the father to allow the creditor to go back on his promise.

3.  Where there is a **composition with creditors**, then no individual creditor can go back on that composition.

4.  Where the **equitable doctrine of promissory estoppel** applies the the debt may be discharged or suspended.

## THE DOCTRINE OF PROMISSORY ESTOPPEL

The doctrine operates to prevent or estop the promisor from reneging on his promise to waive his rights to enforce a debt despite the fact that the promisee has not provided consideration to support the promise. The doctrine originates from the case of Central London Property Trust Ltd v High Trees House Ltd [1947].

**Central London Property Trust Ltd v High Trees House Ltd** [1947]

The claimants let a block of flats to the defendants in 1937 at a rent of £2,500 per annum. The agreement was on the basis that the defendants would sublet individual flats. Owing to the outbreak of war and subsequent bombings of London it was difficult to sublet the flats and in 1940 the claimants agreed to halve the rent. After the end of the war the claimants sued the defendants for the full rent throughout the period of the war. The court held that the claimants were able to reinstate the full rent from the end of the war. However, they could not claim the arrears relating to the war years because the defendant had in good faith relied on the promise and assumed it would be kept, reducing rents to sub tenants accordingly.

The doctrine will only apply in cases where:

1.  The promisor gives a clear statement that he does not wish to enforce his rights and the doctrine only applies where the promise of waiver is entirely voluntary. In the case of **D & C Builders v Rees** [1966] the doctrine could not be used as a defence to the claimant enforcing the whole of a debt despite a promise to accept a lesser sum as the defendant had exploited the claimant's financial difficulties to obtain the promise.

2.  The promisee must have either altered his position or suffered a detriment as a result of the promise. For example in the High Trees case the defendants altered their position once the claimant reduced the rent in the head lease by agreeing to sublet the flats to the subtenants at reduced rents.

3.  It would be inequitable for the promisor to subsequently renege on his promise.

4.  It is used as a defence and not a cause of action (i.e. can only be used as a 'shield and not a sword'). High Trees House could not have brought a claim against Central London Property Trust using the doctrine. The doctrine could only be used in a defence to the claimants claim for the rent arrears.

Note that the doctrine may only suspend the creditor's rights.

# INTENTION TO CREATE LEGAL RELATIONS

## 3.1  Basic rule

The intention of the parties to actually form a legally binding relationship is an essential element of a valid contract.

## 3.2  Domestic and social agreements

THE PRESUMPTION :

**In the context of domestic and social agreements there is a general presumption that there is no intention to create a legal relationship between the parties.**

For example, **Balfour v Balfour** [1919]

The husband agreed to pay his wife £30 per month to support herself and the family while he was away on business. He made some payments but then stopped. His wife sued him for breach of contract. Her action was unsuccessful, as the court found that there was no contract between them. As the parties were acting in a purely domestic context there was presumably no intention to create legal relations and there was no evidence to the contrary to rebut this presumption.

REBUTTING THE PRESUMPTION

The presumption can be rebutted, which means that the presumption can be set aside, where there is sufficient evidence to support or the circumstances show that this was not what was intended by the parties.

Contrast Balfour v Balfour with the case of **Merritt v Merritt** [1970].

A husband who had separated from his wife agreed to transfer the matrimonial home to her if she paid the mortgage. The wife paid off the mortgage but the husband refused to transfer title to the house to her, alleging that his promise was a domestic arrangement not giving rise to legal relations. The agreement was found to be legally enforceable, as there was sufficient evidence to rebut the presumption. The evidence was:

*   the very fact that they were separating; and

*   the agreement was signed.

The case of **Simpkins v Pays** [1955] is an example of a social agreement.

Every week a grandmother, her granddaughter, and their lodger specifically sat down together to enter a competition. On the entry form, which was in the grandmother's name, each made one entry. All three shared the entry fees & postage. They agreed to share any prize. One week the granddaughter's entry won. The lodger asserted that the agreement to share any prize was a contract. The court ruled that there was a contract because the presumption relevant to domestic or social agreements was rebutted by evidence to the contrary. The surrounding facts showed that the parties were engaged in a serious and organised joint enterprise.

## 3.3  Business or Commercial Agreements

THE PRESUMPTION

In the context of business arrangements there is a very strong presumption that there is an intention to create a legal relationship.

REBUTTING THE PRESUMPTION

This presumption can again be rebutted by contrary evidence, but **very clear** evidence will be required.

As in the case of **Rose & Frank v Compton Bros** [1925] the agreement between the parties in very clear terms stated that it was not entered into as a legal agreement. The court held that the very clear wording in the agreement provided evidence to negate any legal relationship between the parties.

The presumption can also be rebutted notably in cases where an agreement is stated to be "binding in honour only" or where similar words are used which negates the intention to create legal relations (**Jones v Vernon's Pools** [1938]).

# Beware

Beware of agreements between relatives or friends that are really business agreements. For example, if a father asks his asks his son who is a qualified accountant to complete work for them in a professional capacity. Despite their relationship this is likely to be considered to be a business arrangement and likely therefore to be a legally enforceable contract.

# 3

# Law of contract – Terms

# Syllabus content

CONTENT OF CONTRACTS

a)   Distinguish terms from mere representations.

b)   Define the various contractual terms.

c)   Explain the effect of exclusion clauses and evaluate their control.

# Chapter contents

SOURCES OF THE TERMS

CONDITIONS, WARRANTIES AND INNOMINATE TERMS

EXEMPTION CLAUSES

Introduction

The two common law rules.

*Unfair Contract Terms Act 1977.*

*The Unfair Terms In Consumer Contracts Regulations 1999.*

# SOURCES OF THE CONTRACT TERMS

The terms of the contract detail the obligations of the parties to the contract. The terms will be a combination of what has been expressly agreed by the parties and terms that are implied into the contract by law.

## 1. EXPRESS TERMS

Express terms are the terms of the contract that have been specifically agreed between the parties and the parties intend these to be included in the contract. A contract can be in a written form or can be oral. In the case of an oral contract the express terms would be the matters agreed between the parties. In the case of a written contract the express terms should be included within the contract itself.

### Terms and Representations

Before the terms of the contract are agreed many matters may be discussed between the parties. It is essential to distinguish contract terms from representations made before the contract is formed.

Representations are inducements to enter into the contract, but do not form part of the actual contract itself. In a written contract it is likely that the terms will be included in the contract itself and any additional matters which have been discussed between the parties are likely to be representations.

The injured party may be able to rescind the contract and can sue for misrepresentation if they have been mislead before entering into the contract by a representation, but there can be no claim for breach of contract unless a term has been breached.

## 2. IMPLIED TERMS

### There are two categories of implied terms

(i)   Terms implied by statute.

Terms implied by statute generally aim to protect the weaker party to the contract.

Examples:

### Contracts for the supply of goods and services

A contract for the supply of goods will be governed by the Sale of Goods Act 1979. This Act is the source of numerous implied terms, for example that the goods supplied are fit for purpose. The parties themselves may not have contemplated any of the matters contained within the Act, but the purchaser nonetheless will benefit from the implied terms.

### Employment contracts

All employment contracts will also have statutory implied terms, for example, those implied by the Equal Pay Act 1970 and a limit on the working hours of employees incorporated by virtue of the Working Time Regulations 1998. Employees' remuneration will be subject to the provisions of the National Minimum Wage Act 1998.

Note that it may be possible for the parties to exclude some of the statutory implied terms by express agreement between the parties, but many of the terms cannot be excluded.

(ii)   Terms implied by the courts

There are various categories of terms implied by the courts.

(i)   Terms implied to give business efficacy

Terms implied by common law are generally incorporated to give business efficacy to the agreement between the parties and to fill in any gaps which have not been covered by the express terms.

The court in such cases decides that it must have been the intention of the parties to include them. The implied terms actually make the agreement workable in practice.

- A term may be implied by the courts as a matter of law. This means terms that are necessitated by the legal nature of the contract.

  For example, the contract of employment necessitates implying that the employee must carry out lawful and reasonable orders of the employer.

- A term may be implied as a matter of fact. This means such terms that are so obvious that the parties did not bother to express them.

  *The Moorcock [1889].*

  W, a wharf owner, contracted to allow a ship owner to unload his ship at the wharf. The ship was damaged when, at low tide, it became grounded on some rocks at the bottom of the river bed. The court implied a term into the contract that the river bottom must be reasonably safe.

  The courts decide what is 'obvious' objectively using the officious bystander test. This means that the courts imagine someone listening to the parties as they are negotiating and ask that bystander – "is the term obvious?"

(ii)   Terms implied by custom or general usage.

Terms can be implied in contracts due to local custom or general use within a particular trade or industry. These customs are likely to be the foundation of the contracts and are therefore implied.

In the case of Hutton v Warren [1836] the court decided that there were implied terms due to local farming customs that a tenant should farm in a particular way and would be entitled to a fair allowance for seeds and labour on quitting the tenancy.

(iii)   Terms implied by previous dealings between the parties

The courts may recognise the existence of a term within the contract as a result of previous regular dealings between the parties.

For example in the case of **Spurling v Bradshaw** [1956] the court decided that an exclusion clause was included in a contract between the parties, despite the fact that the term was not expressly included in contract terms at the time the contract was made, as a result of a regular previous course of dealings between the parties, where such a clause had always been included.

# CONDITIONS, WARRANTIES AND INNOMINATE TERMS

The contract terms can either be classed as conditions, or as warranties, or as innominate terms

## Conditions

**Conditions are the essential terms of the contract. They can be described as going to the root of the contract.**

If a condition is breached the innocent party is deprived of substantially the whole benefit of the contract.

### Remedies for breach of condition

The remedies available to the injured party are discharge of the contract or damages or both.

An example of a breach of condition is provided by the case of **Poussard v Spiers and Pond** (1876) when an opera singer failed to appear on the opening night performance this was held to be a breach of a condition, as presence at the performances was an essential element of the contract. The opera company could therefore discharge the contract and claim damages.

## Warranties

**A warranty is a contract term of lesser importance than a condition.**

It is term which is incidental or collateral to the main purpose of the contract, such that its breach would not destroy the whole purpose of the contract.

### Remedies for breach of warranty

If a warranty is breached the injured party can only claim for damages and cannot bring the contract to an end.

For example, **Bettini v Gye** (1876). In this case an opera singer failed to attend the rehearsals. It was held that the attendance of rehearsals was a warranty, as rehearsals were of secondary importance to the main performances. The only remedy available here was damages, the singer could not be sacked.

## Innominate Terms

An innominate term is a term which cannot be either classed as a warranty or as a condition.

### Remedies for breach of an innominate term

The remedy available to the injured party if an in nominate term is breached will depend upon the seriousness of the breach and the actual effect of the breach.

If the effect of the breach deprives the injured party of the benefit of the contract, as with a breach of condition the injured party will be able to sue for damages and may also discharge the contract. If the breach is incidental to the main purpose of the contract the right to claim damages only will be available.

For example in the case of the **Hansa Nord** [1976] where the ship's cargo which should have arrived in good condition was partly damaged. The cargo could still be used for its intended purpose and so the damage caused could not constitute a serious breach of contract. The only remedy available was damages.

# EXCLUSION/EXEMPTION CLAUSES

## DEFINITION

An exclusion clause is a contract term which seeks to exclude or limit a party's liability for breach of contract.

## VALIDITY OF EXCLUSION CLAUSES

Despite one of the parties to the contract seeking to include an exclusion clause in the contract between the parties, the exclusion clause may not be valid. There are common law rules and statutory provisions which govern the validity of exclusion clauses.

# The Two Common Law Rules

## 1. INCORPORATION INTO THE CONTRACT

In order to be valid the clause must actually form part of the contract terms. This means that the party seeking to rely on the clause must have taken steps to ensure that the clause has been incorporated into the contract.

The courts have recognised three methods of incorporating the exclusion clause.

## BY SIGNATURE

If the document containing the exclusion clause has been signed this is sufficient to incorporate the clause into the contract between the parties.

### L'Estrange v Graucob [1934]

The claimant signed an agreement containing an exclusion clause when she purchased a vending machine from the defendant. The court held that in signing the document containing the exclusion clause the clause was binding upon her even though she was unaware of the exclusion clause not having read the agreement. She was deemed to have agreed to the clause.

Signature is effective **unless** the party seeking to rely on the clause has mislead the other party as to the nature of the clause.

### Curtis v Chemical Cleaning Company [1952]

The claimant took her wedding dress to be cleaned and was asked to sign a document containing an exclusion clause. Mrs Curtis did not read it but asked the shop-assistant to explain the document and was told that it said that the company accepted no liability for damage done to the beads and sequins on the dress. On receipt of the shop-assistant's explanation Mrs Curtis signed the document. The dress was badly stained while being cleaned and the Mrs Curtis sued for damages. The court held that the extent of the clause in the document had been misrepresented to Mrs Curtis and therefore it was not incorporated into the contract.

## BY NOTICE

The exclusion clause can be contained in a notice on documents or displayed at a place where contracts are formed.

If a notice contains the exclusion clause the party who wishes to rely on the clause must take reasonable steps to bring it to the attention of the other party. The nature of reasonable steps depends on the circumstances.

### Thompson v LMS [1930]

The claimant was illiterate and bought an excursion ticket on which was printed "excursion: for conditions see back". On the back it was stated that the ticket was issued subject to conditions contained in the company's timetables. These conditions excluded liability for injury. The court held that in the circumstances reasonable steps had been taken to bring the exclusion clause to Mrs Thompson's attention before the contract was made and was therefore incorporated into the contract.

It is essential that the notice is brought to the attention of the other party **before or at the time that the contract is made**. If it is brought to his attention after the contract is made the clause will not be incorporated into the contract.

An example of the notice being shown to the contractee at the incorrect time was the case of **Olley v Marlborough Court [1949]**. The contract had been made at the hotel reception desk when the claimants paid for their hotel room. The exclusion clause notice was in their hotel room and was therefore only brought to the attention of the claimants at a later time. The court decided that the clause had not been incorporated into the contract and therefore the defendants could not rely on it.

Note that exclusion clauses appearing on receipts or letters of confirmation after an order has been made are not being incorporated at the time the contract is made.

PREVIOUS DEALINGS

Where an exclusion clause is always included in the contract between the parties if this is omitted on one occasion or is brought to the attention of the party against which it is enforced after the contract is formed the party seeking to rely on the clause may be able to establish incorporation by way of a consistent course of dealings between the parties.

### Spurling v Bradshaw [1956]

Each time a contract was made between the parties the defendants always sent a document to the claimants which contained an exclusion clause. There were numerous dealings between the parties over a course of at least 10 years, which the court decided constituted a consistent course of dealings. The court held that even though the clause was only brought to the attention of the defendants after the contract was made this was actually incorporated through the previous consistent course of dealings between the parties.

According to case law, numerous dealings over a period of ten years would amount to a consistent course of dealings (Spurling v Bradshaw) but in the case of **Hollier v Rambler Motors** [1972], the court held that three or four deals between the parties over a period of 5 years could not be seen as a consistent course of dealings. The defendant could not rely on the exclusion clause which was not incorporated into the contract between the parties by signature on this occasion, as it had been in the past.

2.  THE WORDING OF THE EXCLUSION CLAUSE MUST COVER THE LOSS WHICH HAS OCCURRED

The second common law rule relating to the validity of exclusion clauses is that in order to successfully rely on an exclusion clause the clause must definitely exclude liability for the type of loss that has occurred. If there is any question or ambiguity under the **contra proferentem rule**, the courts interpret the wording of the clause narrowly against the interests of the party seeking to rely on the clause.

The leading case in this area is **Photo Production Ltd v Securicor Transport Ltd** [1978]. The claimant entered into a contract with Securicor by which Securicor agreed to provide security services at the claimant's factory, including night patrols. While carrying out a night patrol at the factory an employee of Securicor deliberately lit a fire and as a result the factory and stock inside. The claimant sued Securicor for breach of contract. In its defence Securicor pleaded an exemption clause which stated:" ... under no circumstances shall Securicor be responsible for any injurious act or default by any employee of Securicor ...". The court decided that the exemption clause was clear and unambiguous and protected Securicor from liability.

London
School of Business
& Finance

shaping success in business and finance

## Statutory Provisions

# Unfair Contract Terms Act 1977

The purpose of Unfair Contract Terms Act is to protect consumers from unduly onerous exclusion clauses used in commercial and business contracts. Under the Act clauses will be either deemed void or subject to a reasonableness test.

SUMMARY OF UNFAIR CONTRACT TERMS ACT

Clauses exempting liability for **DEATH** or **PERSONAL INJURY** caused by negligence are **VOID**.

Clauses exempting liability for **OTHER LOSS** caused by negligence are **VOID UNLESS found to be REASONABLE**.

Clauses which exclude or limit liability in all sale contracts regarding the seller's **TITLE TO THE GOODS** and **RIGHT TO SELL THE GOODS** are **VOID**. Clauses in contracts with consumers which exclude or limit liability for **CONFORMITY OF THE GOODS TO THEIR DESCRIPTION OR QUALITY OR FITNESS FOR PURPOSE** are **VOID**.

Any other clauses exempting liability for breach of contract when **DEALING WITH A CONSUMER** or exemption clauses contained within a contract based on **STANDARD TERMS AND CONDITIONS** are **VOID UNLESS found to be REASONABLE**.

THE REASONABLENESS TEST

In trying to establish whether or not the clause is reasonable the court will have regard to the following factors:

(a)    The burden of proving that the clause is reasonable is on the party seeking to rely on the clause.

(b)    The court must consider all the surrounding circumstances in order to establish whether or not the clause is reasonable.

For example in the case of **RW Green v Cade Bros Farms** [1978] an exclusion clause excluded liability for any complaints received after 3 days of delivery of seed potatoes to their destination. The potato seed in question was actually infected by a virus which could not have been identified by inspection on delivery so in these particular circumstances the court found the clause to be unreasonable.

(c)    The Schedule 2 guidelines.

The second schedule to the Act sets out particular guidelines to which the court should have regard to establish reasonableness. The guidelines include:

- the relative bargaining strength of the parties. If the party seeking to rely on the clause is in a much stronger position than the buyer it is unlikely to be reasonable, whereas if the parties bargaining positions are equal or similar the clause is more likely to be found to be reasonable.

- If inducements have been offered to the buyer to enter into the clause the clause is more likely to be found to be reasonable.

- whether the buyer knew or ought to have known of the *existence* and the *extent* of the term. The customer may be more likely to be aware of the term if there has been a number of previous transactions between the parties or if such clauses are customary in a particular trade or industry. If the buyer is aware of the term it is more likely to be found to be reasonable.

- ability to insure. If insurance is readily available to insure against the risks excluded by the clause the clause may be deemed to be reasonable.

In the case of **St Albans City Council v International Computers Ltd** [1995] the court considered the schedule 2 guidelines.

The defendant company supplied a database for the community charge register to a local authority. Owing to an error in the computer software the community charge rate was set too low, causing the authority a shortfall of £1.3 million. The defendant company sought to rely on a clause limiting their liability to £100,000. The court held that the exclusion clause did not satisfy the test of reasonableness under the *Unfair Contract Terms Act 1977* because:

(1) The parties were of unequal bargaining power. ICL was a major international company whereas the claimant was a local authority and was not run by 'businessmen'. There was pressure on the claimant to conclude the contract quickly.

(2) It was normal for a company such as ICL to insure against such losses and in view of its cover worldwide of £50m the limitation of liability to £100,000 for this contract was unjustifiably small. St Albans, as is the case with most local authorities, was not insured for this kind of loss and there was no 'ready-made' policy available.

(3) The practical consequences counted in favour of the authority, including the fact that the company was insured and was well able to pass on the premium to its customers but, if the loss were to be borne by the authority, it would be borne by the local population.

# The Unfair Terms in Consumer Contracts Regulations 1999

The Regulations were originally made in late 1994 to implement a European Community directive. They were re-made in 1999.

OUTLINE OF THE REGULATIONS

The general purpose of the Regulations is to prevent businesses imposing unfair terms on consumers.

THE REGULATIONS APPLY WHERE

- the terms have not been individually negotiated (ie on an overall assessment it is a pre-formulated standard contract), and

- The contract is for the supply of goods or services, and

- the seller/supplier is a business, and

- the other party is a consumer (ie a natural person acting for purposes outside his business).

WHAT IS AN UNFAIR TERM?

(1) Any term which is not expressed in plain, intelligible language.

(2) Any term (but excluding terms as to price or subject-matter) which "contrary to the requirement of good faith causes a significant imbalance in the parties' rights and obligations under the contract to the detriment of the consumer".

*Schedule 3* to the Regulations contains a non-exhaustive list of 17 illustrations of terms which may be regarded as unfair, for example:

- a term which allows the seller to alter the terms of the contract unilaterally without a valid reason which is specified in the contract (eg change of delivery date).

- exclusion clauses (subject to much the same criteria as the *Unfair Contract Terms Act 1977* reasonableness test).

CONSEQUENCES OF THE INCLUSION OF AN UNFAIR TERM

If a term is unfair the particular term is not binding on a consumer. The Regulations also empower the Director-General of Fair Trading and certain other organisations such as *Which?* to obtain an injunction against a business to prevent the use of an unfair term.

# 4

# Law of contract – Breach

# Syllabus content

BREACH OF CONTRACT AND REMEDIES

a)    Explain the meaning and effect of breach of contract.

b)    Explain the rules relating to the award of damages.

c)    Analyse the equitable remedies for breach of contract.

d)    Analyse the doctrine of privity.

# Chapter contents

WHAT IS A BREACH OF CONTRACT?

   Definition.

   Actual breach and anticipatory breach.

REMEDIES FOR BREACH OF CONTRACT

   Damages.

   Specific performance and injunction.

DOCTRINE OF PRIVITY

   Basic principles of the doctrine of privity.

   Important exceptions to the doctrine of privity.

# BREACH OF CONTRACT

## Definition

A party is in breach of contract if, without lawful excuse, he fails to do completely and exactly that which he has agreed to do or if he does it defectively.

For example in a contract for the supply of goods if the seller fails to supply the goods required by the contract he is in breach.

## Actual breach and anticipatory breach

A breach of contract can be actual or anticipatory. The difference between actual breach and anticipatory breach lies in the timing of the breach.

- **Actual breach** arises in a case where the breach occurs on the due date for performance. For example the seller fails to deliver the goods on the required date specified in the contract.

- **Anticipatory breach** occurs when one party to the contract, prior to the due date for performance specified in the contract, shows an intention (expressly or impliedly) that he does not intend to perform his contractual obligations. For example a week prior to the specified delivery date the seller informs the buyer that he will not be delivering the goods.

### EXPRESS ANTICIPATORY BREACH

Express anticipatory breach occurs when one party, prior to the due date for performance actually confirms to the other party that he will not be performing his contractual obligations.

### Hochster v De La Tour [1853].

The defendant agreed in April to employ the claimant as his courier for a foreign tour commencing on June 1. On May 11 he wrote to him saying that he had changed his mind about the tour and therefore would not require a courier. **Held.** The defendant's anticipatory renunciation allowed the claimant to treat the contract as discharged in May and sue for damages immediately. He was not obliged to wait until June.

### IMPLIED ANTICIPATORY BREACH

Implied anticipatory breach occurs where a party carries out some act which makes performance impossible.

### Omnium Enterprises v Sutherland [1919]

The defendant agreed to hire a ship to the claimant. Before the hire period was due to commence he sold the ship. The defendant's act of selling the ship amounted to an implied anticipatory breach and the claimant could sue for damages immediately. He was not obliged to wait until the beginning of the hire period.

### EFFECT OF ANTICIPATORY BREACH

As can be seen by the above two cases when anticipatory breach takes place the innocent party can sue for damages immediately on receipt of the notification of the other party's intention to repudiate the contract, without waiting for the actual contractual date of performance.

Alternatively, the innocent party can wait until the actual time for performance before taking action. He is entitled to actually perform the contract and then claim the agreed contract price as in the case of:

### White & Carter v McGregor [1962].

The claimant agreed to advertise the defendant's business for three years on plates attached to litter bins. The defendant cancelled the contract on the same day that it was made. The claimant nevertheless manufactured and displayed the plates as originally agreed, and claimed the full amount due under the contract. The court held that the claimant was entitled to perform the contract. By cancelling the contract the defendant did not bring it to an end and the claimant still had the option to affirm the contract and continue with performance.

# REMEDIES FOR BREACH OF CONTRACT

## I. TERMINATION OF THE CONTRACT

In certain cases, in the event of breach, the innocent party will be permitted to terminate the contract this will occur:

* Where one party repudiates the contract before the due date for performance or before performance is complete. See for example **Hochster v De La Tour** [1853].

* Where a party commits a fundamental breach of contract by either breaching a condition or an essential innominate term as in the case of **Poussard v Spiers and Pond** [1876].

## 2. DAMAGES

### 2.1 Introduction

Whether or not the innocent party is permitted to terminate the contract where one party to the contract breaches the terms of the contract the innocent party will be entitled to compensation or damages. Damages is a common law remedy and is available as of right.

The aim of damages is to put the innocent party in the position he would have been in had the contract been properly performed. The aim is not to punish the defaulting party nor to allow the injured party to benefit from the breach.

**Surrey County Council v Bredero Homes** [1993] CA.

SCC sold some land to BH and in the contract of sale BH covenanted to build no more than 72 houses on the plot. In deliberate breach of contract BH built 77 houses. SCC claimed damages equal to the profit BH had made on the extra houses. The court held that the purpose of damages at common law for breach of contract is to compensate the innocent party for his loss: its purpose is not to transfer to him any benefit which the wrongdoer has gained by his breach of contract. Since SCC had not suffered any loss, it followed that the damages recoverable had to be nominal.

### 2.2 Liquidated damages clauses and penalty clauses

The contract itself may deal with the innocent party's rights in the event of breach of contract. The contract may even go as far as to provide for details of the sum payable in damages to the innocent party in the event of breach. Such a clause is known as a liquidated damages clause. If a contract contains a liquidated damages clause the sum set out in the clause will be the damages payable, even though in the event the amount of the actual loss is different.

**Cellulose Acetate Silk Co Ltd v Widnes Foundry Ltd** [1933],

W contracted to build a factory for C. The contract provided that W would pay C £20 per week if completion were delayed. There was a delay of 30 weeks. C sued W for £5,850 actual losses. **Held.** The contract sum only need be paid, ie £20 x 30 weeks = £600, as this was in the nature of a genuine liquidated damages clause.

In order to qualify as a liquidated damages clause the sum stated in the contract as the damages payable must be a **genuine pre-estimate** of the probable loss which may be incurred by the innocent party if the contract is breached.

A liquidated damages clause should be contrasted with a penalty clause within the contract which has the aim or purpose of ensuring performance of the contract by imposing a penalty in the form of a fine on the defaulting party in the event of breach. This type of clause will not be enforceable.

Generally the courts will view a damages clause as a penalty clause if:

* the prescribed sum is extravagant in comparison with the maximum loss that could follow from a breach.

* the contract provides for payment of a certain sum but a larger sum is stipulated to be payable on a breach.

* the same sum is fixed as being payable for several breaches which would be likely to cause varying amounts of damage.

## 2.3 Assessment of unliquidated damages

When assessing the compensation to be awarded to the innocent party the court will have regard to the principles of the remoteness of loss and the measure of damages.

### I. Remoteness of loss

Remoteness of loss is an important principle to be considered by the court. Many losses may directly or indirectly arise from another party's breach of contract, but it would not be reasonable for the innocent party to expect to claim damages for everything that could potentially occur, particularly if some losses are incurred owing to exceptional or special circumstances of which the party in breach is not aware. The party in breach can argue that some losses are just too far removed from the original breach that it would not be reasonable or just for the innocent party to be compensated for them. For example, if X makes a contract with Y for the supply of paper for his business if Y then fails to deliver and as a result X is not able to accept a particularly profitable contract with Z, should X be able to claim for all his losses including the loss of profits from the contract with Z, which he could have accepted?

The leading case in this area which sets out the test to apply to identify for which losses damages can be awarded is **Hadley v Baxendale** [1854].

A crank shaft broke at a mill and the owners asked a carrier to transport it to the makers in order to make a new one the same size. The carriers did not deliver it to the makers within the agreed timeframe, which meant that the mill was not in use for a longer period of time than could have been the case had there been no delay. The Claimant claimed for loss of profits whilst the mill was not in use. The judges in the case formulated a two part test ascertain whether or not a loss is too remote.

### A loss is not too remote:

1.  if it arises naturally (ie according to the usual course of things) from the breach; or

2.  if it may reasonably be supposed to be within the contemplation of the parties, at the time they made the contract, as the probable result of breach.

This second limb of the rule deals with abnormal losses.

Where losses occur, which would not generally occur in the usual course of events, the exceptional circumstances, which have created the losses, must be in the knowledge of the defaulting party at the time the contract was formed.

For example, in the case of:

### Victoria Laundry v Newman Industries [1949]

V bought from N a boiler for use in V's laundry. Delivery was agreed for 5 June but was not made until five months later. V sued N, claiming: (a) loss of profit of the laundry during the period of delay on its normal everyday business; and (b) loss of profit from two very unusual and highly profitable dyeing contracts that it was offered but was unable to take. **Held.** V succeeded under (a) because this was normal loss, but the loss under (b) was not recoverable. It was abnormal and neither N (nor V) knew about it nor had they any reason to know about it at the time the boiler contract was made.

Damages for loss of enjoyment or distress or unhappiness

Damages will not generally be awarded by courts for distress arising out of ordinary business contracts.

It is only in exceptional cases where damages can be claimed for loss of enjoyment or distress. Damages can only be claimed for this type of loss or damage in cases where the actual contract itself is selling enjoyment. In the case of **Jarvis v Swan Tours** the court awarded damages for loss of enjoyment for a holiday which was substandard due to a breach of contract. An award for loss of amenity and enjoyment was also made in the case of **Ruxley Electronics v Forsyth** [1995] where a swimming pool in the claimant's garden had not been constructed to the exact specifications of the contract.

## 2. Measure (or quantum) of damages

The measure of damages means the monetary amount of the losses incurred by the injured party. It should be noted that substantial damages will only be awarded where the innocent party has actually suffered loss. If the innocent party has not suffered loss the damages awarded will be nominal.

There are two principal bases of assessment for damages.

### The loss of bargain or loss of expectation basis

The expectation loss represents the profits that have been lost by the innocent party due to breach of contract.

The rule is:

the amount of damages is to put the claimant in the same position that he would have been in had the contract been properly performed.

For example, in **Victoria Laundry V Newman Industries** [1949] the laundry was claiming damages equal to the profits it would have made had the boiler been delivered on time.

There can be difficulties applying the expectation loss basis to construction contracts and teh like because the amount of damages could be calculated in two alternative ways:

1.  the difference between the value of the work if the contract had been properly performed and the value of the work currently due to incorrect performance; or

2.  the cost to the owner of re-doing the work so that it meets the contractual specifications.

It is generally for the claimant to choose which of these two methods of valuing the damages he favours, except where it would be unreasonable to claim for the cost of re-instatement.

For example in the case of **Ruxley Electronics v Forsyth** [1995] where the appellant did not build a swimming pool to the exact specifications of the respondent. If the appellant had been required to rebuild the pool this would have not been proportionate, as the benefit actually obtained by the respondent would not have been great enough to warrant the reconstruction of the pool. The court therefore would only consider basing the level of damages on the difference in value between the proposed pool and the actual pool that was constructed (in this case nil).

### Ruxley Electronics v Forsyth [1995]

RE agreed to build a swimming pool for F at F's house for £17,797.40. The contract specified a pool depth of 7ft 6in. In the event RE built the pool between 6ft and 6ft 9in deep. F claimed damages of £21,560 equal to the cost of re-doing the pool to the agreed depth. RE argued that th edamages should be the difference in value between the pool as specified and as built. (This woud mean £0 since the pool as built was just as suitable for swimming and diving as one built to the agreed specifications). The HL **held** that F would not be awarded damages so as to enable him to re-build the pool as this was unreasonable since the cost was out of all proportion to the benefit to be obtained. Thus his claim would be confirmed to the difference in value. This of course meant £0 – although the HL did uphold the lower court's award of £2,500 for loss of amenity/enjoyment (though they commented that the amount was on the high side).

### Reliance loss or out of pocket basis

This method of assessment is based on the expenditure incurred by the innocent party which has been wasted due to the breach of contract.

This method of assessment may be particularly useful in cases where it is impossible to assess the profits that would have been made if the contract had been properly performed.

In the case of **Anglia Television v Reed** [1972] an actor pulled out of making a film at the last minute, which meant the project was abandoned. The claimants were able to claim for preparatory expenditure. It would have been impossible to assess the profits that could have been made by the claimant if the film had been produced (as it would be impossible to determine whether the film would have been a success or a flop) and to compensate for this.

### The claimant must mitigate his losses

The claimant must always take reasonable steps to **mitigate his loss**.

For example, source goods elsewhere if the seller defaults in supplying goods or sell rejected goods to a new buyer.

If the claimant fails to do this the level of damages that may have been awarded could be reduced by the court.

*Brace v Calder [1895].* The claimant was been employed as a manager in a business with four partners. Two of the partners died. The surviving partners wished to continue in business so they gave the claimant a technical dismissal linked with an offer of re-employment. The claimant resented the dismissal and refused the offer. He sued for wrongful dismissal claiming loss of earnings. **Held.** The claimant would receive nominal damages only. He had not mitigated his loss as if he had accepted their reasonable offer he would have suffered no loss of earnings.

### Loss of an opportunity

As an opportunity has a value, if the claimant is deprived of this opportunity in some cases damages can be awarded by the court if this opportunity is lost due to a breach of contract. It may be difficult to attempt to calculate the appropriate level of damages to be awarded in such cases but nevertheless the courts will be prepared to evaluate an award.

### Chaplin v Hicks [1910].

The defendant, an actor and theatrical manager, agreed with Miss Chaplin that she would attend a meeting (the time and place of which he agreed to give her at a later date) at which he would interview 50 actresses and would then select 12 to whom he would give remunerative employment. In breach of contract he failed to notify Miss Chaplin of the time and place for the interview and thus she lost the chance of obtaining remunerative employment. Miss Chaplin sued for loss of earnings (ie, for the remuneration she would have earned had she been one of the 12 chosen). The defendant contended that she should only get nominal damages since she might not have been chosen – she only had a 1 in 4 chance and moreover a chance that depended amongst other imponderables on his own volition. **Held.** Damages can be awarded for the loss of a chance: Miss Chaplin was therefore awarded substantial damages based on her 1 in 4 chance of having succeeded in the interview. In the case of Chaplin v Hicks 1910 where the claimant was not informed of a time for an interview. Despite the fact that the claimant may not have been successful, she was awarded damages for loss of an opportunity.

## 3. EQUITABLE REMEDIES: SPECIFIC PERFORMANCE AND INJUNCTION

Orders for specific performance and injunction are equitable rather than a common law remedies. The remedies will only be awarded in cases where damages would not be an adequate and equitable way to compensate the injured party.

### 3.1 SPECIFIC PERFORMANCE

An order for specific performance is where the court requires the party in breach to actually perform their positive contractual obligations.

For example, if X fails to transfer a plot of land to Y in breach of their contract damages may not fully compensate X for the loss of the land. The plot of land may have unique features such as a view, which the purchaser may not be able to match in another plot. The only satisfactory remedy would be for Y to be compelled to fulfil his contractual obligations and to transfer the land. This would involve an order for specific performance.

## COURT GUIDELINES

Equitable remedies are not available as of right and are given at the discretion of the court.

The remedies are only available where damages would be an inadequate remedy. Specific performance cannot be granted where this would cause undue hardship for the defendant or where the order would require constant supervision from the court (for example where performance would have to take place over a long period of time).

The usual rules of equity apply for example 'he who comes to equity must come with clean hands' and if the claimant delays in seeking an order this may defeat any claim.

The courts will not make an order for specific performance for employment contracts or contracts for personal service. It would not be practical to force an employee to work for an employer particularly as this would require too much supervision on the part of the court, and it would cause him undue hardship – the equivalent of slavery.

### 3.2 INJUNCTION

An injunction is a court order which prohibits a party to a contract from performing an act which they have contracted to refrain from doing.

For example, if a party has contracted not to sell goods to customers in a certain area the injunction would prevent sale to such customers.

### COURT GUIDELINES

The same discretionary court guidelines used for orders for specific performance apply to the ordering of an **injunction**. However, an injunction can be given of a contract of personal service unless this would be tantamount to specific performance.

**Page One Records Ltd v Britton** [1968]

The claimants requested an injunction to restrain a band, The Troggs, from engaging as their manager anyone other than the claimant. **Held.** The injunction was refused, on the ground that to grant it would in effect compel The Troggs to continue to employ the claimant (and no court would give an order of specific performance to that end).

This case should be contrasted with **Warner Bros Pictures Inc v Nelson** [1937].

A film actress agreed to act for the claimants for a fixed period during which she undertook not to act for any third party, nor to engage in any other occupation, without the claimant's written consent. The court granted an injunction enforcing this, but only to the extent of restraining her from acting for third parties. This would not compel her to act for the claimants because she could earn a living by doing other work.

# DOCTRINE OF PRIVITY

The doctrine of privity of contract determines who can enforce the terms of the contract and against whom can the contract be enforced.

## BASIC PRINCIPLES OF THE DOCTRINE OF PRIVITY

The doctrine of privity of contract comprises three basic principles.

A contract creates rights and obligations only between the parties to it.

A contract cannot impose obligations on, or confer rights on a person who is not a party to the contract.

A person who is not a party to a contract cannot sue or be sued on it.

IMPORTANT EXCEPTIONS TO THE DOCTRINE OF PRIVITY

**Common Law Exceptions**

There are a number of common law exceptions to the operation of the doctrine.

1. In the case of Beswick v Beswick it was established that a personal representative of a party to contract can sue on the contract even though they are not a party to the contract. This is due to the fact that the deceased's rights and liabilities pass to the personal representative on death.

   **Beswick v Beswick** [1968]

   Peter Beswick (PB) sold his business to N. As part of the purchase price N agreed to pay an annuity to PB for his life and thereafter to his widow (MrsB) for her life. When PB died N refused to pay the annuity to MrsB. The court held that (1) In her personal capacity she could not enforce the contract against N as she was not party to the contract; but (2) since she was PB's executor she could enforce the contract in that capacity.

2. According to land law principles restrictive covenants which benefit another piece of land run with the land despite a change in ownership of the land (**Tulk v Moxhay** 1848). Therefore a restrictive covenant agreed between a seller and purchaser of plot of land X which prevents further development of plot X for the benefit of the sellers remaining property will bind a subsequent purchaser plot X. This is because the covenant runs with the land and is not affected by a change in ownership of the land. This exception, however, does not apply to positive covenants for example to maintain a fence which is a personal covenant only (ie between the original parties) and does not attach to the land in order to bind third parties.

3. A third party may be able to bring a claim where there is a collateral contract in existence between the claimant and the defendant and which is essential to the formation of the main contract.

   Example:

   **Shanklin Pier Ltd v Detel Products Ltd** [1951]

   The Claimant had a contract with X co under which the company had agreed to repair and repaint the claimant's pier. X co allowed the claimant to choose the materials, which would be used for the project in particular the choice of paint. The defendant recommended the use of a particular paint to the claimant, which the defendant specifically stated was suitable for the project and of good quality. The claimant followed the defendant's advice and asked X co to use the defendant's product. The paint turned out to be unsatisfactory and the claimant had to spend £4,000 to remedy the problems caused by the paint. The claimant sued the defendant for breach of contract. In its defence the defendant argued that there was no contract between the claimant and the defendant, as it was X co that had purchased the paint not the claimant. The court held that there was a collateral contract between the claimant and the defendant in which the defendant had guaranteed the paint's quality and suitability in return for the claimant specifying that X co used the paint. The main contract would not have come into existence had it not been for the formation of the collateral contract. The claimant therefore had a claim against the defendant.

4. A beneficiary of a trust may enforce the trust. The trust is made between the trustee and the party who creates the trust, but a beneficiary may enforce the trust.

5. An agent is able to create a binding legal relationship between the principal and a third party despite the fact that he has not disclosed to the third party that he is an agent.

6. By valid assignment of the rights under a contract to a third party.

7. By assignment of a right to bring a claim assigned with ownership of property.

Example:

**Linden Gardens Trust Limited v Lenesta Sludge Disposals Limited** [1994]

The claimant was a tenant of a property in Jermyn Street. The claimant had acquired the leasehold interest by assignment from the original tenant. Some years prior to the assignment the original tenant contracted with the defendant to undertake building works including the removal of blue asbestos from the building in which the property was situated. Asbestos was found in the building some years later and yet more asbestos was discovered after the lease assignment to the claimant had taken place. The House of Lords held that the claimant was entitled to recover damages for the cost of remedial works despite there being no contract between the claimant and the defendant. The right to claim against the defendant had also been assigned along with the lease at the time of the assignment. It was foreseeable to the original parties that a later owner of the property could suffer damage due to the defendant's breach of contract (in failing to properly remove the asbestos) and the parties would therefore have contemplated at that time that those who suffered as a result of defective performance should have a right to bring a claim.

## STATUTORY EXCEPTIONS

1. Under insurance law principles a third party is able to take the benefit of a contract of insurance. For example in the case of life insurance.

2. The doctrine can be avoided by the Contracts (Rights of Third Parties) Act 1999.

The Act allows a non-contracting party to enforce a contractual term in his own right in two situations:

* where the contract specifies that he is permitted to do this; or

* where there is no evidence to the contrary, if the term purports to confer a benefit to him.

For example, in the case of Mrs Beswick the annuity purported to confer a benefit on her so the Act should allow her to enforce the terms in her personal capacity as well as in her capacity as personal representative under the common law principles.

For the statute to apply the third party must be expressly identified in the contract. This may be by name or by referring to a class of people or if the third party answers to a particular description.

# 5

## Law of torts

London
School of Business
& Finance

shaping success in business and finance

# Syllabus content

THE LAW OF TORTS

a)      Explain the meaning of tort.

b)      Identify examples of torts including 'passing off' and negligence.

c)      Explain the duty of care and its breach.

d)      Explain the meaning of causality and remoteness of damage.

e)      Discuss defences to actions in negligence.

f)      Professional negligence.

g)      Explain and analyse the duty of care of accountants and auditors.

# Chapter contents

WHAT IS A TORT?

TORT OF NEGLIGENCE

>      The 3 Essential Elements

>      Defences

>      Disclaimers

TORT OF PASSING OFF

>      The 3 Matters to be Proved

>      Remedies of the Claimant

# WHAT IS A TORT?

A tort is a civil wrong which gives rise to a non-contractual claim for damages.

Where a person is a victim of a tort, and has suffered loss, he will be able to sue the wrongdoer in a civil court for compensation, or if he wishes to prevent the tort continuing he is able to seek an injunction from the court. Losses that are suffered can be physical harm, damage to property or pure economic loss. There can be some overlap with tort, contract and criminal law.

## Examples of Commonly Encountered Torts:

### TRESPASS TO LAND

Trespass occurs when without legal excuse the defendant enters stays or places items on the claimant's land. In such circumstances if damage or loss occurs the owner may have a claim for compensation.

### ASSAULT AND BATTERY

The civil offences of assault and battery are distinct from the criminal offences. A civil action for assault and battery may be brought where the victim seeks compensation from the perpetrator. Civil actions may be brought where a criminal action may not succeed as civil offences require a lower standard of proof.

### NUISANCE

Examples of private nuisances are noise pollution from the surrounding properties or environmental pollution from industrial premises. Where damage or loss occurs the victim can sue for compensation.

### OCCUPIERS LIABILITY ACTS CLAIMS

An owner or person in control of a property has a statutory duty to visitors to ensure that the property is not dangerous. Where the owner has not fulfilled his statutory duty a visitor who has suffered injury may be able to claim compensation.

### DEFAMATION

Defamation includes slander and libel which result in damage to a person's reputation.

The F4 syllabus deals with two torts in detail. These are the torts of negligence and passing off.

### NEGLIGENCE

Negligence is the most wide-ranging of all the torts. Negligence is failure to take reasonable care in a situation where a duty to take care is owed to another person which results in harm or loss. The area of professional negligence is particularly relevant to accountants.

### PASSING OFF

Passing off occurs where a business attempts to deceive consumers into believing that they are dealing with another company or business.

# TORT OF NEGLIGENCE

## The 3 essential elements

In order to succeed in the tort of negligence the claimant must prove 3 matters:

1. that the defendant owes him a **duty of care**

2. that the defendant **breached** his duty of care

3. that as a result the claimant suffered **loss**.

## 1. Duty of Care

The first essential element of a negligence claim is to prove that the defendant owed the claimant a duty to take care. Such a duty is not owed to everybody and this will depend on the circumstances and the relationship between the claimant and the defendant.

The leading case in this area is Donoghue v Stevenson.

### Donoghue v Stevenson [1932] HL

Mrs Donoghue became ill after drinking from a bottle of ginger beer which contained the decomposed remains of a snail. She sued the manufacturer. The court held that a manufacturer owes a duty of care to the ultimate consumers of their products despite the fact that there is no contract between them. Manufacturers ought reasonably to foresee that consumers of their products will become ill if the products are contaminated.

The court established a test to determine whether or not a duty of care exists. This test is known as the **neighbour test**. The defendant will owe a duty of care to his neighbour. The defendant's neighbour is:

> "the person who is so closely and directly affected by my act or omission
> that I ought reasonably to have him in contemplation as being so affected
> when I am directing my mind to the acts or omissions in question".

The test is a test of reasonable foreseeability of the damage and proximity between the claimant and the defendant.

### DEVELOPMENT OF THE TEST

The question of whether or not a duty is owed has been further reviewed by the courts since Donoghue v Stevenson.

In the case of **Anns v Merton LBC** [1977] the local authority had allowed builders to construct a block of maisonettes with foundations which were only 2 feet 6 inches deep instead of the required three feet or deeper. The local authority had the power to carry out inspections of the foundation work but had failed to do so. The builder granted 999 year leases of the maisonettes and the claimant was the lessee. Five years later cracks appeared and the floors began to slope. The claimant brought a claim against the local authority for negligence in approving the foundations and failing to carry out the necessary inspections. The court held that the defendant did owe a duty of care to the claimant and was liable. The court established a new two stage test to determine the existence of a duty of care:

1. Whether there is a sufficient relationship of proximity or neighbourhood so that it must be in the reasonable contemplation of the defendant that carelessness on his part may be likely to cause damage to the claimant.

2. Whether there are any considerations which ought to negate, or to reduce or limit the scope of the duty or the class of person to whom it is owed or the damages to which a breach of it may give rise.

Most recently, the test to establish whether a duty is owed has been further refined by the House of Lords in the case of **Caparo Industries v Dickman** 1990 (see next section).

The current test for establishing whether or not a duty exists has three key elements:

1. It must be reasonably foreseeable that, damage will result from the actions of the defendant.

2. There must be proximity, which means a close relationship, between the claimant and the defendant.

3. Thirdly, it must fair just and reasonable to impose a duty and not be contrary to public policy.

## PROFESSIONAL NEGLIGENCE AND NEGLIGENT MISSTATEMENT

The tort of negligent misstatement relates specifically to statements and advice which have been made negligently that generally leads to pure economic loss rather than to any financial losses that actually stem from physical harm or damage to property. The courts have been traditionally reluctant to impose duties relating specifically to pure economic loss.

The courts started to take a different view after the case of Hedley Byrne v Heller and Partners Ltd 1963 was heard by House of Lords.

The general principles relating to the duty of care have been extended to advice given by professionals.

**Professional negligence occurs where the defendant is either acting in a professional capacity or has special skills and he gives advice to others whom he knows will rely on his advice and as a result of that negligent advice financial loss is suffered.** The question here is whether a special relationship exists between the parties. Many of the cases in this area have related to advice given by accountants and auditors.

### Hedley Byrne & Co Ltd v Heller and Partners Ltd [1963]

The claimants started acting for new clients. The claimants requested financial references from the defendants who were bankers. The defendants misstated their client's financial position by giving a favourable reference. The claimants relied on the information and suffered financial loss as a result. The defendants successfully relied on a disclaimer and so avoided liability for the misstatement but the court stated, *obiter dicta*, that the defendants would owe a duty of care to the claimants in the circumstances, mainly due to the fact that a special relationship existed between the parties. The special relationship existed as there was sufficient proximity between the claimant and the defendant as the defendant would have known the purpose for which the information would be used and that in providing the claimant's with inaccurate information they were likely to suffer financial losses.

### Caparo Industries v Dickman [1990] HL

Caparo bought all the shares in a company in reliance on the audited accounts. The court considered whether the auditor owed the claimant a duty of care. The court decided that the auditor in these circumstances did not owe a duty of care to Caparo, as:

(1) the auditors' report is addressed to the members as a body (ie the company) and not to individual members or investors; and

(2) the auditor's report verifies the directors' account of their stewardship of the company for the purpose of a general meeting deciding whether the company should reward (or otherwise) the directors and not for the purpose of people making investment decisions like Caparo.

In the Caparo case it was held that an auditor does not owe a general duty to individual shareholders and potential investors as there is not sufficient proximity between the auditor and such persons and the auditors could not reasonably foresee that the auditors' reports would be relied on by potential investors for the purpose of investing in the company.

The House of Lords in the Caparo case established a new three part test to determine whether or not a duty of care exists. The three key elements that are required to establish that a duty of care in misstatement cases exists are:

1.  It must be reasonably foreseeable that, in the circumstances of the case, the statement would be relied upon by such persons as the claimant. For example ought the auditor to reasonably foresee that Caparo as a potential investor would rely on the report.

2.  There must be proximity, which means a close relationship, between the maker and the recipient. This will be established if the statement is made to persons known to the maker for a known purpose and the information is used for that purpose.

3.  Thirdly, it must not be contrary to public policy to impose a duty. This part of the test considers the fairness of imposing a duty. In the Caparo case it would probably have not have been fair to impose a duty on auditors acting for the company to owe duties to any potential investors in the company, and by setting such a precedent would lead to a significant amount of litigation in the future.

Contrast the Caparo case in which it was found that the auditors did not owe a duty of care with ADT v BDO Binder Hamlyn 1995.

## ADT v Binder Hamlyn [1995]

The defendant firm was the auditors of a company called Britannia Securities Group (BSG) and the claimant was the purchaser of all the shares of BSG. The 1989 accounts were published with an unqualified audit report.

At a subsequent meeting between the Binder Hamlyn audit partner and a director of ADT (a meeting which was known to both to be the final hurdle before ADT finalised its bid for BSG) the Binder Hamlyn audit partner specifically confirmed that he 'stood by' the 1989 accounts. ADT then bought BSG for £105m. It was subsequently discovered that BSG's true value was only £65m.

The High Court **held** that Binder Hamlyn owed a duty of care to ADT in relation to the statement by the Binder Hamlyn partner confirming the accuracy of the accounts. Sufficient proximity was established in this case because that statement was made to a known person for a known purpose. Caparo was therefore distinguished.

## AUDITORS' DUTIES TO CREDITORS

In the case of Al Saudi Bank v Clarke Pixley the court decided that auditors do not owe a general duty of care to either existing or potential creditors.

## Al Saudi Bank v Clarke Pixley [1989]

In reliance on annual accounts audited by Clarke Pixley, Al Saudi Banque loaned money to a company called Gallic Credit International Ltd. Later Gallic went into insolvent liquidation with an estimated deficiency of £8.6m – meaning that Al Saudi Banque was not able to recover all of the loan that it had made to Gallic. So Al Saudi Banque (and other lenders) sued Clarke Pixley in the tort of negligence. The court held that auditors of a company do not owe a duty of care to a bank which lends money to that company, regardless of whether the bank is an existing creditor making further advances or is a potential creditor making new advances. There is no proximity between existing or potential creditors of a company and its auditors.

## AUDITORS' DUTIES TO THIRD PARTIES

It may generally be difficult to establish sufficient proximity between the auditors and third parties for there to be a duty.

Example:

## James McNaughton Paper v Hicks Anderson [1991]

JMP entered into negotiations with MK paper for an agreed take-over of MK. The chairman of MK asked its accountants, HA, to prepare draft accounts for MK to use in the negotiations. The accounts were shown by MK to JMP. After the take-over was completed JMP discovered certain discrepancies in the accounts – which meant that it had paid too much for MK. JMP brought an action against MK's accountants in the tort of negligence. Held. No duty of care was owed because of lack of proximity between JMP and HA. The prime reason being that the accounts were produced for MK's use in the negotiations, not for JMP's.

# 2. Breach of Duty (standard of care)

Once the claimant has established that the defendant owed him a duty of care the next stage in establishing tortious liability is to establish that this duty was broken. This is the fault element of negligence. It means that the claimant must prove that the defendant failed to exercise **reasonable care**.

The test for establishing whether or not there has been a breach of duty was developed in the case of **Blyth v Birmingham Waterworks Company** [1856]. The judges concluded that **failing to exercise reasonable care** means that the defendant has not done "what a reasonable man guided upon those considerations which ordinarily regulate the conduct of human affairs would do or would not do".

What amounts to reasonable conduct on the part of the defendant depends objectively on the circumstances. The following factors may have an impact on what is reasonable conduct.

(i) Whether it is practical to take preventative measures to protect against the risks.

Example:

**Latimer v AEC** [1953]

Factory premises became slippery when oil mixed with water on the floor. To deal with this the employer ensured that this was brushed up as far as possible and put down sawdust. Some patches remained on which the claimant slipped and sustained an injury. The court held that the employer had not breached his duty of care as he had done what could be expected of a reasonable employer to ensure the safety of the employees.

(ii) The seriousness of the potential damage to the claimant.

If the defendant knows that the claimant has an increased risk of serious injury if he should have an accident, extra measures should be taken to fulfil his duty to take care.

**Paris v Stepney Borough Council** [1951]

The claimant only had sight in one eye. He worked in a garage. While using a hammer metal entered his good eye and as a result he became totally blind. The claimant was not using protective goggles at the time and none were supplied by his employer as was common practice in this trade. The court held that the defendant should have taken into account the condition of the claimant's eyes and the gravity of the consequences if anything should happen to his good eye. In not providing goggles the defendant was in breach of his duty of care.

(iii) The expertise and experience of the defendant

Previous cases have shown that lack of experience or skill is irrelevant to establishing whether there has been a breach of duty. The standard which is expected is the standard expected of a reasonably skilled and competent doctor or driver etc.

Examples:

**Nettleship v Weston** [1971]

In this case the claimant who was giving driving lessons to a learner driver was injured in an accident. Despite the fact that a learner driver would not have the driving capabilities of a qualified driver the court held that the defendant had breached his duty of care to the claimant in failing to reach the standard of driving expected of a reasonably competent driver.

**Wilsher v Essex Area Health Authority [1988]**

The fact that a doctor had limited experience was not taken into account by the court in assessing whether or not the duty of care had been breached, as the patient should expect to be treated by a suitably experienced and competent doctor.

(iv) Professionals

The standard care of a professional man acting in that capacity is that of a competent member of his profession. Therefore, the standard of care expected of an accountant is that expected of a reasonably competent qualified accountant. Professionals will be expected to meet the standards required by any professional bodies such as the

law society for solicitors or ACCA etc for accountants. Professionals may be subject to codes of conduct laid down by professional bodies or also statutory provisions. Reasonably competent professionals would be expected to abide by such codes and provisions.

(v)   General knowledge of the risks

Examples:

**Roe v Minister of Health** 1954

An anaesthetic was contaminated as a result of there being invisible cracks in a glass vial. Two patients were left paralysed as a result. The court held that the defendant was not liable. The cracks were not foreseeable given the state of knowledge at the time amongst anaesthetists. As the cracks were not foreseeable within the profession, a reasonable anaesthetist would not have taken any precautions to prevent damage and injury arising.

**Haley v London Electricity Board** [1965]

A blind man tripped over a hammer which was being used to protect pedestrians from a trench on the pavement being excavated by workmen. The man was unable to detect the hammer with his stick and was injured as a result of tripping. The court held that the defendant should have been able to foresee that blind people may use the pavement and the hammer was not adequate protection for the blind. The defendant was liable as less able users of the pavement should have been in the defendant's contemplation when creating a barrier around the trench to protect pedestrians.

## RES IPSA LOQUITUR (THE ACT SPEAKS FOR ITSELF)

Res ipsa loquitur can be used in certain cases to prove a breach of duty. In cases where the only explanation for what has occurred is that the defendant has been negligent res ipsa loquitur may be relevant. In these circumstances it will be up to the defendant to prove that he has not been negligent.

# 3.   Resultant Loss (remoteness of damage)

The third element of the negligence claim is that the claimant must have suffered loss as a result of the defendant's breach of the duty of care.

The losses recoverable can be in respect of:

*   personal injury (e.g. physical or mental injury to the body, death)

*   damage to property (e.g. a wrecked car)

*   financial loss directly connected to personal injury or to property damage (eg loss of earnings, loss of profits)

*   pure financial loss is only recoverable for negligent misstatements.

## CAUSATION AND REMOTENESS OF DAMAGE

These are two important concepts in determining whether or not the breach of duty has caused the claimant's losses.

(i)   Causation

In order for the court to award compensation to the claimant he must satisfy the court that the loss or injury must have been **caused** by the defendant's breach of duty.

**The 'but for' test**

The 'but for' test is a simple test to establish whether or not the defendant's actions or act caused the claimant's injury or loss. The question to ask is but for the defendant's actions would the claimant have suffered his loss or damage?

A case example where the 'but for' test was employed by the court is **Barnett v Chelsea and Kensington Hospital** [1969].

A doctor sent home a patient from hospital and told him to see his GP in the morning. The patient died of arsenic poisoning a few hours later. The court held on applying the 'but for' test that it was not the doctor who had caused the patient's death, it was the arsenic poisoning. The doctor could have done nothing to save him in the circumstances.

Note that the use of the 'but for' test may be problematic in circumstances where there may have been more than one reason for the damage or some act of the claimant or a third party may break the chain of causation.

(ii) Remoteness of Damage

The claimant must prove that the damage sustained is not too remote. Not every loss can be recovered by the claimant, the damage has to be of a type that is foreseeable.

The damage caused by the defendant must be reasonably foreseeable to the defendant in order for the court to award compensation. If the loss or injury is not reasonably foreseeable the defendant would be unable to take steps to avoid it

The test for establishing whether or not the damage is too remote was established by the court in **The Wagon Mound No 1** [1961] HL.

The Wagon Mound was a tanker belonging to the defendant which leaked oil. Cotton debris became entangled in the oil and sparks from some welding equipment ignited the oil. A fire resulted that caused extensive damage. Expert evidence showed that the particular type of oil did not normally burn. The court held that the defendant was not liable for the fire damage which was not foreseeable.

# Defences

Once the claimant has proved the three essential elements, the defendant will be liable unless he can prove a defence.

## 1. VOLENTI NON FIT INJURIA

The literal translation of volenti non fit injuria is to he who consents no injury is done. Volenti non fit injuria is also known as consent or volenti.

Volenti is a complete defence to a tortious claim for damages. Therefore, if the defendant can establish volenti, the claimant will receive no compensation. The basis of the defence is that if the claimant has accepted the risk of injury to himself and has freely consented to the risk he should not receive damages for any loss or injury sustained.

### Imperial Chemical Industries v Shatwell [1964]

The Claimant and his brother worked for the defendant in a quarry. They used working methods when dealing with detonators which were considered to be unsafe and which had been specifically forbidden by the defendant. As a result of the claimant's actions there was an explosion in which he was injured. The court held that the defendant could rely on the defence of volenti to avoid liability. The claimant was an expert in this type of work, he had freely decided to adopt this method of testing the detonator and despite safety warnings from the defendant had continued.

Note that consent must be freely given. A claimant does not freely consent if he is under pressure (social, economic, moral).

For example, if an employee is under economic pressure to continue in an unsafe workplace this is not volenti on the part of the employee.

In the case of **Smith v Baker** [1891] quarrymen were held not to have consented to the risk of injury merely because they continued to work on quarry floor whilst a crane was swinging nets of stones over their heads. The employer had created the dangerous working environment and was negligent in doing so. By simply continuing to work there the employee had not consented to the risks.

Note that volenti should be distinguished from mere awareness of risks as in Smith v Baker. The claimant needs to truly have accepted the risks.

## 2. CONTRIBUTORY NEGLIGENCE

Contributory negligence serves to reduce the amount of damages awarded to the claimant. Unlike volenti this is not a complete defence.

The principle of contributory negligence is that if the claimant by his own negligence has contributed to his loss or injuries the claimant's damages should be reduced to take account of his own negligence.

In the case of **Sayers v Harlow Urban District Council** [1958] when the claimant became trapped in a public toilet she decided to climb out placing one foot on the toilet seat and the other on the toilet roll. As a result of trying to escape she injured herself. The court held that the council had been negligent but the claimant had contributed to her injuries.

If the defendant proves contributory negligence the court will reduce the claimant's damages by a reasonable proportion to reflect the extent to which he has contributed to the injuries.

In the case of Sayers above, the claimant's damages were reduced by 25% as she was found to be 25% to blame for her injuries.

In the case of **Froom v Butcher** [1976] involving a road traffic accident the victim's damages reduced by 25% because of failure to wear a seatbelt.

# Disclaimers

Even where the claimant establishes that the defendant is liable for the damage caused, the defendant may avoid liability by relying on a disclaimer of liability. This occurred in Hedley Byrne v Heller. Such clauses will be subject to the provisions of The Unfair Contract Terms Act 1977 which states that:

- any exclusion of liability for **death** or **personal injury** caused by failure to take reasonable care (contractual or tortious) is **void**

- any exclusion of liability for **other loss** (eg damage to property, financial loss) caused by failure to take reasonable care is **void unless reasonable**.

See chapter 3 on contract terms.

# TORT OF PASSING OFF

This tort arises when a defendant business passes off itself (or its products) as another business. The defendant intends to deceive customers by leading customers to believe that they are purchasing another company's goods and services. In these circumstances the claimant business can seek remedies to stop the defendant passing itself off as the claimant's to protect the claimant's business and goodwill.

# The 3 Matters to be Proved

In order to bring a successful claim in the tort of passing off the claimant must prove 3 matters:

1.  that the defendant's business is using a name (or selling products) which is similar to that of the claimant. (There has been a misrepresentation by the defendant).

2.  that prospective customers are mislead into believing that the defendant's business (or products) is the claimant's business (or products)

3.  that this has caused damage to the claimant's business or goodwill, or will probably do so.

# Remedies of the Claimant

If the tort is proved the court may issue an injunction stopping the defendant from using the name (or selling the products). It may also award damages.

# Case Illustration

### Ewing v Buttercup Margarine Company [1917].

Ewing ran the Buttercup Dairy Company. He successfully obtained an injunction stopping the defendant from using the word "Buttercup" in its name, as there was evidence to show that people would confuse the two businesses.

# 6

## Law of employment

## Syllabus Content

### 1. Contract of employment

a) Distinguish between employees and the self-employed.

b) Explain the nature of the contract of employment and give examples of the main duties placed on the parties to such a contract.

### 2. Dismissal and redundancy

a) Distinguish between wrongful and unfair dismissal including constructive dismissal.

b) Explain what is meant by redundancy.

c) Discuss the remedies available to those who have been subject to unfair dismissal or redundancy.

## Law of Employment Contents

THE TWO TYPES OF WORKER

Definitions

How To Make The Distinction

Importance Of The Distinction

THE CONTRACT OF EMPLOYMENT

Formation

ERA 1996 Written Particulars

Sources Of Terms

Common Law Duties Of Employees

Common Law Duties Of Employers

DISMISSAL

Introduction

Wrongful Dismissal

Unfair Dismissal

Redundancy

# THE TWO TYPES OF WORKER

## Definitions

An **employee** is a worker who works under a contract of service. The employee will usually contract to work for the employer for a specified amount of hours to work in a particular role for an agreed salary at a specified location of the employer.

An **independent contractor** is a worker who works under a contract for services. The independent contractor will generally have a contract to perform a particular service.

## How to make the distinction

It its simplest form an employee has a contract of service, whereas an independent contractor has a contract for services. However, in our increasingly complex society it is not always easy to determine the difference. The courts have developed a number of tests to distinguish between the two.

The three common law tests are:

### 1. The control test

The first test to develop (back in 1880) was the control test. This test was set out in *Yewens v Noakes* where it was said "a servant is a person subject to the command of his master as to the manner in which he shall do his work". In other words, if the employer instructs the worker not only when and where to do his job but more importantly in the manner of doing it then the worker is an employee.

This test was appropriate to a society where most workers were unskilled and therefore the employer was able to tell the worker how to do his job. For example, a heart surgeon can be an employee of a hospital, but due to the complexity of the work involved the hospital is very unlikely to exert control over how operations are carried out, as nobody would have the required expertise.

However, with increasing specialisation and technological expertise this test is not appropriate for today's skilled workers because the employer himself will not have the necessary knowledge to be able to tell the worker how to do his job.

Due to the limitations with this test the courts have developed further tests.

### 2. The integration test (or organisational test)

This test requires the court to consider how the worker's work fits into the employer's business. If the work being done is fully integrated into the employer's business they are likely to be an employee. If, however, the work is accessory to the employer's business they are likely to be an independent contractor.

In *Cassidy v Ministry of Health* a surgeon was held to be an employee as, amongst other matters, he was part of the institution of the hospital.

This test overcomes the problems of the control test when dealing with skilled workers but has proved difficult to apply particularly as it may be difficult to establish the degree of integration of the work which is required to meet the standard of the test.

### 3. The multiple test (or economic reality test or entrepreneurial test)

Difficulties with the 2 tests, set out above, have led the courts to develop the multiple test. This test goes beyond solely considering control or integration or both.

With the multiple test the court takes into account all the circumstances surrounding the relationship between the parties and not just control and integration.

For example, the court may consider the following:

### 1. Provision of tools

If the worker provides his own tools or equipment the court is more likely to categorise the worker as an independent contractor. An employer may be more likely to provide tools to his employee.

## 2. Regularity of hours

An employee is more likely to work set hours on a regular basis, whereas an independent contractor is more likely to work irregular hours or on an irregular basis.

## 3. Regularity of payment (both in terms of timing and amount)

If a worker is paid a fixed sum at regular intervals (weekly/monthly) he is likely to be an employee. On the other hand an independent contractor is more likely to be paid varying amounts on submission of an invoice.

## 4. Number of employers

Independent contractors may work for various employers whereas an employee will generally work full or part time for one employer only.

## 5. Mutuality of obligation

There is normally lack of mutuality of obligation between an independent contractor and an employer: in the sense that the employer is not obliged to offer the contractor work, and if offered it the contractor is not obliged to take up the offer. Whereas employees are obliged to obey an order to do a task (assuming it is a lawful order).

In *Carmichael v National Power* some tour guides who were engaged on a 'casual as required' basis were classified as independent contractors largely because of lack of mutuality of obligation, in that the employer was not bound to offer them work nor were they bound to accept it.

## 6. Ability to delegate (provide a substitute)

An independent contractor is more likely to be able to provide a substitute or delegate tasks whereas an employee will not.

If the worker has not merely the ability to provide a substitute, but the duty to provide a substitute, this is a very weighty factor in favour of independent contractor status.

## 7. Degree of financial risk (profit motive)

An independent contractor is more likely to assume financial risk whereas an employee will generally work for the employer in return for a wage only: as was said in the leading case of *Ready Mixed Concrete v Ministry of Social Security* an independent contractor is, in effect, a 'small businessman'.

## 8. Opinion of the parties.

Overall, each relationship is looked at on its own individual facts and no one factor is conclusive.

# Importance of the distinction

Whether a worker is classified as an employee or independent contractor has important implications in a number of areas of law:

## 1. Employment Rights Act 1996 protection

The *Employment Rights Act 1996* provides employee with rights and protection, for example, with regard to unfair dismissal and redundancy and provides for minimum notice periods to be given on dismissal.

The *Employment Rights Act 1996* does not apply to independent contractors.

## 2. Insolvency of employer

Employees rank as preferential creditors in relation to a certain amount of unpaid wages

Independent contractors rank as ordinary unsecured creditors.

Thus employees of an insolvent employer are more likely to get payment than are the self-employed.

### 3. Tax

There are certain tax benefits for the independent contractor as he is taxable under Schedule D giving him certain favourable allowances, whereas an employee is taxable under Schedule E which is more restrictive.

Further, employees but not independent contractors are subject to the PAYE system. Thus an employee must receive his wages or salary net of income tax and his national insurance contributions. An independent contractor is entitled to be paid gross: he will at a later date account for tax and national insurance.

### 4. National Insurance Contributions

In much the same way as the PAYE system for tax, employees must receive their pay net of their national insurance contributions. Whereas independent contractors are paid gross any ay their self-employed contributions at a later date.

An important factor today is the employer's national insurance contributions. Every employer must make a contribution in respect of each employee. No such contribution arises in respect of independent contractors he employs.

### 5. State benefits

Only employees have rights to certain social security benefits such as statutory sick pay.

### 6. Vicarious liability

Employers may be vicariously liable for acts committed by employees in the course of their employment if, for example, the employee has been negligent.

There can never be vicarious liability for acts of an independent contractor.

### 7. Common law implied contractual terms

There are extensive provisions for employees (see next section). For example, an employee has a right to be reimbursed by the employer for properly incurred expenses and he has a duty to obey all lawful and reasonable orders of the employer. There are no equivalent provisions for independent contractors.

# THE CONTRACT OF EMPLOYMENT

## Formation

A contract of employment is an example of an ordinary commercial contract and will be subject to the general contract rules detailed in the contract chapters. There is no requirement for employment contracts to be in writing and many such contracts will be oral.

## ERA 1996 written particulars

Except where a written contract deals with all the required matters, under the provisions of the *Employment Rights Act 1996* a **statement of particulars** must be given by the employer to the employee within two months of the commencement of employment. This written statement (perhaps in the form of a letter of engagement or as part of an actual written contract) must include the following:

* The names of the employer and employee;
* The date on which employment began;
* Pay – how it is to be calculated and how it is to be paid;
* Job title and nature of the work;
* Hours of work;
* Holidays and holiday pay entitlement;
* Sick leave and sick pay;
* Any pension rights;
* Place or places of work;
* Disciplinary and grievance procedures (if any);

- Any collective agreement relating to the employment;
- Length of notice to be given by each party to terminate the agreement.

If any change is made to these written details, the employer must give the employee a written statement of the change within one month.

The statement is not the employee's contract. Its purpose is to bring to the attention of the employee at an early stage what the employer believes to be the terms of the contract. This should thus assist the vast majority of employees who have no formal written contract to know their obligations may be and, if the written particulars are inaccurate, to bring to the attention of the employer what was differently actually agreed.

## Sources of terms of the employment contact

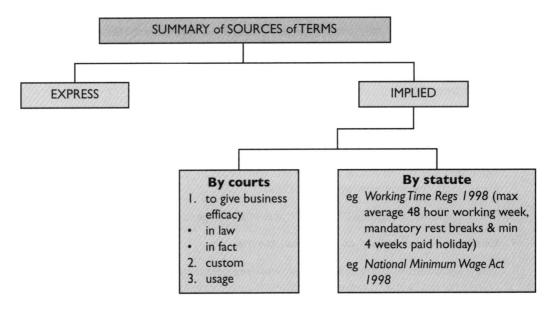

The employment contract will consist of express terms, which have been agreed between the parties, and terms implied by common law and statute.

## Common law implied terms

The common law imposes duties on both employees and employers.

## 1.   Common law duties of employees

Employees owe the following duties to their employers:

If an employee is in breach of an implied term (or indeed express term) the employer may sue him for damages to recover any loss. If the breach is serious the employer may terminate the contract without notice (ie dismiss the employee summarily).

### 1. Personal service.

This means that the employee must not delegate the performance of his job (unless the employer expressly or impliedly gives permission).

### 2. Reasonable care and skill.

The employee must act with reasonable care in performing his duties. The standard of care will depend on the circumstances.

Although an isolated act of negligence is not normally regarded as sufficiently serious so as to entitle the employer to terminate the contract (ie, dismiss the employee), repeated acts do, as does a single act of gross negligence – *Lister v Romford Ice [1957]*.

In the *Lister* case an employee was found to be in breach of this duty, and therefore in breach of contract, when he negligently ran over another employee with a fork-lift truck.

### 3. Obedience

This means that the employee must perform the work in a reasonable manner. In the case of *Pepper v Webb [1968]* a gardener was found to be in breach of the common law duty of obedience when he refused to plant the plants where instructed by his employer.

An employee is not obliged to follow an order that is unlawful or unreasonable. An order is unlawful not only where the carrying out of it would result in a criminal offence but also if it is outside the terms of the contract. What is a reasonable order will depend on the circumstances.

### 4. Fidelity

This is a duty of good faith and requires a high degree of honesty by the employee.

This is a wide duty which includes:

* not to make a profit or benefit from the employment in a way that is detrimental to the employer.

For example:

### Sinclair v Neighbour [1967].

An employee secretly borrowed from the shop till. He repaid the money the next day. The court held that he was in breach of the duty of good faith and, since this was a serious breach of contract, the employer was justified in summarily dismissing him.

* not to compete with the employer's business. For example, running a rival company in the employee's spare time.

For example:

### Hivac Limited v Park Royal Scientific Instruments Limited [1946].

Two employees of a company which manufactured sophisticated components for hearing aids worked at the weekends for a rival company. The court granted an injunction to prevent the employees working for the rival company, as there was potential for misuse of the secret information.

* not to disclose or use confidential information and trade secrets regarding the employer or the employer's business.

### 5. Mutual co-operation.

This means that the employee must perform the work in a reasonable manner.

This is a wide and flexible duty and can encompass matters such as appropriate dress at work, use of appropriate language at work and "go-slows' (the latter as in *Secretary of State for Employment v ASLEF*).

In the case of **Secretary of State for Employment v ASLEF [1972]**, some employees, who were railway workers, 'worked to rule' ie, they obeyed the British Rail rulebook to the letter. This resulted in considerable delays to the train service. **Held**. They were in breach of contract since, although they were performing the work, they were doing so in a wholly unreasonable way in that their actions had the effect of disrupting the service they were there to provide.

## 2. Common law duties of employers

Employers owe the following duties to their employees:

### 1. To pay reasonable remuneration.

It will be rare for the parties to not agree the wage to be paid to the employee and the level of remuneration should be included in the employees written particulars to which all employees are entitled, but in the absence of any express term dealing with this there is a duty for the employer to provide reasonable remuneration. The employer must, however, comply with the provisions of the *National Minimum Wage Act 1998* and the *Equal Pay Act 1970*.

## 2. To indemnify employee for properly incurred expenses.

The employee must be indemnified for expenses properly incurred on behalf of the employer which arise during the course of employment.

## 3. To give reasonable notice of termination of employment

This duty only applies where the length of the notice has not been expressly agreed.

Most contracts of employment will expressly set out the period of notice – and these expressly agreed periods are subject to statutory minima (covered later in this chapter).

This duty does not apply to fixed term contracts.

## 4. To provide a reasonably safe and healthy workplace.

To provide a reasonably safe and healthy workplace. The employer must have a safe system of work in place. There are also numerous statutory provisions relating to this duty, for example, the Health and Safety at Work Act 1974.

## 5. Mutual co-operation/respect.

The employer should not act in any way that may damage the relationship of mutual cooperation and respect that should exist between employer and employee, for example being abusive to the employee.

### Provision of work

An employer has no common law duty to provide the employee with work to do. But exceptionally there may be such a duty arising from the facts of the particular case.

For example, if the employee is a skilled worker or has been engaged in a situation where he is a trainee and contemplates that he will develop his skills as a result of working this duty will apply.

In the case of *William Hill Organisation v Tucker [1998]* in a situation where the employee was on garden leave, the employer was in breach of this duty in not providing work because the employee had particular skills that had to be used to maintain these skills.

This duty will also apply to employees who are remunerated on a piece work or commission basis. In these cases a reasonable amount of work must be provided.

## Terms implied by statute

The following statutes are the main sources of statutory implied terms for employment contracts:

### 1. Employment Rights Act 1996

*   This statute provides employees rights regarding redundancy and unfair dismissal. These will be dealt with in the following sections.

*   Employees are entitled to a written itemised pay slip. Deductions must be authorised either by law (for example, PAYE) or in advance in writing by the employee.

*   The Act gives pregnant employees a right to maternity leave, a right to paid time off for ante-natal care and protection against dismissal. The Act also gives parental leave rights to both men and women.

*   The Act provides for minimum notice periods

The period of notice is usually agreed between the employer and the employee. However, the *Employment Rights Act 1996* sets out minimum notice periods as follows.

| Continuous employment of employee | Minimum notice to be given by employer |
| --- | --- |
| Between one month and two years | One week |
| Between two and twelve years | One week for each complete year of employment |
| Twelve years or more | Twelve weeks |

An employee who has worked for his employer for a continuous period of at least 4 weeks must give his employer at least one week's notice prior to terminating his contract.

## 2. Health and Safety at Work Act 1974

Under health and safety legislation employers must –

The main duties under the Act are:

- To take all practicable steps to ensure the health, safety and welfare of employees

- To provide safe plant and systems of work

- To provide sufficient information, training and supervision to ensure employees safety

- To maintain the place of work to a satisfactory standard to ensure safety

## 3. The National Minimum Wage Act 1998

- Provides for a minimum hourly pay to which an employee is entitled currently £5.80 per hour for employees aged over 22.

## 4. The Working Time Regulations 1998

- Limits the working week to 48 hours unless the worker agrees in writing otherwise.

- Provides for a minimum four week holiday entitlement.

- Provides for daily and weekly rest breaks.

- Contains special provisions for young workers and night workers.

## 5. Equal Pay Act 1970

- The Act makes it unlawful for an employer to discriminate between men and women, doing similar or equal work, with regard to pay, conditions or benefits.

# DISMISSAL

# Introduction

An employee who has been dismissed may have any one or more of the following three legal actions against his employer

- **wrongful dismissal.** This is a common law action claiming damages for breach of contract. The most common allegation of breach is that the employer summarily dismissed the employee (ie, he dismissed him without giving the contractually due length of notice). The action can be brought by both employees and independent contractors.

- **unfair dismissal.** This is a statutory action under the *Employment Rights Act 1996* on the basis that the employer did not have a fair reason for the dismissal or that he acted unreasonably. There are three statutory remedies: re-instatement, re-engagement and the monetary award. The action can only be brought by employees, not by independent contractors.

- **redundancy.** This is a statutory action under the *Employment Rights Act 1996* on the basis that the employee is redundant (eg, there is no work for the employee). The remedy is a redundancy payment. The action can only be brought by employees, not by independent contractors.

Before examining these three actions in detail you need first to grasp the important concept of constructive dismissal.

### Constructive Dismissal

In principle, an employee who resigns cannot sue for wrongful dismissal, unfair dismissal, or redundancy. The concept of constructive dismissal is a modification of this principle.

Constructive dismissal occurs where the employer commits a serious breach of contract and as a direct result of this breach the employee resigns. By resigning the employee is treating the contract as discharged.

An example of such a repudiatory breach of contract by the employer was seen in the case of **Simmonds v Dowty Seals [1978]**. The employer ordered the employee to change from a day to a night shift and the employee resigned. The court decided that this was a repudiatory breach by the employer and the employee had been constructively dismissed.

# Wrongful dismissal

### 1. Definition

Wrongful dismissal occurs when the employee, without breaching the employment contract himself, has either been dismissed without notice or the employer has terminated his fixed term contract before the end of the fixed term.

**Note that independent contractors are also able to claim for wrongful dismissal as well as employees. Independent contractors are, however, unable to bring claims for unfair dismissal or redundancy as the *Employment Rights Act 1996* only applies to employees.**

### 2. Employee's breach of contract

The employer can be justified in summarily dismissing an employee if the employee has committed a serious breach of contract such as:

- Dishonesty;
- Disclosure of confidential information;
- Violence;
- Persistent neglect or carelessness;
- Gross or repeated negligence; or
- Serious misconduct.

### 3. Remedies

A wrongful dismissal claim is a common law action for breach of contract. The only remedy available to the employee will be damages.

The employee will claim damages for loss of earnings for either the notice period or the remainder of the fixed term of his contract. The employee will have a duty to mitigate his loss and must therefore try to find alternative employment. If the employee fails to do this it may affect the level of damages awarded.

An action can be brought in the county court or high court depending on the value of the claim. The action must be brought within I have six years of the dismissal.

Alternatively, employees can bring a claim for wrongful dismissal in an employment tribunal provided the damages claim is £25,000 or less. The limitation period is 3 months.

# Unfair dismissal

The right for an employee to claim for unfair dismissal is a right established by the *Employment Rights Act 1996*. Unfair dismissal occurs where an employee is dismissed without a justifiable reason.

### Complaint

Any claim for unfair dismissal must be made to the Employment Tribunal and normally within three months of the dismissal.

### Qualifying condition

In order to bring a claim the employee must have been continuously employed by his employer for a period of one year, **except where the employee has been dismissed for one of the inadmissible grounds.**

## Dismissal

The employee must first prove that they have been dismissed.

According to the *Employment Rights Act 1996* there are three ways of proving dismissal:

(i) The employer has terminated the employee's contract.

(ii) Where a fixed term employment contract is not renewed on expiry.

(iii) Where the employer has breached the employment contract and the employee has terminated the contract as a result of the employer's breach (constructive dismissal).

If the employee resigns, except where this is due to constructive dismissal, the employee will not be able to bring a claim for unfair dismissal.

Example:

**Morton Sundour Fabrics v Shaw [1966].** An employee was warned that it was likely that he would be dismissed at some unspecified date in the future. He then left (because he had found another job). The court held that he had not been dismissed and therefore had no actions under the *Employment Rights Act 1996*.

### Presumption that the dismissal was unfair

There is a presumption that the dismissal is unfair. Like all presumptions, this can be rebutted by the employer.

### Rebuttal by the employer

*Step 1*

The employer must prove to the tribunal that he had a reason for dismissing the employee and what it was.

Example:

**Devis v Atkins [1977].** Mr Devis was dismissed at a time when the employer had no reason for the dismissal. Subsequent to Mr Devis's departure the employer discovered that he had been embezzling funds. Mr Devis brought an action for unfair dismissal. **Held.** His action succeeded. The employer was not able to rely on the after discovered facts of dishonesty to justify the dismissal as fair since the dishonesty was not the reason for the dismissal. Since the employer had no reason for the dismissal at the date of the dismissal, it was an unfair dismissal. *Note:* such after discovered facts are relevant to assessing the amount of any monetary award.

*Step 2*

The employer must prove that the reason for the dismissal related to one or more of the following **five fair reasons**:

1. That the employee lacked sufficient capability or qualifications to perform his duties. The employer must, however, give the employee adequate training.

2. The conduct of employee justified the dismissal. For example, in the case of **Stevenson v Golden Wonder [1977]**. where the employee assaulted another employee this was found to be sufficient misconduct to justify dismissal

3. There is a redundancy situation, which means that the employer ceases to trade (completely or at the employee's usual place of work) or where the usual kind of work that the employee is employed to undertake ceases or diminishes altogether or at the employee's usual place of work.

   Employees need to be fairly and objectively selected for redundancy and procedures need to be followed properly. If this is not the case or there is any question of discrimination the employee may have a claim for unfair dismissal (see redundancy section for further details).

4. Illegality of continued employment (i.e. it would contravene statute to continue to employ him). For example, if an employee does not have a work permit (where required).

5. Some other substantial reason

The most common instance involves behaviour by the employee that results in the employer no longer being able to trust the employee.

For example:

In the case of **Foot v Eastern Counties Timber [1972]** dismissal was held to be justified when an employee married an employee of a direct competitor.

In the case of **Singh v London Bus Service** dismissal was held to be justified when an employee whose job was in a position of trust was convicted of a criminal offence involving dishonesty.

## Reasonableness

Once the employer has proved a fair reason, it is then for the tribunal to decide whether or not it was a fair dismissal using the reasonableness test.

Case law shows that the reasonableness test has 2 aspects:

(i) Was the reason given sufficiently serious to justify dismissing the employee? (ie was dismissal a reasonable reaction to the fair reason proved?)

(ii) Did the employer act reasonably both in coming to the decision to dismiss and in the manner of the dismissal?

In order to prove reasonableness the employer should have complied with the ACAS Codes of Practice where possible. For example, investigate complaints of misconduct fully and do not dismiss on mere suspicion; in cases of bad work, give warnings and time to improve).

Example:

In the case of **Polkey v A E Drayton Services[1987] HL** the court held that it was unreasonable to sack a long-serving employee without any warning even though for the fair reason of redundancy.

## Remedies

### 1. Reinstatement.

This means that the employment tribunal makes an order requiring the employer to allow the employee to return to his old job on exactly the same terms and assuming that the employee has never left the employment.

### 2. Re-engagement.

This means that the tribunal makes an order requiring the employer to re-employ the employee but this can be to a different role provided that the new role is equivalent to the old role and suitable for the employee. The tribunal may specify further terms that it sees fit.

### 3. Compensation or monetary award.

This can be awarded by the tribunal as an alternative remedy to either reinstatement or re-engagement.

The award can be made up of three possible components, which together make up the total award made to the employee.

(i) First, the basic award.

The award is calculated according to the age of the employee and the length of the employee's service.

1½ weeks' pay for each complete year aged ≥ 41, plus

I week's pay for each complete year aged ≥ 22 < 41, plus

½ week's pay for each complete year aged < 22.

The maximum weekly pay that can be used for the calculation is £350 per week and the maximum ervice period that can be used is 20 years.

The basic award may be reduced by the tribunal where the claimant has already received a redundancy payment, has contributed in some way to his dismissal or has unreasonably refused an offer of reinstatement from the employer.

(ii) Second, the compensatory award.

This aims to provide just and equitable compensation to the claimant for the loss of employment. It may compensate the applicant for any additional loss of earnings which may be due to, for example, the loss of a benefit in kind or a bonus payment or pension rights and contributions. The maximum compensatory award is £66,200.

The compensatory award may be reduced if the claimant has failed to mitigate his loss; and, as with the basic award, has in some way contributed to his dismissal.

(iii) Finally, an additional or higher award can be made by the tribunal in cases where:

- the employer fails to comply with a previous order for reinstatement or re-engagement; or
- there is evidence of race, sex or disability discrimination on the part of the employer; or
- the employee has been dismissed for one of the inadmissible grounds.

### Inadmissible reasons

If an employee is dismissed for one of the following inadmissible reasons the tribunal will find that the dismissal will be automatically unfair.

**Note that when an employee is dismissed for one of the inadmissible reasons there is no qualifying period of employment necessary. Therefore, an employee that has been employed for a period of less than one year can still bring a claim.**

The inadmissible grounds are:

1. For any reason connected with pregnancy, childbirth or the exercise of maternity leave rights.

2. For any reason connected with trade union membership or trade union activities.

3. For any reason relating to a complaint about health and safety matters.

4. In the event that the employee is unfairly selected for redundancy by an employer using unfair or non-objective criteria (see section on redundancy).

5. In the event that the employee is dismissed following the making of a protected disclosure regarding their employer. For example, if the employee reports the employer to the authorities for certain activities such as criminal activity or breach of health and safety regulations. This is commonly called 'whistle blowing'.

6. If the employee refuses to work more than 48 hours per week or the exercise of rights established by the *Working Time Regulations 1998*.

7. Where the employee is asserting statutory rights under the *Employment Rights Act 1996*.

# Redundancy

### Basic right and meaning of redundancy

Under the provisions of the *Employment Rights Act 1996* every employee who is dismissed by reason of redundancy is entitled to receive a redundancy payment from his employer.

Redundancy is defined by *Employment Rights Act 1996*.

An employee is redundant if he has been dismissed by his employer and the dismissal is attributable wholly or mainly to:

either

1. the fact that the employer ceases to trade (completely or at the employee's usual place of work);

or

2. the fact that the usual kind of work that the employee is employed to undertake ceases or diminishes altogether or at the employee's usual place of work.

A redundancy situation does not exist where an employer wishes to replace an employee.

Example:

In the case of **Vaux and Associated Breweries v Ward [1969]** the court held that the employee was not redundant where the employer sought to employ a more glamourous and younger barmaid following a pub refurbishment. This was not a redundancy situation even though the nature of the workplace had changed because the employer still needed a barmaid so the position itself was not redundant.

Mobility Clauses

If an employee is required to move to a different location to work where the work in the employees usual place of work diminishes and the employee's contract of employment contains a mobility clause (a clause which states that the employee may be required to work in a choice of different locations at the option of the employer from time to time) the employee will not be redundant if he is required to work in a different location.

## Procedures

1. The claimant must be an employee. Redundancy is only relevant for employees. An independent contractor will have no rights under the *Employment Rights Act 1996*.

2. Any complaint in relation to redundancy must be made to an employment tribunal within six months of the dismissal.

3. The employee must have been employed by his employer for a continuous period of at least two years.

4. The employee must prove that he has been dismissed. According to the *Employment Rights Act 1996* there are three ways of proving dismissal. Firstly, the employer has terminated the employee's contract. Secondly, where a fixed term employment contract is not renewed on expiry. Thirdly, where the employer has breached the employment contract and the employee has terminated the contract as a result of the employer's breach (constructive dismissal).

## Employer's duties in redundancy situations

Employers will need to comply with the following if they take the decision to make redundancies.

1. To consult with employees and trade union representatives or elected employees' representatives over any redundancy proposals at the earliest possible point.

2. To attempt to avoid making employees redundant where possible, for example, making cost savings elsewhere.

3. To use fair criteria to select employees for redundancy from a pool of employees who are at risk (for example, skills, attendance record or standard of work of the employees). Any employee who is selected for redundancy for reasons connected with sex, race, disability, trade unionism, action taken against the employer for health and safety breaches or any other unfair selection criteria will have a claim for unfair dismissal.

4. To attempt to find alternative employment for redundant employees.

## Calculation of redundancy payment

Employees who have been dismissed by reason of redundancy will be entitled to a redundancy payment.

The payment is calculated in the same way as the unfair dismissal basic award according to the age of the employee, the employee's salary and the length of service.

If the employee is aged 41 or over he will receive 1½ weeks pay for each complete year's service. Employees aged between 22 and 41 will receive 1 week's pay for each complete year's service. Employees aged under 22 will receive ½ week's pay for each complete year's service.

The maximum weekly pay that can be used for the calculation is £350 per week and the maximum service period that can be used is 20 years.

### Loss of the right to a redundancy payment

The right to a redundancy payment is lost if the employee unreasonably refuses an 'offer of suitable alternative employment'.

The alternative employment must be suitable and must be equivalent employment to the employee's previous position.

Example:

In the case of **Taylor v Kent County Council** the court held that it was not unreasonable for a redundant headmaster to refuse alternative job as a supply teacher because of loss of status even though new job at same pay and conditions.

### Taylor v Kent County Council [1969].

Taylor was the headmaster of a school. The school was amalgamated with another school and a new head was appointed to the combined school. Taylor was offered employment in a pool of new teachers, standing in for short periods in understaffed schools. He would retain his current salary. **Held.** Taylor was entitled to reject this offer and to claim a redundancy payment. The reduction in status made it reasonable for him to refuse the alternative employment.

# 7

## Law of agency

London
School of Business
& Finance

shaping success in business and finance

# SYLLABUS CONTENT

a) Define the role of the agent and give examples of such relationships paying particular regard to partners and company directors.

b) Explain how the agency relationship is established.

c) Define the authority of the agent.

d) Explain the potential liability of both principal and agent.

# Chapter contents

INTRODUCTION

HOW THE AGENCY RELATIONSHIP ARISES

    Express Agreement

    Implied Agreement

    Necessity

    Ratification

    Estoppel

AUTHORITY

    Express

    Implied

    Apparent

EXAMPLES OF AGENTS IN BUSINESS

PERSONAL LIABILITY OF AGENTS

# INTRODUCTION

The role of the agent is to create a contractual relationship between his principal and a third party. The agent is a representative of the principal.

The most important agency relationships for the purposes of the syllabus are the relationships between company officers (directors/company secretary) and the company and between individual partners and the firm.

Once an agent has formed a contract with a third party, the role of the agent is complete. The contract he has negotiated is between the principal and the third party only.

# HOW THE AGENCY RELATIONSHIP ARISES

The relationship between a principal (P) and an agent (A) may arise in any of the following situations.

## 1. Express Agreement

This is where the principal (P) actually appoints someone (A) to be his agent, whether orally or in writing.

## 2. Implied Agreement

Where the parties have not expressly agreed to become principal and agent, it may be possible to find an implied agreement based on their conduct or relationship. See section below on implied authority.

## 3. Necessity

For the relationship to be created by necessity four conditions need to be satisfied:

(i) The principal must have entrusted his property to the person (A) who is alleging that he is an agent of necessity.

Example:

**Great Northern Railway v Swaffield** [1874]

Swaffield sent his horse by rail and on its arrival at its destination there was no one to collect it. GNR was unable to contact Swaffield. GNR incurred the expense of stabling the horse in a livery stable for the night. The court held that GNR was an agent of necessity and therefore had authority to incur the expense of stabling it overnight.

(ii) An emergency situation arises making it necessary for A to take action.

Example:

**Prager v Blatspiel** [1924]

A bought skins as agent for P but was unable to send them to P because of prevailing war conditions. Being unable to communicate with P he sold the skins. The court held that A was not an agent of necessity in these circumstances, because he could have stored skins until the end of the war. There was no real emergency.

(iii) The action taken by the agent must be in the principal's interests.

Example:

**Sachs v Miklos** [1948]

M agreed to store S's furniture. Some considerable time later M decided that he needed the storage space for his own use. He tried to contact S to get the furniture removed but was unable to do so, so he sold the furniture. When S found out he sued M for wrongfully disposing of the furniture. The court held that the defendant was liable. M's argument that he had acted as an agent of necessity in disposing of the furniture was dismissed since he had sold it merely for his own convenience, rather than acting in S's interests.

(iv)    It must be impossible for the agent to contact or communicate with the principal.

Example:

**Springer v Great Western Railway** [1921]

A consignment of fruit was found by the carrier to be going bad. The carrier sold the consignment locally instead of delivering it to its destination. The court held that the carrier was not an agent of necessity because he could have obtained new instructions from the owner of the fruit. He was therefore liable in damages to the owner.

# 4   Ratification

The effect of ratification is to backdate A's authority to act as agent.

Six conditions must be satisfied for agency to arise through ratification:

(i)    A purports to act as agent for a principal (P) who is named or otherwise identified.

Example:

**Keighley, Maxsted v Durant** [1901] **HL**

X agreed to buy some wheat from T. Although X intended this to be on behalf of P, X did not tell T this nor did he indicate to T that he was dealing as an agent, and nor did X have any authority from P. When X told P what he had done P purported to ratify, but he later changed his mind and refused to take delivery of the wheat. The court held that he was not bound to do so. His 'ratification' was inoperative because T did not know of the existence of P.

(ii)    P has capacity and exists both at the date the contract is made and at the date of ratification.

Example:

In the case of **Kelner v Baxter** [1866]

Three promoters of a company bought goods from K on the company's behalf before it was incorporated. Once the company was incorporated it then purported to ratify the contract with K. The court held that the company was not able to do so since it did not exist at the date the contract was made. Thus K had no claim against the company for payment.

(iii)    P has been fully informed of the terms of the contract (or is prepared to ratify in any event).

(iv)    P ratifies the whole contract.

(v)    P ratifies within a reasonable time.

(vi)    P clearly signifies his intention to ratify to TP

A void or illegal contract cannot be ratified because it is of no legal effect from its inception.

# 5.   Estoppel

Agency by estoppel arises where the principal makes a representation to the third party that the agent is his agent, even though he is not. In this situation the principal is then estopped from denying this representation. See following section on apparent authority.

# AUTHORITY

This is the key agency topic: it overlaps into partnership law and company law.

**BASIC RULE:**

An agent can only create a legally binding relationship between the principal and the third party if the agent is acting within his authority given to him by the principal.

This authority may be express, implied or apparent.

# Express authority

Where an is agent specifically appointed and given explicit instructions by the principal as to the contracts that he is able to enter into on behalf of the principal he will be acting with express authority.

Express authority is the authority that the principal has explicitly given to his agent. Express authority is actual authority given to the agent.

The principal will be bound by any agreements entered into by the agent with a third party where the agent is acting with express authority.

# Implied Authority

Implied authority like express authority is actual authority. Implied authority arises in cases where the agent has not expressly been given authority by the principal, but this can be implied by certain circumstances.

An agent will have implied authority to:

1. undertake matters which are reasonably incidental to the performance of any authority, which is expressly given to the agent; or

2. to undertake matters which a person in that position would normally have authority to undertake.

The agent themselves cannot exceed their authority and engage in activities that have been specifically prohibited by the principal, but implied authority is particularly relevant when considering whether the principal can be bound to an agreement with a third party. A binding agreement will be created between the principal and the third party where the agent is acting with implied authority.

Examples:

**Watteau v Fenwick** [1893]

The agent (an innkeeper) and bought cigars for resale, which was expressly prohibited by the principal. The court decided that there was a binding agreement between the principal and the agreement between the principal and the third party as the purchase of cigars would be within the usual authority of an innkeeper and it could be assumed he would have this authority even though this had been prohibited, as the third party was not aware of this prohibition.

**Hely-Hutchinson v Brayhead Ltd** [1968]

A company appointed one of the directors as chairman of the board and chief executive. The director was not appointed as the managing director, but acted as if he had been. When the company tried to deny that it had a contract with a third party the court held that the third party was entitled to assume that he had the necessary authority of the company to bind the company to contracts, which was a consequence of his appointment as chief executive, although no authority could be implied from his position as chairman of the board.

# Apparent/Ostensible Authority

Apparent authority arises in a situation where the agent does not have actual authority (either express or implied), but the **principal** has represented to a third party that the agent does have authority. The principal may make the representation by words or by conduct.

The representation by the principal arises in two main ways:

1. By the very appointment of the agent by the principal it may appear to a third party that the agent has the authority to undertake matters which are usually undertaken by an agent in that position.

Example:

**Freeman & Lockyer v Buckhurst Park Properties** [1964]

Two directors of a company left X, the third director, for some years to run the company's business of property development. X engaged some architects on the company's behalf although he had no express authority to do so. Later the company refused to pay the architects on the ground that X had no authority. The court decided that (1) X's position as a director did not give him usual authority to enter into commercial contracts such as the engaging of architects; but (2) the position of a managing director does carry such usual authority; and (3) even though X was not managing director the company had led third parties to believe that he was. Thus the company was estopped from denying that X had authority as if he were managing director. The result, therefore, was that the company had to pay the architects.

2. Authority may arise from previous dealings between the agent and the third party.

For example, if the principal had previously allowed the agent to exceed his authority and form a contract with the third party, which was not within his actual authority this is representing to the third party that the agent has the authority to continue to make this type of contracts in the future.

The effect of the representation by the principal is that if a third party relies on this representation, the agent acting with apparent authority can create a legal relationship between the principal and the third party.

If the third party knows that the agent does not have authority, the third party cannot claim that there a binding agreement is formed between him and the principal by virtue of apparent authority.

# EXAMPLES OF AGENTS IN BUSINESS

# Company agents

### DIRECTORS

A company is a corporate body and can therefore only act through its agents. The directors can be agents of the company. They can form a binding contract between the principal (the company) and a third party. For example, entering into a contract to purchase goods on behalf of the company. The position of a general director does not give implied authority. The company articles will generally delegate the running of the company's business to the board of directors. Individual directors may be given either express, implied or apparent authority from the board to enter into binding contractual relationships with third parties.

As can be seen from the case of **Hely-Hutchinson v Brayhead Ltd** above implied authority may arise from a director being appointed in a position such as chief executive or managing director.

Apparent authority may arise in a situation where the company leads third parties to believe that a director has been appointed as managing director or some similar position when they have not actually been so appointed. See **Freeman & Lockyer v Buckhurst Park Properties** above.

### COMPANY SECRETARY

The extent of the company secretary's implied authority was assessed by the court in the case of **Panorama Developments v Fidelis Furnishing Fabrics** [1971]. In this case a company secretary hired a car in the name of the company which was actually to be used for his own purposes. He did not have authority from the company to enter into this agreement. The court held that there was a binding agreement between the company and the car hire company as a company secretary would **usually** have the authority of the company to enter into contracts of an administrative nature such as the ordering of cars and the hiring of staff.

**Note** it appears from other cases, for example, **Re Maidstone Buildings** [1971] and **Re Cleadon Trust** [1968] that the implied/apparent authority of the company secretary will not extend to entering into commercial contracts or entering into loan agreements.

# Partnership agents

Individual partners are agents of the firm and the other partners to carry on the partnership business and can bind the partnership in contracts with third parties where:

1    The partner has express authority from the other partners. For example, he has authority in the partnership agreement.

2    A partner in such a position as the partner in this firm would usually have authority to enter into this type of contract (implied authority).

3    A partner has apparent authority to enter into contracts of the **usual** type which would be entered into to conduct the business engaged in by the partnership.

Example:

**Mercantile Credit v Garrod** [1962]

P was a partner in a firm carrying on a garage business mainly concerned with lettting lock-up garages and repairing cars. G was a sleeping partner. A clause in the partnership agreement excluded the buying and selling of cars. P, without G's authority, sold a car, to which he had no title, to the claimant for £700. When the claimant found out that P had had no title to the car, it claimed the £700 from G. The court held that the sale of the car was "an act for carrying on in the usual way business of the kind carried on by the firm", and thus the firm was bound, and therefore G was accountable for the money. The court was of the view that the outside world in general would think that persons trading as a garage would usually buy and sell cars.

See following chapter on partnership for further examples.

# PERSONAL LIABILITY OF AGENTS

# Breach of warranty of authority

An agent who acts outside his authority is liable to the third party in damages for breach of warranty of authority.

# Breach of duty

Where an agent acts contrary to his principal's instructions the principal can sue him for damages (for breach of the agency agreement). If serious breach, the principal can dismiss the agent.

8

# Partnership law

# Syllabus content

a)   Demonstrate a knowledge of the legislation governing the partnership, both unlimited and limited.

b)   Discuss how partnerships are established.

c)   Explain the authority of partners in relation to partnership activity.

d)   Analyse the liability of various partners for partnership debts.

e)   Explain the way in which partnerships can be brought to an end.

# Chapter contents

INTRODUCTION

THE PARTNERSHIP ACT 1890 PARTNERSHIP

THE LIMITED PARTNERSHIP

THE LIMITED LIABILITY PARTNERSHIP (LLP)

# INTRODUCTION

This chapter will deal with three types of partnership:

- *The Partnership Act 1890* partnership, which is an ordinary partnership. The partners are collectively referred to as a 'firm'.

- The Limited partnership, governed by the *Limited Partnership Act 1907*, which is a modified ordinary partnership. The partners are collectively referred to as a 'firm'.

- Limited liability partnership, governed by the *Limited Liability Partnerships Act 2000*, which is a cross between a partnership and a company. The persons involved are correctly called members – not partners; and an LLP is not a firm.

# THE PARTNERSHIP ACT 1890 PARTNERSHIP

## Definition of Partnership *s1 Partnership Act 1890*

All unlimited liability partnerships will be governed by the provisions of the *Partnership Act 1890*.

*s1 Partnership Act 1890* states that it is the relationship between two or more persons carrying on business in common with a view to profit.

- **Relationship**

  A partnership is not a legal entity – it is nothing more than the relationship between the partners. This means that the partners *are* the partnership and it follows that they together personally own the assets of the business and are personally liable for the debts.

- **Two or more**

  There must be at least two partners. One person alone cannot be in partnership with himself – he will be a sole trader.

  There is no legal maximum number of partners.

- **Persons**

  Normally the partners are human persons. But they can be artificial persons, such as companies.

- **Carrying on a business**

  This generally means that there has to be some sort of business activity taking place. The mere co-ownership of a property is not sufficient to constitute business activity.

- **In common**

  This means that the partners must be engaged in and participating in some way in the business together, this especially refers to financial participation. Note that a partnership may include sleeping partners who will not take part in the management of the firm, but are still partners.

- **With a view to profit**

  This means that the partners generally intend to have a business that generates some sort of financial return. Profit usually refers to net profit rather than gross returns.

There are no prescribed formalities for the creation of a partnership. If what the parties are doing fits the *s1 Partnership Act 1890* definition of partnership, they are partners.

**A partnership** (which **is a contractual relationship** between the partners) can be implied or it may be express. An express agreement may be in any form, for example oral, in writing, by deed, etc. The partners may or not have a partnership agreement which sets out how the partners have agreed to run their affairs.

# Liability of the partners for partnership debts

The liability of the partners for partnership debts in this type of partnership is unlimited and is joint and several – *s9 Partnership Act 1890*. A creditor can therefore pursue all the partners, or some or, just one of the partners for the debts of the business.

Unlimited liability means that a partner can be liable up to the full amount of his personal wealth: there is no limit on his liability.

Joint liability means that each partner is fully liable for all the debts of the firm.

Several liability means that a creditor can sue the partners simultaneously in one legal action or he may choose to bring successive actions.

# Agency position of the partners

### AUTHORITY OF PARTNERS – s5 PARTNERSHIP ACT 1890

If one partner within the partnership enters into a contract are the partnership and the other partners bound by that contract?

The law of agency applies to partners and therefore whether they have the necessary authority to the partnership in contract with a third party.

s5 Partnership Act 1890 states that:

'Every partner is an agent of the firm and of his other partners for the purpose of the business of the partnership; and the acts of every partner who does any act for the carrying on in the usual way business of the kind carried on by the firm bind the firm and his partners, unless the partner so acting has in fact no authority to act for the firm in the particular matter, and the person with whom he is dealing either knows that he has no authority, or does not know or believe him to be a partner'.

Therefore:

An individual partner is an agent of the firm and his other partners to carry on the partnership business and can bind the partnership in contracts with third parties where:

1.   The partner has **actual** authority from the other partners. For example, he has express authority set out in the partnership agreement.

2.   A partner has **apparent** authority to enter into contracts of the usual type which would be entered into to conduct the kind of business engaged in by the partnership.

     Example:

     **Mercantile Credit v Garrod** [1962]

     P was a partner in a firm carrying on a garage business mainly concerned with lettting lock-up garages and repairing cars. G was a sleeping partner. A clause in the partnership agreement excluded the buying and selling of cars. P, without G's authority, sold a car, to which he had no title, to the claimant for £700. When the claimant found out that P had had no title to the car, it claimed the £700 from G. The court held that the sale of the car was "an act for carrying on in the usual way business of the kind carried on by the firm", and thus the firm was bound, and therefore G was accountable for the money. The court was of the view that the outside world in general would think that persons trading as a garage would usually buy and sell cars.

     In a non-trading partnership it is not usual for a partner to have authority to borrow money.

Example:

**Higgins v Beauchamp** [1914]

B and M were in partnership as proprietors and managers of cinemas. Without the consent of B, M borrowed money from H, who subsequently sued B for its return. The court held that the character of the firm was non-trading (because it provided services, rather than buying and selling goods) and therefore no partner had any implied power to borrow. Thus the action failed.

If the partnership is bound by the contract all the individual partners will have joint and several liability for any debts owed under this contract.

There may be personal liability for the partner and not the partnership where:

1.   The third party knows that the partner has no actual authority, or

2.   The partner has no actual authority and the third party does not know or believe him to be a partner.

The partners within the partnership can change from time to time as partners retire or new partners join the partnership. It is therefore important to establish the liabilities of partners for debts incurred by the partnership before and after the partner joins the partnership. The rules are as follows:

1.   An incoming partner is not liable for debts incurred before he became a partner.

2.   An incoming partner becomes fully liable for debts incurred after he becomes a partner.

3.   An outgoing partner remains liable for debts incurred while he was a partner.

4.   An outgoing partner becomes liable for debts incurred after he has ceased to be a partner, unless the third party with whom the partnership is dealing has been given notice of his retirement in accordance with s36 *Partnership Act 1890*.

   s36 provides that:

   •   actual notice of the partner leaving the partnership must be given to third parties who were customers of the firm prior to his retirement

   •   constructive notice of the partner leaving the partnership published in the London Gazette is sufficient notice for those parties who were not existing customers, but who knew the outgoing partner to be a partner

   •   it is not necessary to give notice to those third parties who were not existing customers of the firm and who did not know the outgoing partner to be a partner **unless** it can be shown that the retired partner represented himself or knowingly suffered himself to be represented as a continuing partner of the firm (this is known as holding out, see below).

   Example:

   **Tower Cabinet v Ingram** [1949]

   C and I carried on a business of household furnishers under the name "Merry's". The partnership was dissolved in 1947, with C continuing the business alone under the same name. One year later the claimant, which had not previously dealt with Merry's, received an order to supply six suites of furniture. This order was confirmed on some old headed notepaper, with I's name on it as well as C's, which was inadvertently used by C without I's authority. The price of the goods was not paid and the claimant obtained judgement against Merry's. The claimant then sought to enforce the judgement against I. The court held that I was not liable. This was because (1) prior to his retirement he was not known to the claimant to be a member of the firm, and accordingly I was under no obligation to give any notice of his retirement to the claimant; and (2) he had not knowingly allowed C to hold him out as a partner under s14 *Partnership Act 1890*.

5.   Indemnity.

The continuing (and incoming) partners may agree to indemnify the outgoing partner against debts incurred pre-retirement or post-retirement or both.

**Liability of a person who is not a partner as if he were (holding out) – s14 Partnership Act 1890**

s14 Partnership Act 1890 states that every person who either by his words or by his conduct represents himself to be a partner of a firm (or knowingly allows himself to be represented as being a partner by others) is liable as if he were a partner to anyone who thereby gives credit to the firm.

This is known as holding out. The person holding themselves out to be a partner is therefore jointly and severally liable for the partnership debts to the third party and can be pursued personally for the debt.

Example:

**Martyn v Gray [1863]**

G went down to Cornwall to discuss possibly investing in a tin mine belonging to X. Nothing came of the discussions but while G was down in Cornwall G was introduced to M by X as "a gentleman down from London, a man of capital". Thus giving M the impression that G was in partnership with X. G did not deny the statement. M later gave X credit believing he was in partnership with G. The court held that although the introduction was oblique it amounted to a representation that G was in partnership with X; and so G was liable for the debt incurred subsequent to the introduction. He should have made the true position clear to M by correcting the impression made that he was a partner.

This case can be contrasted with the above case of **Tower Cabinet v Ingram** where the defendant was not himself aware of the holding out (his name appearing on the partnership notepaper as a partner) and could therefore do nothing to prevent it.

Note that although such a person incurs liability to outsiders as if he were a partner, he acquires no rights as a partner vis-à-vis the other partners.

# Dissolution of the Partnership

A partnership can always be terminated by agreement between the partners.

The grounds upon which the partnership will be automatically dissolved under the provisions of the Partnership Act are as follows:

1.   On the expiry of any fixed term if the partners have agreed that the partnership should only exist for a set amount of time.

2.   If the partnership has accomplished its venture, which was the purpose for which the partnership was established, as there will be no need for it to continue.

3.   The death or bankruptcy of any of the partners (this provision can be excluded in the partnership agreement).

4.   If the carrying on of the partnership becomes illegal (for example if the business carried on by the partners becomes illegal after a change in the law).

Under the provisions of the Partnership Act 1890 the partners or any one partner may dissolve the partnership in the following ways:

1.   In any way which is authorised by the partnership agreement.

2.   By a partner giving notice. (This right can be excluded in a partnership agreement). This right is only relevant so long as the partnership is to carry on for an indefinite duration and not for an agreed fixed term.

3.   If one of the partner's shares becomes the subject of a charging order the others have the option of dissolution.

Any of the partners can apply to the court to dissolve the partnership on any of the grounds set out in s35 *Partnership Act 1890*. The grounds are as follows:

1.  If any partner becomes a mental patient.

2.  If a partner is incapacitated and therefore becomes incapable of performing his part in the partnership business.

3.  If the activities of any of the partners are prejudicial to the business carried on by the partnership.

4.  If a partner wilfully breaches the partnership agreement or in some way by his conduct makes it impossible or unreasonable for the joint enterprise to be continued.

5.  Where the partnership business can only be carried on at a loss.

6.  Any other reason for which it would be just and equitable to dissolve the partnership.

## THE LIMITED PARTNERSHIP

A partnership that is governed by the *Limited Partnership Act 1907* is known as a limited partnership. In practice, this type of partnership is not commonly encountered.

A limited partnership has the following characteristics:

1.  A limited partnership is a variant of the ordinary partnership. In this type of partnership the liability of one or more of the partners is limited to the amount of his capital contribution to the partnership. These partners therefore enjoy limited liability.

2.  A partnership cannot be a limited partnership unless 2 conditions are fulfilled:

    *   There must be at least one general partner with unlimited liability, and therefore as with the *Partnership Act 1890* partnership, creditors can pursue this partner for debts and claim against all his personal assets. Therefore, not all the partners can enjoy limited liability within the partnership.

    *   If a *Limited Partnership Act* partnership is formed Companies House must be informed of its creation and limited liability status.

3.  A limited partner is not permitted to participate at all in the partnership management and is thus a sleeping partner. If he does take part in the management of the partnership at all he will forfeit his right to his limited liability status.

4.  The limited partner has no power to bind the firm to contracts and he is, therefore, not an agent of the firm.

5.  If a limited partner draws out all or any of his capital contribution he remains liable for the firm's debts up to the amount so drawn out.

## THE LIMITED LIABILITY PARTNERSHIP (LLP)

The LLP has only been possible from April 2001 and is now a popular form of business arrangement for professional partnerships such as solicitors and accountants.

LLPs are governed by the provisions of the *Limited Liability Partnerships Act 2000*.

The LLP was invented to address the issue of lack of limited liability particularly within large partnerships. Its members benefit from limited liability as the LLP is a separate legal person. In general, the LLP and not its members are liable to third parties.

LLPs are subject to the income tax regime applicable to partnerships, rather than to the corporation tax regime applicable to companies. Apart from tax, very few partnership provisions apply to LLPs. Many provisions applicable to companies apply, with modifications, to LLPs.

Different terminology is used to describe LLPs, as they are completely different in nature to the ordinary partnership. The individuals in the LLP are known as 'members' rather than 'partners'. The word 'firm' cannot be used to describe an LLP.

# Nature

An LLP is neither a partnership nor a company, but is a mixture of the two forms of business organisation.

The *Limited Liability Partnerships Act 2000* states that the law relating to partnerships does not apply to limited liability partnerships.

A limited liability partnership is a body corporate with a legal personality separate from its members, which is formed in accordance with the provisions of the *Limited Liability Partnerships Act 2000*.

This means that it is a person in law and, in the same way as a company, it:

- is an artificial legal entity with perpetual succession.
- can hold property in its own right.
- enters into contracts in its own name.
- sues and is sued in its own name.
- can create floating charges.

It is created by registering an incorporation document with the Registrar of Companies.

# Incorporation of an LLP

An LLP is brought into existence by registration by the Registrar of Companies – *s2 Limited Liability Partnerships Act 2000*.

The Registrar of Companies will not register an LLP unless an incorporation document is delivered to him together with a declaration of compliance made either by a solicitor or by someone who subscribed his name to the incorporation document as agreeing to become an initial member of the LLP. The incorporation document must:

- state the name of the LLP. The last three words in the name of an LLP must be 'limited liability partnership' or the abbreviation LLP;
- state whether the registered office (ie, the official legal address) of the LLP is to be situated in England and Wales, in Wales or in Scotland;
- state the actual address of the registered office;
- state the name and address of each of the persons who are to be members of the LLP on incorporation. (There must be at least two members); and
- either specify which of those members are to be designated members or state that every person who from time to time is a member of the LLP is a designated member. (The significance of 'designated member' is covered below).

Provided the incorporation document is complete and correct the Registrar will register the incorporation document and will give a certificate that the LLP is incorporated by the name specified in the incorporation document.

# Membership of an LLP

The first members of an LLP are those named in the incorporation document.

After incorporation, any person may become a member of an LLP by agreement with the existing members.

An LLP must have at least two designated members. The role of designated members is to perform the administrative and filing duties of the LLP. They are also responsible in law for such matters as the appointment of auditors and the signing of the annual accounts. If no member is specified as a designated member, then in default, all members are deemed to be designated members. Similarly if the number of designated members falls below two.

A person may cease to be a member by death, dissolution and in accordance with any agreement with the other members of the LLP. Where there is no agreement a member may cease to be a member by giving reasonable notice to the other members.

Any change in the membership of an LLP (or who are the designated members) must be notified to the Registrar of Companies.

# Agency position of the members

Each member of the LLP is an agent of the LLP.

This means that the LLP is liable to third parties on contracts made by members acting within their actual and apparent authority. However the LLP is not bound where the third party knows of the lack of actual authority or does not know or believe him to be a member of the LLP.

In relation to torts committed by members: not only is the member personally liable but the LLP is also.

# Liability of the members

1. Generally, the liability of a member of an LLP to contribute to its debts is limited to his capital contribution (if any). There is no requirement for a capital contribution and if there has been one it can be withdrawn at any time.

2. Under *s214A Insolvency Act 1986* in the event that a LLP does go into liquidation the liquidator can apply to the court for an order compelling a member to repay any drawings that have been made in the previous two years if:

   - the member knew or had reasonable grounds to believe that at the time the LLP was unable to pay its debts; or

   - by taking funds out of the LLP the LLP became unable to repay its debts.

3. Sections *213* and *214 Insolvency Act 1986* creating the offences of fraudulent trading and wrongful trading apply to members of LLPs as in much the same way as to companies.

   - A member will be liable for fraudulent trading if he has knowingly carried on the business with the intent to defraud creditors or for fraudulent purposes.

   - A member will be liable for wrongful trading where the LLP is in insolvent liquidation and if it can be established that, firstly, he knew or ought to have known that there was no reasonable prospect of avoiding the insolvent liquidation and secondly, the member did not take all the steps that he could take in order to minimise the potential loss to creditors.

   In the case of either offence an order can be made by the court requiring him to contribute to the assets of the LLP.

   Both fraudulent trading and wrongful trading are covered in detail in Chapter 17.

9

Company law –
legal personality
and company
formation

# Syllabus Content

### Legal personality

a) Distinguish between sole traders, partnerships and companies.

b) Explain the meaning and effect of limited liability.

c) Analyse different types of companies, especially private and public companies.

d) Illustrate the effect of separate personality.

e) Recognise instances where separate personality will be ignored.

### Company formation

a) Explain the role and duties of company promoters.

b) Describe the procedure for registering companies, both public and private.

c) Analyse the effect of a company's constitutional documents.

d) Describe the contents of model articles of association.

e) Explain how articles of association can be changed.

f) Describe the statutory books, records and returns that companies must keep or make.

g) Explain the controls over names that companies may or may not use.

# Chapter Contents

INTRODUCTION TO COMPANY LAW

DOCTRINE & VEIL OF INCORPORATION

    Doctrine of Incorporation

    Consequences of Incorporation

    Lifting the Veil of Incorporation

TYPES OF COMPANY

    *Companies Act 2006* Definitions

    Basic Classification

    Public and Private Companies : Major Differences

SHOULD A BUSINESS BE A COMPANY OR A PARTNERSHIP?

    Differences Between Companies And Partnerships

    Advantages & Disadvantages of Incorporation

COMPANY REGISTRATION

    Registration Procedures

    Trading Certificate

    Promoters

    Pre-Incorporation Contracts

London
School of Business
& Finance

shaping success in business and finance

# INTRODUCTION TO COMPANY LAW

UK company law can trace its origins back to the 19th century. Prior to this, companies had to obtain a Royal Charter from the ruling Monarch. This in itself was problematic to obtain and therefore many 'companies' existed without any form of incorporation with little or no investor protection leading to crises such as the South Sea Bubble in the early 18th Century.

In the 19th Century, the growth of railways that needed investment, and the existence of limited companies in the USA, meant that the UK had little choice but to follow, with major Acts passed by Parliament in 1844, 1855 and 1862. These aimed to provide a suitable structure for the formation of companies and enshrined the principal that a company's members have limited liability but also that they have key responsibilities and rights. These basic principals still hold true today with the current Companies Act.

In the 20th Century a further nine Companies Acts were passed by Parliament including the 1985 and 1989 Companies Acts. The *Companies Act 2006* is the largest ever with over 1300 sections. The Act's main objective was to make it easier to set up and run a company,
particularly smaller companies, whilst ensuring shareholder engagement and a long term investment culture.

Although the *Companies Act 2006* received the Royal Assent on 8th November 2006, much of it did not come into force until October 2009. Nevertheless, though it has been examinable by ACCA since June 2008.

The ACCA syllabus for Company Law is:

- The formation and constitution of business organisations.
- Capital and the financing of companies.
- Management, administration and regulation of companies.
- Legal implications relating to companies in difficulty or in crisis.

As Company Law such a large topic, this manual splits it into seven chapters as follows:

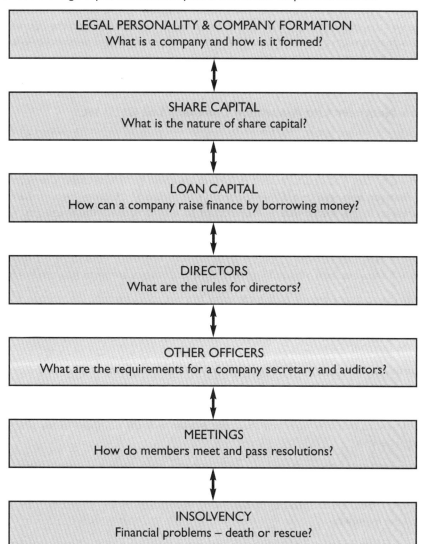

| LEGAL PERSONALITY & COMPANY FORMATION |
| :---: |
| What is a company and how is it formed? |

| SHARE CAPITAL |
| :---: |
| What is the nature of share capital? |

| LOAN CAPITAL |
| :---: |
| How can a company raise finance by borrowing money? |

| DIRECTORS |
| :---: |
| What are the rules for directors? |

| OTHER OFFICERS |
| :---: |
| What are the requirements for a company secretary and auditors? |

| MEETINGS |
| :---: |
| How do members meet and pass resolutions? |

| INSOLVENCY |
| :---: |
| Financial problems – death or rescue? |

# DOCTRINE AND VEIL OF INCORPORATION

## Doctrine of incorporation

The basic rule of the doctrine of incorporation states that a company is a separate legal person, which has an identity distinct from its owners, the members, and its directors who manage the company.

This is expressed in law by imagining aa 'veil of incorporation' that is drawn down between the company and those others.

The leading case from which the doctrine originates is the case of *Salomon v Salomon*.

### Salomon v Salomon & Company Limited [1897] **HL**

S owned a boot and shoe business, as a sole trader. He then formed a company and sold his business to the company in return for shares and a loan secured on the company's assets. Subsequently, the company became insolvent and went into liquidation. It was argued that (a) S was personally liable for the debts of the company, and (b) S had no right to repayment of the loan on the basis that since he was the company he could not be a creditor of it. The court held that a company is a separate person from its shareholders. This therefore meant (1) the company was liable for its debts, not S; and (2) he could be a creditor of it and therefore he had a right to repayment of the loan from it.

Further examples:

- A sole director & majority shareholder can be an employee of company.

### Lee v Lee's Air Farming Ltd [1960]

A small company was formed to run an aerial crop spraying business. Mr Lee was the sole shareholder, managing director and pilot for the company. He was killed in a flying accident while crop spraying. Mrs Lee claimed payment under the Workmens Compensation Acts for the death of her husband in his capacity as an employee. The court held that Mr Lee and the company were two separate entities. Acting in one capacity he was the employee of the company. Since he died whilst acting in the course of his employment, Mrs Lee was able to claim compensation. The concept of separate legal personality enabled Mr Lee to be both owner and employee simultaneously.

- Members/directors do not have any interest in the company's property.

### Macaura v Northern Life Assurance Company Ltd [1925] **HL**

Macaura owned a timber estate. He formed a limited company, in which he owned all the shares, and sold the timber estate to it. Before he sold the estate to the company it had been insured in his own name. After the sale he neglected to transfer the insurance policy to the company. Some years later the estate was destroyed by fire. The court decided that Macaura could not claim under the policy because the assets that were damaged belonged to a different person, the company. Macaura even as the only member had no insurable interest in the timber estate. All he could do was to recover the premiums.

## Consequences of incorporation

1. A company is a separate legal person in its own right and is separate from its shareholders and directors.

2. The debts of the company belong to the company and not to its owners, the members. In companies either limited by guarantee or by shares members can enjoy the benefit of limited liability. This means that the liability of the individual members will be limited to the agreed amount of the guarantee or the amount left unpaid on the members' shares.

3. A sole shareholder can make loans to the company and so become a creditor of the company and have a right to repayment of the debt.

4. A company has perpetual succession, which means that even though the owners of the company may change from time to time this does not affect the existence of the company in any way, as the company is a separate legal person.

5. As a separate legal entity the company can own property, make contracts, incur liabilities, sue or be sued all in its own name.

6. In a company it is possible to separate management, undertaken by the directors, from ownership of the company by the members.

7. On incorporation, the company becomes subject to the provisions of the *Companies Act 2006*.

# Lifting the veil of incorporation

*Exceptionally* the corporate veil will be lifted.

Lifting the veil means that, despite the concept of separate legal identity, when required the separation of the company from its owners and directors can be set aside. The actions of the company are then treated as the actions of the members and directors. This will only occur in exceptional circumstances.

The following are important examples of where the law directs the 'veil to be lifted'.

## Statutory examples

1. **Public company is trading without a trading certificate** – *s767 Companies Act 2006.*

   A public company is required by *s767 Companies Act 2006* to obtain a trading certificate before it can start trading.

   If the company directors fail to obtain the certificate before commencing business and the company defaults on any of its obligations to creditors within 21 days of being required to do so, the directors will become personally liable for the debts to third parties by virtue of *s767 Companies Act 2006*. The directors have joint and several liability to third parties in this instance.

2. **Fraudulent trading and wrongful trading** – *Insolvency Act 1986*

   **Fraudulent trading** (s213 Insolvency Act 1986). A director will be liable for fraudulent trading if he has knowingly carried on a business with the intent to defraud creditors or for fraudulent purposes.

   **Wrongful trading** (s214 Insolvency Act 1986). A director or shadow director will be liable for wrongful trading where a company is in insolvent liquidation and if it can be established that, firstly, he knew or ought to have known that there was no reasonable prospect of avoiding the insolvent liquidation and secondly, the director or shadow director did not take all the steps that he could take in order to minimise the potential loss to creditors.

   In either case a director who is liable for these offences may be called upon to contribute to the assets of the company.

   Both fraudulent trading and wrongful trading are covered in detail in chapter 17 – Fraudulent behaviour

3. **The phoenix company (restriction on re-use of name of insolvent company)** – *Insolvency Act 1986*

   If a director of a company that has gone into insolvent liquidation re-uses its name within 5 years, he is personally liable for the debts of the phoenix company. In the event of breach of this legislation the director will have personal liability for the debts of the phoenix company.

   See later, chapter 17 on Fraudulent behaviour.

## Common law examples

The veil may be lifted in circumstances where the veil is a façade concealing the true facts – **Woolfson v Strathclyde Regional Council** [1978]

Examples:

### Woolfson v Strathclyde Regional Council [1978] **HL**

Mr Woolfson owned the premises which he leased to a company, Woolfson Ltd, of which he was the director and controlling shareholder. Strathclyde Regional Council compulsorily purchased the premises and refused to pay the level of compensation that is statutorily due to an owner-occupier, arguing that there was no one person who was both owner and occupier of the premises. Mr Woolfson argued that the veil of incorporation between he and his company should be lifted so as to treat them as one. The court held that the veil will be lifted only where special circumstances exist indicating the veil is a mere façade concealing the true facts. This was not such a special circumstance since it is a common business arrangement for a major shareholder to lease property to his company.

### Jones v Lipman [1962]

Lipman agreed to sell some land to Jones. Lipman then changed his mind and, in order to evade specific performance of the contract, sold the land to a company of which he was the controlling member. The court held that the company was a sham and therefore the veil would be lifted. This meant that the order of specific performance extended not only to Lipman but also to the company.

### Gilford Motor Co v Horne [1933]

H entered into a covenant, as part of his employment contract with GM, not to solicit customers from GM in the five years after he had left. When he left he formed a company and the company itself solicited customers. The court held that the veil of incorporation was lifted and thus an injunction would be granted against both H and his company. The company was a sham since H was using the façade of the company to enable him to act in breach of the covenant.

Whether a court decides to lift the veil will depend on the individual circumstances of the case. There has to be good reason for the lifting of the veil not simply so that justice can be done. The courts will respect the principle of separate legal personality unless there is sufficient reason to lift the veil, for example if a subsidiary company is acting as an agent of a holding company or where a company is a mere façade .

### Adams v Cape Industries [1990] CA

A holding company (Cape), which mined asbestos in South Africa, marketed the asbestos world-wide through subsidiaries which it incorporated in the different countries. Adams obtained a court judgement against the US subsidiary. Adams sought to make Cape, the English holding company, liable for the judgement debt. The court held that the holding company was not liable. The veil of incorporation would not be lifted since the veil between Cape and its various subsidiaries was not a mere façade. Each subsidiary had its own autonomous board of directors and was not subject to the day-to-day control of Cape.

### Ord and another v Belhaven Pubs Ltd [1998]

The defendant made various misrepresentations to the claimant regarding the profitability of a pub, which had been renovated. The claimant took on the pub lease. By the time the claimant became aware of the misrepresentations the defendant had all but ceased trading, and therefore had virtually no assets thus making it not worthwhile bringing a claim. The claimant therefore sought leave of the court to bring the claim against the defendant company's holding company rather than the company, which made the misrepresentations. The court held that the claimant could not bring a claim against the holding company, as the original company had not been a mere façade for the holding company, nor vice versa. The two companies were completely independent trading companies and neither company had been created as a sham to avoid some liability. There had been no element of asset stripping and so the veil should not be lifted in the circumstances.

# TYPES OF COMPANY

## Companies Act 2006 definitions

1. A **private company** is any company which is not a public company.

2. A **public company** is a company which meets the following conditions:

   (i) is limited by shares, and

   (ii) its Certificate of Incorporation states that it is a public company, and

   (iii) it has been properly registered or re-registered as a public company.

## Basic classification

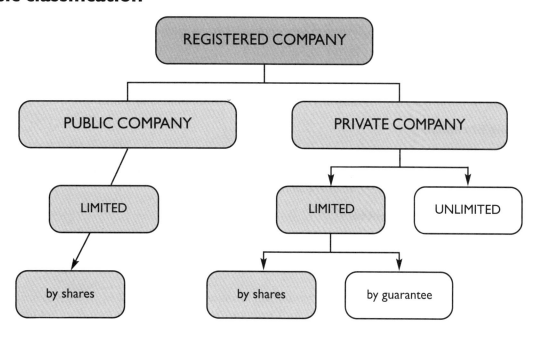

The Companies Act 2006 provides for the formation of three different types of company. These are an unlimited company, a company limited by guarantee and a company limited by shares. In the three different types of company the liability of the members to contribute to the debts of the company differs.

- **Unlimited Companies**

   Unlimited companies are companies in which the liabilities of the shareholders for the debts of the company have not been limited in any way.

   The debts of the company do still belong to the company and not to the members themselves, but the members are liable to contribute to the debts of the company without limitation.

   Only a private company can be incorporated with unlimited liability. A public company cannot be an unlimited company.

   The main advantage of this type of company over limited liability companies is that the company (unless it is a member of a group) is not required by the provisions of the *Companies Act 2006* to file accounts, which means that the company can keep its financial affairs, for example the level of profits, private.

- **Companies limited by guarantee**

   A company limited by guarantee is a form of Limited Liability Company.

   The liability of the individual members is limited to an agreed amount, which can be called on in the event that the company goes into insolvent liquidation. The members will not be called upon to contribute anything in excess of the agreed amount and so their liabilities are limited.

   A company limited by guarantee can only be a private company and not a public company. In general, only non trading companies such as charities or a property management company can be companies limited by guarantee.

- **Companies limited by shares**

   A company limited by shares is a form of Limited Liability Company. This is the most common form of company.

   On incorporation (and later) the company issues shares to its members. A shareholder is liable to pay the issue price – this is the nominal value plus any premium. Thus the liabilities of the individual members is limited to the amount unpaid (if any) on their shares. Once the shares are fully paid there will be no further liability to contribute towards the company's debts in the future.

   A company limited by shares can be either a private or public company.

# Public and private companies: major differences

The main differences between public and private companies are as follows:

### Limitation of liability

A private company may be either registered as an unlimited company or a company limited by shares or guarantee. A public company may only be registered as a company limited by shares.

### Raising of capital

It is illegal for the shares of a private company to be advertised (by anyone) as being available for public subscription. Thus private companies cannot raise capital from the public: whereas public companies can (and this is why private and public companies are so named).

### Minimum number of directors

A public company must have at least two directors whereas a private company can have just one director.

### Company secretary

A public company must have a company secretary and he must be suitably qualified. Private companies are not required to have a company secretary; and if such a company chooses to have one, he does not need to be qualified.

### Commencement of business

A private company can begin business immediately it is incorporated (ie from date on its certificate of incorporation). A public company cannot begin business immediately on incorporation, must get a further certificate from the Registrar, commonly called a trading certificate.

### Minimum capital

A public company must have a minimum share capital of £50,000 in nominal value and each share must be paid up to at least ¼ on the nominal value plus the whole of any premium. There is no minimum or maximum requirement for a private company.

### Administrative requirements of the *Companies Act 2006*

Some of the burdensome administrative requirements of the *Companies Act 2006* are relaxed, in certain circumstances, for private companies. For example, a private company is not required to hold annual general meetings.

### Audit

The statutory audit requirement does not apply to *private* companies with a turnover below £5.6m. The audit requirements apply to all non-dormant public companies.

### Level of financial disclosure

All limited companies are required to file accounts. But certain small and medium-sized *private* limited companies do not have to file full accounts.

# SHOULD A BUSINESS BE A COMPANY OR A PARTNERSHIP?

## Differences between companies and ordinary partnerships

*Reminder:* a partnership is defined as "the relationship which subsists between persons carrying on business in common with a view to profit" – *Partnership Act 1890.*

| COMPANY | PARTNERSHIP |
|---|---|
| **1. Legal personality** | **1. No legal personality** |
| • company owns property in its own name | • partners own property |
| • company contracts in its own name | • partners are personally party to contracts |
| • company sues and is sued in its own name | • partners are jointly and severally liable |
| • possibility of limited liability | • partners have personal unlimited liability |
| • company unaffected by death or bankruptcy of members/directors – formal procedure required for dissolution, called liquidation | • death or bankruptcy of any partner means the partnership is dissolved automatically |
| **2. Transferability of shares** | **2. No transferability of shares** |
| • member can freely sell his shares of co-partners | • partner cannot sell his share without consent |
| **3. Borrowing** | **3. Charges** |
| • can create debentures | |
| • can create floating charges | • cannot create debentures |
| • cannot create floating charges | |
| **4. Participation in management** | **4. Participation in management** |
| • members have no right to participate, directors run the business | • every partner has the right to take part in<br>• management |
| **5. *CA 2006*** | **5. *PA 1890*** |
| • all must be complied with | • much can be disapplied by agreement between the partners |
| • formalities of registration to incorporate | • partnership may be created informally |
| • company cannot return capital to members | • partners may withdraw capital |
| • restrictions on distributable profits | • partners agree profit-sharing ratios |
| • must prepare annual accounts | • no partnership law requirement for accounts |
| • public financial disclosure (limited companies) | • no financial disclosure to public |
| • administrative requirements eg the holding of general meetings, audit, and returns to Registrar of Companies | • no such administrative requirements |
| **6. Tax** | **6. Tax** |
| • company pays corporation tax | • partners pay income tax |

# Advantages and disadvantages of incorporation

### Advantages of incorporation as a company

#### 1. Perpetual succession

The company will be unaffected by changes in membership and will continue as a legal entity until the company is formally liquidated. A partnership does not have perpetual succession and will automatically dissolve on the death or bankruptcy of a partner.

#### 2. Limited liability

As a company is a separate legal entity it is the company that is responsible for the company's debts to creditors rather than its members. The liability of shareholders is limited to the amount unpaid on their shares. The company enters into contracts in its own name and can sue and be sued on these contracts. Partners on the other hand are joint and severally liable for partnership debts without liability.

#### 3. Wider range of borrowing options

Companies are able to create debentures whereas partnerships cannot create debentures. If a creditor wishes to take security for a loan companies are able to create floating charges which will provide a further security option for a company which is not available to partnerships.

#### 4. Transferability of shares

Members are able to transfer shares in a company freely (except where there may be restrictions in place in a private company). To withdraw capital from a partnership would require the approval of the partners and may be subject to further restrictions.

#### 5. Ability to separate ownership from management

In a company it is possible to separate management, undertaken by the directors from ownership of the company, by the members. This can bring benefits to the company. In a partnership all the partners will be able to participate in the management of the firm as well as owing the business.

### Disadvantages of incorporation as a company

#### 1. Registration formalities

A partnership can start trading with no initial formalities saving time and expense, for example the need for professional advice. A company must be registered and a public company will require a trading certificate.

#### 2. Ongoing administrative requirements

Once a company is registered there are ongoing obligations such as completing an annual return, calling meetings including holding an AGM for public companies and complying with the accounts requirements. It may be necessary to appoint auditors. There are restrictions on paying dividends. Partnerships do not have to comply with these provisions.

#### 3. Publicity

Limited companies are required to file accounts and therefore the financial affairs of the company are in the public domain. Partnerships do not have to file accounts and therefore can keep the financial affairs of the partnership private.

# COMPANY REGISTRATION

## Registration procedures

A company is incorporated which means that it is brought into legal existence by registration by the Registrar of Companies. *s15 Companies Act 2006* provides that the certificate of incorporation issued by the Registrar is conclusive evidence of all matters stated on it.

The matters stated on the certificate will be the type of company, fact & date of incorporation.

London
School of Business
& Finance

shaping success in business and finance

**Jubilee Cotton Mills v Lewis** [1925]

The Registrar of Companies registered a company on the 8th January. In error he dated the certificate the 6th January. On the 7th January the directors had allotted shares on behalf of the company. Later the allottees refused to pay, arguing that the company did not exist on that date. The court held that the date on the certificate was conclusive evidence as to the date of incorporation of the company. Therefore the allottees had to pay for the shares.

In order to register a company the following items have to be submitted to the registrar of companies:

**(i)    An application for registration**

Application form IN01 must be completed. The form requires details of:

1. The company's proposed name.

2. Whether the location of the company's registered office is to be in either England and Wales, in Scotland or in Northern Ireland.

3. The address of the registered office.

4. Whether the company is to be unlimited or limited, and if so whether by shares or by guarantee. If it is to be limited by guarantee, there must be a statement of the amount of the guarantee.

5. Whether the company is to be public or private.

6. Whether the company is adopting the model articles of association and whether there are to be any entrenched articles.

7. Particulars of the company secretary and an address for service if the company is to have one. Public companies must have a company secretary who must be qualified. Private companies may have a company secretary.

8. Particulars of the company's first director(s). A public company must have at least two directors, one of which is an individual. A private company can have just one director, who must be an individual. An address for service for the director must be included; this does not have to be the director's residential address.

9. A statement of capital and initial shareholdings, if the company is to be limited by shares. This must state:

   (a)    The class of share.
   (b)    The amount paid up on each share.
   (c)    The amount unpaid on each share.
   (d)    The number of shares.
   (e)    The aggregate nominal value.
   (f)    Particulars of rights attached to each class of share (for example different dividend or voting rights.

10. A statement of guarantee for a company limited by guarantee.

11. A statement of compliance which confirms that the requirements of the Companies Act have been complied with.

**(ii)    A Memorandum of Association.** The person or persons who intend to form the company must sign a memorandum of association agreeing to become members. If the company is limited by shares the subscribers must agree to become shareholders and to take at least one share in the company.

**(iii)    The Articles of Association of the company** in the event that the company chooses not to adopt the model articles or only adopt the model articles in part.

**(iv)    A Registration fee,** which is currently £15 (or £50 to guarantee that the company is registered the same day as the application is received).

**Practice note:** instead of forming a company from scratch it is possible to buy a company 'off the shelf'. There are a number of businesses (generally called company formation agents) that offer this service, and do so cheaply. Although you then have the advantage of an 'instant' company it is very probable that the name and the Articles of the off-the-shelf company are unsuitable for your purposes and will have to be changed.

# Trading certificate (PLCs only)

By virtue of s761 *Companies Act 2006* a newly incorporated public company is not able to commence business (including the borrowing of money) immediately on incorporation. The company must obtain a further certificate from the Registrar called the **Trading Certificate**.

In order to obtain a trading certificate an application is made to the Registrar stating:

1.  that the company has issued shares totalling at least £50,000 in nominal value.

2.  that each share is paid up to at least $\frac{1}{4}$ on the nominal value plus the whole of any premium.

3.  the amount of the preliminary expenses, and who has paid or is to pay them.

4.  any benefits given or to be given to promoters.

If a public company commences trading without a trading certificate:

1.  the company and any officer who is in default is liable to a fine.

2.  the validity of any transaction with the company is not affected: but if the company fails to honour its obligations within 21 days of being required to do so, the directors become jointly and severally liable to third parties.

Under s122 *Insolvency Act 1986* if a public company fails to obtain a trading certificate within a year of incorporation, a petition may be presented by the Government for the winding up of the company.

# Promoters

Q.41 A promoter was defined in the case of **Twycross v Grant** [1877] as a person who 'undertakes to form a company and who takes the necessary steps to accomplish that purpose'

The definition excludes persons acting in a purely professional capacity.

Promoters of the company owe **fiduciary duties** to the company in the event that there are other owners of the company when it is incorporated. The promoter will owe a duty not to obtain advantages or a profit through being a promoter of the company and must make a disclosure of any personal interest he may have to the intended post incorporation company members or board of directors.

If a promoter makes a secret profit from his position as promoter, for example by selling property to the company, the company may:

*   rescind the contract; and
*   claim damages for any loss caused; and
*   require him to account for any profit.

# Pre-incorporation contracts

### What is a pre-incorporation contract?

A pre-incorporation contract is a contract purportedly entered into on behalf of a company before it is incorporated.

### What is the legal effect of a pre-incorporation contract?

1.  The legal difficulty with pre-incorporation contracts is that one of the parties to the contract (the company)

London
School of Business
& Finance

shaping success in business and finance

did not actually exist when the contract was created so the contract will be void. This therefore means:

- The company cannot enforce a pre-incorporation contract (even after incorporation).
- The company cannot, once incorporated, ratify (ie unilaterally adopt) the contract

Example:

**Kelner v Baxter** [1866]

Three promoters of a company bought goods from K on the company's behalf before it was incorporated. Once the company was incorporated it then purported to ratify the contract with K. The court held that the company was not able to ratify the contract since it did not exist at the date the contract was made. Thus K had no claim against the company for payment.

- The third party cannot enforce the contract against the company (even after incorporation and even though the company has benefited from the contract

Example:

Again in the case of *Kelner v Baxter* the company had benefited from and used the goods bought from the third party prior to incorporation, but the third party could not enforce payment.

2. The promoter of the company is purporting to act as an agent for the company in entering into pre-incorporation contracts. *s51(1) Companies Act 2006* provides that the third party can enforce the contract against the promoter personally, although he has no rights against the company. The promoter himself also has the right to enforce the contract against the third party.

In the case of *Phonogram v Lane* the court held that very clear wording in a contract would be needed to avoid the promoter being personally liable under the pre-incorporation contract.

**Phonogram v Lane** [1982]

A company was to be formed to manage a rock band. Phonogram loaned the 'company' £6,000 for business expenses. The promoter signed the loan document "for and on behalf" of the company. The company was never incorporated and Phonogram sued the promoter for the £6,000. The court held that the promoter was personally liable under *s51 Companies Act 2006*. The words "for and behalf of" were not sufficient to negate personal liability on the contract.

**Note** *s51 Companies Act 2006* is a statutory exception to the basic common law rule that agents (or persons purporting to be agents) are not personally liable on the contracts they make.

3. It is possible, once the company is incorporated, for the company, the promoter and the third party to get together and to agree to 'transfer' the contract to the company. This is called "novation".

## COMPANY NAMES

Many companies choose to carry on business under a 'trading' or 'business' name.

However, the *Companies Act 2006* requires every company to have a **registered** name. This name will be the company's name for all company law purposes.

A company's initial registered name must be filed with the registrar of companies on application for registration of the company.

## Restrictions on the choice of a company's registered name

### Positive restrictions

1. If the company is a public company the last words in its name must be 'public limited company' or the abbreviation 'plc' or the equivalent in Welsh.

2. If the company is a private company and limited the last word in its name must be 'limited' or the abbreviation 'ltd' or the equivalent in Welsh.

**Note:** there are no positive requirements for a private unlimited company.

### Negative restrictions

Companies cannot use:

1. plc or ltd except as appropriate.

2. a name that is the same as a name already on the index of names maintained by the Registrar.

3. a name that is the name of a criminal offence (under other legislation).

4. a name that is offensive in the opinion of the Secretary of State.

### Approval restrictions

Approval is needed (primarily from the Secretary of State) for the use of:

1. any name suggesting connection with the Government or any local authority;

2. any word or phrase contained in a Statutory Instrument called the *The Company, Limited Liability Partnership and Business Names (Sensitive Words and Expressions) Regulations 2009* (examples of regulated names include National, British, European; University, Charity, Group, Insurance; Royal, King, Queen, Prince).

### Unwise choices

Companies could encounter significant difficulties if a company name is selected that:

1. Is the name of a company that has recently gone into liquidation. See chapter 17 for further details on the Phoenix company restriction.

2. Is a similar name and the business is simiilar to that of an existing business. See chapter 5 for further details on the tort of passing off.

3. Is a name too like that of an existing registered name. (See below, 'Compulsory change').

4. Is a name which gives a misleading impression of the nature of its business. (See below, 'Compulsory change').

## Alteration of the registered name

**Procedures** – *s77 Companies Act 2006*

The company can change its name at any time by way of special resolution or by any other means provided for in the articles.

By *s78 Companies Act 2006* notice of the name change and a copy of the resolution must be sent to the Registrar of Companies.

Once satisfied that the correct procedures have been followed and the provisions of the *Companies Act 2006* have been complied with the Registrar will enter the new name of the company on the register of companies and will issue a new certificate of incorporation for the company (*s80 Companies Act 2006*).

### Circumstances in which a company may change its name

### 1. Voluntary change

A company may decide to change its name on a voluntary basis at any time for any reason.

### 2. Compulsory change

The Secretary of State and the Names Adjudicators have statutory powers to compel a company to change its name.

A company may also be required to change its name as a result of a **common law** tort action for passing off where a company is cashing in on another's goodwill by having a similar name (see chapter 5 for further details).

**Summary of Secretary of State's statutory powers:**

(i) Name same as, or too like, an existing registered name Secretary of State can require change within a 12 month time period.

(ii) Name is misleading as an indication of the nature of its activities as to be likely to cause harm to the public there is no time period within which the Secretary of State can require a change of name.

(iii) Misleading information/undertakings given when applying for a name requiring approval – Secretary of State has a 5 year time period.

**The Company Names Adjudicators**

The *Companies Act 2006* provides for the creation of the Company Names Adjudicators. The Names Adjudicators work from the UK Intellectual Property Office operating a tribunal to deal with complaints regarding company names. Under the provisions of the *Companies Act 2006* objections can be filed with the Company Names Adjudicator if a new company is registered with a name, which is the same or similar to the name of an existing company with the aim of benefiting from the goodwill built up by the existing company and misleading customers.

**Summary of the Names Adjudicators' statutory powers:**

If Company B is using a similar registered name to Company A in order to cash-in on Company A's goodwill, then Company A can complain to the Names Adjudicators. The Names Adjudicators can then order Company B to change its name; if Company B does not comply, then the Names Adjudicators can change its name.

# ARTICLES OF ASSOCIATION

## Characteristics

Every company must have articles of association.

A company's articles of association are a major constitutional document of the company. The articles set out the rules and regulations relating to the management and running of the company.

There are no statutory mandatory contents of the articles but the articles of most companies will deal with matters such as the procedures for board and general meetings, the appointment of directors and the powers and duties of the directors.

## Model articles

A company may opt to create its own articles of association, but in the event that the company does not wish to create its own set of tailor made articles completely from scratch it may simply adopt the model articles.

The statutory model articles can also be adopted by the company in part to fill in any gaps in its own tailor made articles.

If a company does not submit articles with its application for registration the statutory articles will apply in their entirety.

There are 3 statutory models:

- one for private companies limited by shares;
- one for private companies limited by guarantee;
- one for public companies.

The statutory model articles for public companies is given as an appendix at the end of this manual.

## Legal effect of the articles

*s33 Companies Act 2006* provides that the company's articles are a contract between the company and its members.

Case law shows the articles are a contract which binds:

## 1. the members to the company

Members are bound by the articles to the company and must comply with the procedures laid out in the articles.

Example:

### Hickman v Kent or Romney Marsh Sheep Breeders Association [1915]

Under the company articles, differences between a company and any of the members had to be referred to arbitration. Hickman, a shareholder with a dispute with the company relating to his expulsion from the company, sued the company without referring the matter to arbitration. The court held that Hickman in his capacity as a member was contractually bound by the articles. He could not avoid the procedures for settling disputes laid down by the articles. The company was therefore entitled to have the action stayed and the matter referred to arbitration.

## 2. the company to the members

The company is bound by the articles of association. The company must comply with the provisions of the articles and cannot deny members rights set out in the articles.

Example:

### Pender v Lushington [1877]

The articles gave members a right to vote according to the value of their shareholdings. The company attempted to deny the shareholders the right to vote. The court held that the right to vote provided for in the articles could be enforced against the company.

## 3. the members to the members

Members are able to enforce the provisions of the articles against other members.

Example:

### Rayfield v Hands [1960] HL

The articles of a private company stated "every member who intends to transfer shares shall inform the directors who will take the shares equally between them at a fair value". The directors were also obliged by the articles to become members. The claimant member told the defendant directors that he wanted to transfer his shares but the directors denied liability to take and pay for them. The court held that the articles created a contractual relationship between the claimant as a member and the defendant directors in their capacity as members, therefore a contractual relationship between members.

## BUT

The articles cannot bind the company to any third parties who are non-members (for example directors), nor any member who is acting in a different capacity.

Examples:

### Eley's case, Eley v Positive Life Assurance Company [1876]

The articles appointed E as a solicitor of the company for life. While employed in this capacity E became a member. He was later dismissed as solicitor and brought an action against the company for damages for breach of contract (ie, loss of earnings) contained in the articles. The court held that he could not enforce the provisions of the articles against the company. There was no contract between the company and E as solicitor under the articles. E was an outsider in his capacity as a solicitor. The articles gave him rights only in his capacity as a member and here he was suing to enforce rights as solicitor, not membership rights.

**Beattie v E F Beattie** [1938]

Under the articles, any disputes between a company and any of the members had to be referred to arbitration. Beattie, a shareholder and a director had a dispute with the company relating to access to minutes of board meetings and he sued the company without referring the matter to arbitration. The court held that Beattie in his capacity as a director was not contractually bound by the articles an was thus not bound to refer the dispute to arbitration. The company was therefore not entitled to have the court action stayed.

# Amendment of the articles

s21 *Companies Act 2006* states that the company can alter the articles at any time by way of special resolution (75% of members voting agree). There are, however, both statutory and common law restrictions on the general ability of the company to change its articles.

## Restrictions

1. **Entrenched articles** – *Companies Act 2006*

   A company's articles may entrench specified articles by requiring procedures for amendment that are more restrictive than a special resolution.

   Any provision for entrenchment may only be made:

   (a) in the company's articles on formation, or

   (b) by an amendment to the articles agreed to by all the members.

   Even though an article is entrenched, it may still be amended by agreement of all the members or by court order.

2. **Increase of a member's liability** – *Companies Act 2006*

   A member is not bound by an alteration that increases his liability, unless he agrees to it in writing.

3. **Common law restriction**

   Under common law rules a member will be able to challenge an amendment to the company articles in cases where the amendment was not made **bona fide for the benefit of the company as a whole.**

   The meaning of the common law 'bona fide for the benefit of the company as a whole test' laid down in *Allen v Gold Reefs of Africa* was explained by Evershed MR in **Greenhalgh v Arderne Cinemas** [1951] when he said:

   *".....it is now plain that 'bona fide for the benefit of the company as a whole' means not two things, but one thing. It means that the shareholder must proceed on what, in his honest opinion, is for the benefit of the company as a whole. The phrase, 'the company as a whole' does not (at any rate in such a case as the present) mean the company as a commercial entity distinct from the corporators: it means the corporators as a general body. That is to say the case may be taken of an individual hypothetical member and it may be asked whether what is proposed is, in the honest opinion of those who voted in its favour, for that person's benefit."*

   The test has both subjective and objective elements. Firstly, the subjective test is that whoever proposes the amendment must believe that it is in the interests of the company. Secondly, the objective test is whether the amendment is in the interests of an 'individual hypothetical member'.

   Case law applications of the 'bona fide for the benefit of the company as a whole' test:

   • **Allen v Gold Reefs of Africa** [1900].

   The company's articles gave the company a lien on partly paid shares for debts owing to it. Allen was the only member who had fully paid shares and was the only member who owed money to the company. The company altered its articles to extend the lien to fully paid shares to enable it to collect monies from Allen. Allen objected to the alteration. The court dismissed Allen's objection. The alteration was made to benefit the company as a whole and therefore done bona fide for the benefit of the company as a whole. The hypothetical member would agree to an alteration allowing a company to collect monies owing to it

- **Sidebottom v Kershaw, Leese and Company Limited** [1920].

    The articles were altered to enable directors to purchase at "a fair price the shareholding of any member who competed with the company in its business". A minority shareholder who was in competition sought a declaration that the resolution was invalid. The court held that this amendment was a bona fide alteration in the interests of the company as a whole. This was because (1) the power of expulsion in the articles was only

    exercisable for a stated reason (and not just to acquire minority shareholder's shares) and (2) that stated reason was a reason a hypothetical member would agree was for the benefit of the company (ie not to have a competitor as a shareholder).

- An example of a case where the court held that the amendment could not be justified was the case of **Brown v British Abrasive Wheel** [1920].

    The articles were altered to enable the majority shareholders to purchase at "a fair value the shares of the minority". The intention was to invoke the clause against some minority members who were refusing to inject further capital into the company – capital that the company needed. The minority shareholders objected to the alteration. The court held that this was a not a bona fide alteration in the interests of the company as a whole. This was because no specific reason or objective was stated in the new article for the exercise of the power of expulsion.

# Objects clause and ultra vires

### Introduction

The articles of some companies can contain an article known as the objects clause, which sets out the purpose for which the company was created and the type of business to be conducted by the company.

An objects clause will usually be included in the articles where the company's activities are to be restricted. If the company does not have an objects clause its activities will be completely unrestricted and can be involved in any type of business.

The objects clause can be amended at any time by way of special resolution.

A company has acted ultra vires where it engages in a business or enters into a contract that is outside its objects.

Examples:

### Ashbury Railway Carriage v Riche [1875]

The company had a very restrictive objects clause, which limited the objects of the company to the building of rolling stock only. When the company entered into a contract to build a railway line this was held to be ultra vires.

### Re German Date Coffee [1882]

The company's objects clause stated its business to be "the working of a German patent for the manufacture of coffee from dates". The company was unable to obtain a German patent. However, it obtained a Swedish patent from which it successfully made coffee from dates. A minority member petitioned for the winding up of the company on the ground that it would be just and equitable under s122(g) Insolvency Act 1986. The court held that the entire business of the company was ultra vires. Since it was not possible for the company to carry on business within the confines of its objects clause (as a German patent was not forthcoming) it was just and equitable to wind the company up. (Note: at the date of the case, the law did not allow a company to alter its objects clause).

### What is the effect of an ultra vires act?

The *Companies Act 2006* provides as follows:

1. Under the provisions of ss39 and 40 *Companies Act 2006*, if the company has entered into an ultra vires contract with a third party the third party can enforce the contract against the company (provided that the third party has acted in good faith).

2. The company members can ratify an ultra vires contract entered into by the directors by way of a special resolution (75% of members voting agree).

3. Any member is entitled to obtain an injunction to prevent the company entering into an ultra vires transaction.

4. If directors have caused the company to act ultra vires, for example by entering into an ultra vires contract, this is a breach of duty to the company on the part of the director by virtue of *s171 Companies Act 2006*. (see later, directors' duties, in chapter 12).

5. If a company is unable to carry on business within the limits of its objects clause any member can apply to the court for a winding up order on the 'just and equitable ground' of *s122(g) Insolvency Act 1986*. This is the failure of the substratum rule established in **Re German Date Coffee** [1882] see above.

# STATUTORY BOOKS, RECORDS AND RETURNS

## The registered office

Every company must at all times have a registered office.

It must always be situated within the country as stated in the application for registration as a company.

Initially the address must be notified to the Registrar of Companies when applying for registration of the company.

Subsequently it can be changed (by board resolution). The change is not effective until it has been notified to the Registrar and has been gazetted by him.

## Statutory registers

**All companies** must keep the following **statutory registers** at its registered office:

1. Register of Members, which gives the names and addresses of the members, details of the member's shareholding (the number of shares he holds and the class of share).

2. Register of Debenture holders providing details of any debentures

3. Register of Charges, which gives details of any fixed or floating charges, the chargee, the amount of the charges and any encumbered property.

4. Register of Directors and the Company Secretary, which provides details of the officers names and addresses.

5. Register of Directors' Interests. This is a record of dealings in shares and debentures by the company.

- **PLCs only:**

  Register of Notifiable Interests.

- **Private companies only:**

  Register of Written Resolutions.

## Statutory records

Apart from the statutory registers there are other **statutory records** that must be kept at the registered office:

### 1. A copy of the annual accounts & reports

The items that are required are the:

- balance sheet;
- profit & loss account;
- cash-flow statement (plcs & certain private companies);
- directors' report;
- auditors' report;
- group accounts (parent companies only).

### 2. **Accounting records**

The company's accounting records must be sufficient:

1. to show and explain the company's transactions & to disclose the company's financial position at any time, and
2. to enable the directors to ensure that the annual accounts give a true & fair view.

In particular the accounting records must show:

- day-to-day entries of receipts & expenditure
- a record of assets & liabilities

and where the company deals in goods:

- statements of stock held at the end of each financial year
- all statements of stocktaking
- statements of all goods sold & purchased including identities of the buyers and sellers (except in the case of retail sales).

### 3. **Copies of any instruments creating charges**

### 4. **Minutes of board & general meetings**

### 5. **Copies of directors' service contracts**

## Statutory returns

The following are examples of returns that must be made to the Registrar:

- The annual accounts and reports.
- Special resolutions. Copies of any special resolutions made by the company must be filed with the registrar.
- Changes of directors and in their particulars.
- The annual return. This is a return made on an annual basis by the company which deals matters such as the address of the registered office, details of the members and their shareholdings, details of the directors and company secretary.

# 10

Company law –
share capital

# Syllabus Content

### Share capital

a) Examine the different meanings of capital.
b) Illustrate the difference between various classes of shares.
c) Explain the procedure for altering class rights.

### Capital maintenance and dividend law

a) Explain the doctrine of capital maintenance and capital reduction.
b) Examine the effect of issuing shares at either a discount, or at a premium.
c) Explain the rules governing the distribution of dividends in both private and public companies.

# Chapter contents

# INTRODUCTION TO CAPITAL

Companies can raise two forms of capital to finance the business: share capital and loan capital.

This chapter deals with share capital and the next chapter deals with loan capital.

# MEANING OF SHARE CAPITAL

Issued share capital represents the value of shares that have actually been allotted to shareholders. The company is not obliged to issue all its share capital at once. Some of its capital can be left unissued. The company can increase its issued capital by various means for example the issue of bonus shares or rights issues. The company cannot, however, reduce its issued capital except where it follows the procedures set out at *s641 Companies Act 2006*.

All public limited companies must have a minimum issued share capital of £50,000 in nominal value and each share must be paid up to at least one quarter of the nominal value plus the whole of any premium. There are no minimum or maximum requirements for a private company.

The paid up capital is the amount which the company has raised through the issue of shares. For example if the company has issued 1,000 £1 shares, which are fully paid up the company will have paid up capital of £1,000.

As shares can be issued part paid or unpaid it may agree to only require the shareholder to pay 75p per share at the time of issue, which would give paid up capital of £750. The company can call on the shareholders to pay the remaining £250 at any time or the shareholders may be required to do so by a liquidator on liquidation of the company.

# SHARES

## Nature of a share

All public companies and some private companies will have members who are called shareholders. Companies are able to raise capital through the issue of shares.

A share is a fraction of ownership in a company held by a shareholder or more formally "the interest of a shareholder in the company defined by a sum of money".

A share carries both obligations (for example, the shareholder must pay for his shares) and rights (right to dividends and to vote at meetings). The company articles will detail these rights and obligations. In addition the *Companies Act 2006* details many rights, for example every shareholder has a right to receive a copy of the annual accounts.

# Terminology

### 1. Nominal value

The nominal value of a share is a fixed monetary value given to a share, which the company establishes, when the shares are first issued to shareholders.

For example, the nominal value of each share may be set at £1 by the company. Shareholders must pay for the shares that have been issued to them. Shares cannot be issued below their nominal value (s580 Companies Act 2006 see below), but can be issued to shareholders partly paid. If shares are issued at a higher value than nominal value the shares have been issued at a premium (see below).

### 2. Partly paid shares

If the shareholder is not required to pay the full nominal value of the shares at the time of issue, the shares have been issued partly paid. The company can call on the shareholder to pay the amount outstanding at any time and a liquidator can request payment, should the company go into liquidation.

### 3. Paid up share capital

The company's paid up share capital is the aggregate amount of money paid up on shares which have been issued, ie, the amount actually received by the company on account of the nominal value.

For example, if the company has issued 1,000 £1 shares, which are fully paid up the company will have paid up capital of £1,000. As shares can be issued partly paid it may agree to only require the shareholder to pay 75p per share at the time of issue, which would give paid up capital of £750.

### 4. Called up share capital

The company's called up share capital is the aggregate amount of nominal value that members have been called upon to pay. Full payment might not always be due at the time that the shares are issued (the shares are issued partly paid). Instead, the company may require payment by a number of instalments (this is called making a 'call on shares').

### 5. Market value

Shares in public companies may be transferred to a new shareholder. Once the shares have been issued to the original shareholder at nominal value the shareholder is able to sell them for a different value. The value at which a share can be bought and sold is its market value. This value will depend on demand for the share which can be affected by the success or failure of the company and other market conditions.

### 6. Issued capital

Issued share capital is the shares that have actually be allotted to shareholders. The company can increase its issued capital by various means for example the issue of bonus shares or rights issues. The company cannot, however, reduce its issued capital except where it follows the procedures set out at s641 Companies Act 2006 (see below).

All public limited companies must have a minimum issued share capital of £50,000 in nominal value and each share must be paid up to at least one quarter of the nominal value plus the whole of any premium. There are no minimum or maximum requirements for a private company.

# Classes of share

WHAT IS MEANT BY "CLASS OF SHARE"?

According to *s629 Companies Act 2006* shares are of a class if the rights attached to them are in all respects uniform.

WHAT CLASSES OF SHARES ARE FOUND IN PRACTICE?

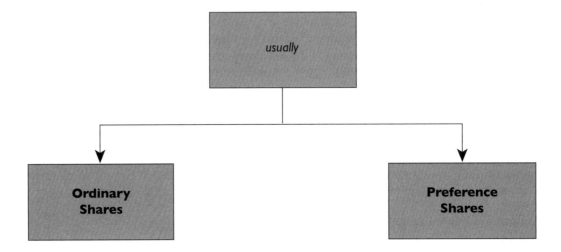

usually

**Ordinary Shares**

**Preference Shares**

# Class rights

CLASS RIGHTS

Class rights are the rights attaching to different classes of shares. The company's articles will set out the different rights and so will vary from company to company.

CLASS RIGHTS ASSOCIATED WITH ORDINARY SHARES AND PREFERENCE SHARES

These rights will vary from company to company but generally the difference between ordinary and preference shares lies in the voting rights, dividend rights and right to return of investment in the shares on a winding up of the company.

The *usual* position is:

## ✓Preference shares

Preference shares are a form of company shares. The company's articles of association will provide full details of the status and rights of the shareholders. Generally, the holders of preference shares will have no or very restricted voting rights and so their participation in the company is limited.

However, preference shareholders may attend class meetings. A class meeting is a meeting for members who hold a particular class of share for example where the company has issued both ordinary and preference shares separate meetings may be required as some company matters may only affect members who hold the preference shares. As with the general meetings, class meetings will be called when they are required and the formalities involved in convening such meetings are the same as they are for general meetings.

Preference shareholders may have priority fixed rights in respect of dividends. Such dividend rights may also so be cumulative, so in the event that the company does not perform as expected one year and is unable to declare a dividend the rights will be carried over to the next year. It is not lawful to make any payment of dividend unless the company has profits.

In the event of the company being wound up preference shareholders will have a prior fixed right to the return of the nominal value paid for the shares ahead of any claim by the ordinary shareholders.

## Ordinary shares

Generally, the holders of ordinary shares have full voting rights in direct proportion to their shareholding and so have full participation in the company. This includes the right to attend the Annual General Meeting (AGM) and vote for any proposed resolutions. All public companies are required to hold an AGM on an annual basis and are required by s337 CA 2006 to hold the meeting on a date which is not more that six months after the accounting reference date. Private companies are not required to hold an AGM. The agenda for the AGM can be dictated by the company as there are no statutory requirements, but may include such matters as the appointment of directors, the election of auditors or the declaration of a dividend. By virtue of s338 Companies Act 2006 members are able to require a item to be included on the agenda if they hold 5% of the voting rights or if together 100 members who each hold an average of £100 paid up share capital request this

Ordinary shareholders generally have the right to fully participate any dividend, after payment of dividend on preference shares. In some cases the performance of the company may mean that dividends are not declared for some period of time. It is not lawful to make any payment of dividend unless the company has profits.

In the case of any surplus of assets given the liquidation of the company, ordinary shareholders can fully participate after return of nominal value to preference shareholders.

## VARIATION OF CLASS RIGHTS - s630 Companies Act 2006

In companies with share capital in order to vary class rights the s630 procedures must be followed. s630 Companies Act 2006 states that:

1. If a method of variation is set out in the company articles this must be followed in order to vary the rights.
2. If no method of variation is set out in the articles class consent must be obtained by either:
   - special resolution at a separate class meeting for holders of the particular class of shares to be varied; or
   - by written consent of the holders of the class of shares if approval is given by the holders of ¾ of the shares issued of that class in nominal value.

## Shareholders rights to object to the variation - s633 Companies Act 2006

Where class rights have been varied under s630 Companies Act 2006 shareholders may have the right to object to the variation, provided three conditions are satisfied. The purpose of this section is to protect minority shareholders.

To object to the variation the following conditions must be satisfied:

1. An application must be made to court on behalf of shareholders which make up at least 15% of the shares issued in that class in terms of nominal value
2. The shareholders objecting must not have consented to the variation
3. The application must be made to the court within 21 days of the date the special resolution was passed or consent was given.

The court may confirm or cancel the variation. Once an application has been made to court, the variation will not take effect until it has been confirmed by the court.

The court will cancel the variation if on the evidence presented the court is satisfied that the variation is unfairly prejudicial to the members of that class of share.

### What is meant by a variation of class rights?

The provisions of *s630 Companies Act 2006* and *s633 Companies Act 2006* come into play only where class rights have been **varied**.

A variation only occurs when the rights attached to shares has actually been changed, for example, if the percentage dividend to be received by a class of shares is changed.

Case law shows that a distinction must be drawn between a variation which merely affects the value, enjoyment or power which is derived from the rights, which would not constitute a variation for the purposes of *s630 Companies Act 2006* and *s633 Companies Act 2006* and a variation which actually **changes** the rights themselves.

Examples:

* A sub-division of shares does not amount to a variation of voting rights.

### Greenhalgh v Arderne Cinemas [1946]

The company's shares were divided into 2 classes: 50p shares and 10p. All shares carried 1 vote. The 50p shares were held by the Mallard family and carried ordinary resolution control. The 10p shares were held by Greenhalgh. There was a proposal to subdivide each 50p share into 5 x 10p shares. Greenhalgh objected on the basis that the proposal varied his voting rights and therefore s630 and s633 must be complied with. The court held that s630 and s633 did not have to be complied with. His voting rights had not been varied since both before and after the share-split he still had one vote per share

* A new issue of shares (whether same class as existing or new class) does not vary the rights of any existing shares, even though the effect may be to dilute the dividend/voting rights of the existing shareholders.

### White v Bristol Aeroplane [1953]

The company issued bonus preference shares to ordinary shareholders. The court held that this was not a variation of the rights of the existing preference shareholders even though the effect was that the ordinary shareholders now had control at class meetings of preference shareholders.

# ISSUE OF SHARES – the payment rules

## Basic common law rule

Payment can be made in any form by the shareholder. The consideration could therefore be cash, goods, services, etc. It is for the company to value any non-cash consideration.

## Statutory rules: all companies

1.  THE NO DISCOUNT RULE – *s580 Companies Act 2006*

    *s580 Companies Act 2006* states that shares cannot be issued by a company at a discount. Issuing shares at a discount means that the share has been issued at a value which is below the nominal value of the share. This prohibition is intended to protect the interests of creditors so the company's share capital is not less than it seems.

    For example, a share has been issued at a discount if the share has been allotted to the shareholder fully paid in return for payment of 75p where the nominal value of the share is £1. This differs from a company issuing shares partly paid where the shareholder remains liable to pay the extra 25p per share if called upon to do so.

    If a company does breach *s580 Companies Act 2006* and does issue shares at a discount the shares are treated as if they had been issued at nominal value and the shareholder must pay the value of any discount plus interest to the company (*s588 Companies Act 2006*). If the share has been sold on to a new shareholder the new shareholder is also liable to pay the value of the discount provided that they were aware of the original discount.

    Under common law principles it is also unlawful for a company to allot a share at less than its nominal value.

    The common law prohibition of the issue of shares at a discount was established in the case of **Ooregum Gold Mining Co of India v Roper** [1892]. In this case the market share of the shares in question was well below the nominal value and to try to obtain new finance the company issued shares with at a discount but still higher than the market value (The company issued £1 shares, credited as fully paid, for 25p). When the company went into liquidation the court held that the shareholders must be required to pay the full nominal value of the shares to the company, ie the 75p discount plus interest.

    In the case of private companies it may be possible to issue shares at a discount if the shareholder makes payment for the shares in the form of goods and services and the value of the goods and services is inflated. This would only be effective, however, if the valuation does seem reasonable. This would not be possible in the case of a public company (see below).

2.  SHARE PREMIUMS – *s610 Companies Act 2006*

    s610 states that "If a company issues shares at a premium, whether for cash or otherwise, a sum equal to the aggregate amount or value of the premiums on those shares shall be transferred to an account called 'the share premium account'."

    The issue of shares at a premium means that the price paid for the shares exceeds the nominal value of the shares at the time of the issue. The premium (the amount by which the price paid exceeds the nominal value) may be in the form of cash or may be other consideration (for example goods or services). In either case the general rule is that the additional consideration paid must be valued and paid into a separate share premium account.

    *s610 Companies Act 2006* provides that the shares premium account may not be reduced and must be treated as if it were part of the company's paid up share capital.

Exceptionally, *s610 Companies Act 2006* permits the share premium account to be applied for the following purposes:

- to pay for bonus issues

  A bonus share issue is defined as a free issue of shares to existing shareholders in direct proportion to the number of shares that they currently own. No new funds for the company are raised and hence the value of the company remains the same as before the bonus issue but the total number of shares in issue increases.

- to pay for expenses etc of an issue of shares

# Additional statutory rules for Public Limited Companies

1. **The one-quarter rule – *s586 Companies Act 2006***

   *s586 Companies Act 2006* states that a public company must not allot a share unless it is paid up to at least one quarter on the nominal value plus the whole of any premium. If shares are allotted in contravention of this section the shareholder must pay the minimum amount required under this rule together with interest.

2. **Subscribers' shares – *s584 Companies Act 2006***

   Subscribers to the memorandum of a public company must pay cash for their subscription shares together with any premium.

3. **Payment for shares must not be in the form of work or services – *s585 Companies Act 2006***

   *s585 Companies Act 2006* states that a public company must at no time accept an undertaking to perform work or services in payment for the shares or any premium payable.

4. **Non-cash consideration must be received within 5 years – *s587 Companies Act 2006***

   *s587 Companies Act 2006* states that a public company is not permitted to accept non-cash payment for shares unless it is certain that performance of the undertaking to give consideration will be complete within five years of the date of allotment.

5. **Non-cash consideration must be independently valued and reported on – *s593 Companies Act 2006***

   *s593 Companies Act 2006* states that the public company may only accept non cash consideration for shares if the consideration is independently valued within six months of the allotment. Independence is achieved by the requirement that the report be made by a person qualified to be the company's auditor and by the requirement that the valuation be done by him or by someone outside the company appointed by him.

# MAINTENANCE OF CAPITAL

## The maintenance principle

**Capital must be maintained. This is to protect creditors.**

The general rule is that company must not reduce capital by returning it to shareholders.

The purpose of the maintenance principle is to protect creditors by treating capital as a guarantee or buffer fund for creditors.

The principle ensures that the capital of solvent companies is not returned to members to the detriment of creditors. The principle applies to capital contributed to the company by shareholders. This generally applies to issued share capital, the share premium account and the capital redemption reserve. The principle has no relevance to loan capital.

An exception to the rule is that capital can be reduced provided that the *s641 Companies Act 2006* procedures are complied with (see below).

## Reduction of Capital – *s641 Companies Act 2006*

### Exception provided by *s641 Companies Act 2006*

Any company may reduce any capital at any time, for any reason.

### Particular situations envisaged by *s641 Companies Act 2006* in which a company may wish to reduce captial:

The first situation allows a company to return paid up capital to shareholders that it no longer has a use for.

The second situation is used where a company can foresee that it is not going to need to raise further capital by making calls on partly paid shares.

The third situation allows a company to write off losses to capital.

### Procedures required for a private company to reduce capital under *s641 Companies Act 2006*

1. The company must hold a General Meeting to pass a special resolution or pass a written resolution to resolve to reduce capital.

2. The directors must make a solvency statement confirming that the company can pay its debts, and will be so able for at least the next 12 months. The statement must be made not more than 15 days before the special resolution is passed. It is a criminal offence for directors to make the statement without having reasonable grounds to do so.

   If the directors are unable to make a solvency statement, the sanction of the court must be obtained in the same way as for a public company to proceed with the reduction of capital.

3. The company must send to the Registrar of companies:
   i)  A copy of the solvency statement;
   ii) A statement of capital as reduced by the resolution;
   iii) A copy of the resolution.

**Procedures required for a public company to reduce capital under _s641 Companies Act 2006_**

1. The company must hold a General Meeting to pass a special resolution to resolve to reduce capital.

2. The company must make an application to the court to sanction the capital reduction.

    The court will consider:

    i) The interests of members

    Members must be treated fairly and equally, and in accordance with class rights as if it were a liquidation.

    ii) The interests of the company creditors

    In situations 1 & 2 the court must (in situation 3 normally will) require the company to settle a list of creditors.

    The court must be satisfied that every creditor of the company who is entitled to object to the reduction of capital has either:

    1) given his consent to the reduction; or

    2) his debt has been discharged or has determined or has been secured.

    iii) The court will not approve a reduction that takes the issued capital below £50,000 (unless it also orders conversion to a private company).

3. The company must send to the Registrar of companies:

    i) A copy of the court order authorising the reduction of capital;

    ii) A statement of capital as reduced by the resolution;

    iii) A copy of the resolution.

# DISTRIBUTIONS

_Exam papes_

## Introduction

A dividend is a payment made to shareholders out of distributable profits of the company, which is a return for their investment in the company shares.

The basic statutory rule regarding dividends is that the company shall not make a distribution except out of profits for the purpose. A company cannot, therefore, pay a dividend out of capital. The procedures for the declaration of dividends will be set out in the company's articles, but it is generally the directors who will recommend the level of dividend payment and the members who will vote by ordinary resolution to declare the dividend.

Additional rules which apply to public limited companies are set out in _s831 Companies Act 2006_. This section is sometimes called the 'net assets' test or the 'full net worth' test. The section provides that both before and after the distribution the company's net assets must be at least equal to the aggregate of its called-up share capital and undistributable reserves.

## Distributable profit

1. The profit that is available for distribution to members is defined by _s830 Companies Act 2006_ as accumulated realised profits (which have not been previously utilised by distribution or capitalisation) less accumulated realised losses (which have not been previously written off in reduction of capital).

    'Accumulated' means that profits and losses from previous years must be included in the calculations.

    A profit or a loss is 'realised' when, for example, the company has actually sold an asset. This is in contrast to an unrealised profit or loss when, for example, the company has re-valued an asset in its books.

**Example**

DEF was incorporated 11 years ago and made net losses of £10,000 for each of the first 10 years. This year it makes a net trading profit of £10,000 and manages to sell a piece of land at a net profit of £130,000. It also re-values another asset upwards by £20,000.

How much, if anything, is available for distribution?

**A** £10,000.

**B** £40,000.

**C** £60,000.

**D** £140,000.

The correct answer is **B**.

The losses of the previous 10 years (totalling £100,000) must be set off against this year's realised profits (£130,000 + £10,000). The unrealised profit (£20,000) arising on the re-valuation is not distributable.

2.  There is an additional rule which applies to public companies is set out in *s831 Companies Act 2006*.

    The overall effect of the rule is to restrict the amount of distributable profit calculated under *s830 Companies Act 2006*.

    This section is sometimes called the 'net assets' test or the 'full net worth' test.

    The section provides that both before and after the distribution the company's net assets must be at least equal to the aggregate of its called-up share capital and undistributable reserves.

    The undistributable reserves are defined by *s831 Companies Act 2006* as:

    i)   The share premium account.
    ii)  The capital redemption reserve.
    iii) The amount by which its accumulated unrealised profits exceed its accumulated unrealised losses (the revaluation reserve).
         The effect of this latter is that a public company must net-off unrealised losses.

3.  The calculation of distributable profit must be made using the latest audited accounts.

    If the auditors qualified the accounts then any distribution is unlawful unless the auditors have stated that the qualification is not material to the calculation of distributable profit.

# Consequences of the payment of an unlawful dividend

In the event of payment of an unlawful dividend the company has the following possible claims to recover the unlawful distribution:

1.  From any member who at the time he received it knew, or had reasonable grounds for knowing, that it was unlawful.
2.  From any director unless he can show he exercised reasonable care in relying on properly prepared accounts
3.  From its auditors if the dividend was paid in reliance of erroneous accounts and the auditors negligently failed to report this.

Any member is able to apply for a court injunction preventing the company from paying an unlawful dividend.

# SUMMARY OF THE MAINTENANCE RULES

1. The **no discount rule** ensures that a company raises capital when it issues shares.

2. **The share premium rule** ensures premiums are credited to a share premium account which is not distributable.

3. **Capital may not be reduced (returned to members).** There is an exception under the formal procedures of *s641 Companies Act 2006* for a reduction of capital.

   There are also other exceptions. These are not covered in this Manual because they are not within the ACCA syllabus.

4. It is unlawful for a company to pay **dividends** except out of profits available for distribution – *s830-831 Companies Act 2006.*

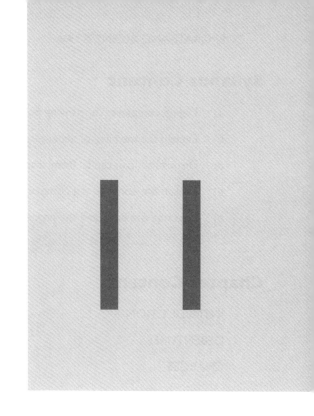

# Company Law –
# Loan capital

## Syllabus Content

a) Define companies' borrowing powers.

b) Explain the meaning of debenture.

c) Distinguish loan capital from share capital.

d) Explain the concept of a company charge and distinguish between fixed and floating charges.

e) Describe the need and the procedure for registering company charges.

## Chapter Contents

INTRODUCTION

DEBENTURES

CHARGES

Types of Charge

Crystallisation of Floating Charges

Advantages of the Floating Charge

Disadvantages of the Floating Charge

Priority of Charges

Registration of Charges

London
School of Business
& Finance

shaping success in business and finance

# INTRODUCTION

Companies may wish to raise capital by borrowing from creditors.  Borrowing can take place in various forms.  This could be in the form of an overdraft with a bank, small loans, or a large mortgage from a bank to fund the purchase of the company's offices, factory or warehouse premises.

Raising finance through borrowing is a very different method of raising finance compared to raising capital through the issue of share capital.  Creditors will not become members of the company and regardless of the performance of the company, the creditor will be entitled to the payment of interest on the loan and repayment of the loan at an agreed time.  In the event of liquidation, creditors will be repaid ahead of shareholders.

Companies incorporated under the 2006 Act will have an implied power to borrow whether or not the company is a trading company.  The company will usually delegate its borrowing powers to the board of directors, who will have the responsibility of dealing with the company's borrowing requirements and will have the power to enter into agreements with lenders.  The company articles may limit these powers.

Debentures are generally created between the company and lender to acknowledge the loan between the two parties.  The debenture document will set out the terms of the loan and particularly the terms regarding repayment.

Some lenders may wish to take security for the loan from the company to attempt to ensure repayment in the event of default by the company or the company entering into liquidation.  A lender can legally take security over a large range of company assets. This chapter will deal with fixed and floating charges.

# DEBENTURES   _Exam paper_

A debenture can be defined as "a document issued by or on behalf of a company containing an acknowledgement of its indebtedness whether charged on the company's assets or not".  The debenture is a contract between the company and the lender.  The lender can therefore enforce the debenture as a contract in the event of default by the borrower.

The debenture document will be set out the terms for interest and repayment. Commonly encountered terms deal with:

- Interest.  The terms regarding interest will determine the rate of interest payable. This may be a fixed or variable rate and may be linked to the Bank of England base rate.  The terms will set out when interest is payable, for example on a monthly basis. In some cases no interest will be payable.

- Date of repayment.  The loan will usually be made for a fixed period of time and will therefore be repayable to the lender in full by the company on a specified date.

- Whether or not secured and, if so, what type of charge.

Debentures may be issued as a single debenture, as a series of debentures or as debenture stock.

Debentures usually rank in the order of creation and so the company will have to pay off the earlier debentures first as they have priority over later debentures.  If the debentures are issued as part of a series a pari passu clause within the debenture will mean that all the loans will rank equally irrespective of the date of creation.

Debentures can either be secured against company assets or not. Where the loan is secured the debenture will create a charge over one or more of the company assets. The two types of charges are fixed and floating charges.

# CHARGES

A lender may take a charge over certain company assets as security for re-payment of the loan that has been made to the company.

A charge creates a prior right over other creditors for the lender to obtain repayment of the loan from the value of the asset over which the charge has been taken. For example, if a lender takes a charge over the company's commercial premises, if the company defaults on the loan, the lender may sell the commercial premises and can obtain repayment of the loan from the proceeds of sale. This is particularly important where the company not only defaults on the loan but also goes into liquidation: if no security had been taken the lender would be an unsecured creditor and would have no prior claim ahead of any other creditor, and it would therefore be far less certain that the lender would be repaid.

Charges may be either fixed or floating charges depending on the type of asset over which the charge is taken.

# Types of Charge

### THE FIXED CHARGE

A fixed charge can be defined as a legal or equitable mortgage on a specific asset(s).

### CHARACTERISTICS:

1.  A fixed charge is created where the company's debt is secured over a particular identified asset belonging to the company.

2.  The effect of the charge is the company may no longer sell or deal with the property without the prior consent of the chargee who will wish to ensure that the asset is not disposed of nor devalued in any way. For example, in the case of land the company will not be able to sell, grant leases or create further charges over the land without the consent of the lender.

3.  In the event that the company defaults on the terms of the loan the charge may provide the right for the lender to sell the property or take possession of the property.

On liquidation the charge will give the lender priority for repayment of their debt from the value of the charged asset ahead of payment to other creditors.

Theoretically fixed charges over any asset whatsoever.

But there are practical considerations. For example consider the practical problems if a company were to create a fixed charge over items of stock-in-trade (inventory) – the company would not be able to sell those items without the consent of the chargee! Therefore in practice fixed charges are often taken over fixed assets that are intended to be owned long-term by the company, such as land, and plant and machinery. It is also common in practice for a chargee that is a bank to take a fixed charge on book debts (ie, debtors) and to require the proceeds of the debts to be paid into a special bank account, from which the company cannot make drawings except with the consent of the that bank.

### THE FLOATING CHARGE

### CHARACTERISTICS:

In the case of *Re Yorkshire Woolcombers Ltd [1903]* a floating charge was identified as having three characteristics.

1.  It is a charge on a class of assets present and future.

2.  The assets within the charge will change from time to time in the ordinary course of the company's business.

3.  The company has the general freedom to deal with the assets in the ordinary course of its business.

As long as the floating charge has not crystallised the company can deal with the charged assets in the ordinary course of its business as it sees fit. This means that a floating charge can be taken over the company's stock in trade. And in practice a floating charge is commonly taken over the whole of the company's business.

Only corporate bodies (eg companies and LLPs) are permitted to create floating charges, which are not available for sole traders or partnerships.

# Crystallisation of floating charges

### What is the Effect of Crystallisation?

Crystallisation means that the floating charge ceases to float over present and future assets and attaches to the assets which are the subject of the charge at the time of crystallisation. The company will no longer be able to deal with the assets freely and consent will be needed from the chargee.

### When Do Floating Charges Crystallise?

The charge document itself will detail the trigger events for crystallisation and will generally include any default on the terms of the charge, for example, non-payment of interest. Otherwise, trigger events will generally include:

*   cessation of business; or

*   liquidation.

# Advantages of the Floating Charge (as opposed to the fixed charge)

1.  The company is free to use the charged assets in the ordinary course of its business, without needing the consent of the lender. Therefore, the company can for example buy and sell stock subject to a floating charge as it requires for its business without requiring permission from the lender. It is only when the charge crystallises that the company is no longer free to deal with the assets.

2.  In the case of a floating charge a wider class of assets can be charged, as the assets do not have to be long term assets of the company and can be assets that change on a day to day basis such as stock in trade.

# Disadvantages of the Floating Charge (as opposed to the fixed charge)

1.  It will be impossible to predict the value of the charged assets until crystallisation, as the assets within the charge will be changing on a day to day basis. Contrast this with a fixed charge over freehold property of which the value will remain relatively constant enabling the lender to predict whether or not this is adequate security for the value of the loan.

2.  By virtue of *s245 Insolvency Act 1986* a floating charge will be invalid if it was created within the 12 months immediately preceding commencement of winding up and at a time when the company was unable to pay its debts. This is not applicable to fixed charges.

3.  Fixed charges take priority over floating charges and therefore the fixed chargee will have their loan repaid ahead of the floating charge if, for example, the company goes into liquidation.

4.  The Insolvency Act requires preferential creditors (employees owed wages in an insolvency) to be paid out of floating charge assets prior to the floating chargee.

# Priority of Charges

Where a company has created a number of charges over the same asset, for example, a first and a second charge over the company's business premises it may be necessary to ascertain which charge has priority and therefore which of the lenders will have the right to be repaid first, particularly in the event of liquidation.

There are two basic rules:

1.   With equal charges, where the charges are of the same type, the charge that was created first in time takes priority.

2.   With unequal charges (for example, a fixed charge and a floating charge) fixed charges will always have priority over floating charges, except where the charge document provides that the floating charge will have priority over any subsequent fixed charges. This is known as a negative pledge clause. However, in order for the floating chargee to retain priority over a later fixed chargee the fixed chargee must have actual knowledge of the negative pledge clause. If the fixed chargee has no knowledge of the clause it will have no effect.

An unregistered charge that is registerable does not obtain priority over a registered charge.

## Registration of charges

There are two places where charges must be registered:

### I. REGISTRATION AT COMPANIES HOUSE: s860 Companies Act 2006

Nearly all charges must be registered with the Registrar of Companies within 21 days of creation.

Registration of the charge must be effected by the company or any person interested in the charge. This latter is the chargee.

If the company fails to register the charge:

*   The company and every officer in default may be fined.

*   Any monies secured under the charge become immediately repayable by the company.

*   An unregistered charge is void as against a liquidator: therefore on liquidation the chargee will be an unsecured creditor.

### 2. REGISTRATION AT THE COMPANY'S OWN REGISTERED OFFICE

Under the provisions of the *Companies Act 2006* the company must:

(i)    Keep a copy of every instrument creating a charge at the company's registered office (*s875*); and

(ii)   Enter short particulars of the charge in the company's Register of Charges (*s876*).

If the company fails to comply with either *s875* or *s876*, the company and every officer in default is liable to a fine.

In addition, all charges over land must be registered at the land registry.

# 12

## Company law – directors

# Syllabus Content

a) Explain the role of directors in the operation of a company.

b) Discuss the ways in which directors are appointed, can lose their office or be subject to a disqualification order.

c) Distinguish between the powers of the board of directors, the managing director and individual directors to bind their company.

d) Explain the duties that directors owe to their companies.

e) Demonstrate an understanding of the way in which statute law has attempted to control directors.

# Chapter Contents

INTRODUCTION

THE OFFICE OF DIRECTOR

APPOINTMENT OF DIRECTORS

    Qualification And Disqualification

    Appointment & Reappointment Procedures

    Service Contracts of Directors

TERMINATION OF OFFICE OF DIRECTORS

    Methods Of Termination Of Office

    *s168 Companies Act 2006*

GENERAL DUTIES OF DIRECTORS

    To Whom Are The Duties Owed?

    What Are The Duties?

    Further Add-Ons

AGENCY POSITION OF DIRECTORS

    Common Law Rules

    Statutory Rules

# Introduction

This chapter deals with the important topic of the company directors who have responsibility for the running and management of the company.

There are statutory rules contained in the *Companies Act 2006* regarding the appointment and removal of directors which will be considered in detail.

Directors owe statutory duties to the company in performing their roles. The main duties are set out at *s171-s177 Companies Act 2006*. These duties will be dealt with later in the chapter.

The agency position of directors to bind the company in contract with third parties will also be considered.

This chapter covers the law regarding directors. Non-legal recommendations by the Combined Code on Corporate Governance of best practice regarding directors is covered in Chapter 16.

# The Office of Director

### What is meant by the term 'director'?

The board of directors is responsible for the general direction and management of the company. Directors derive their powers from the company's articles and statutory provisions. The exercise of these powers is carried out at Board meetings. The legal function of directors is to attend Board meetings and participate in strategic decision-making.

*s250 Companies Act 2006* states that the term director "includes any person occupying the position of director by whatever name called". A de jure director will have been properly appointed by the company to act as a director in accordance with the company's articles of association and will have agreed to act as director.

The test to determine whether a person is actually a director is thus a test of function, not of title. Therefore, a person may be performing the role of a director may be a director even if he has not been given the title of director, he will be a de facto director in this case. Conversely, a person may well be given the title of director (eg 'Director of Publishing' – this is often done to upgrade an employee's status): such a person is not a director in the legal sense unless he participates in strategic decision-making at Board meetings.

Larger companies may have a number of directors serving specific roles in the company and may also benefit from the expertise of non-executive directors.

### What is meant by the term 'non-executive' director?

There is no general legal requirement for a company to have non-executive directors. However, all companies that are listed on the London Stock Exchange are required by the listing rules to comply with the Combined Code on corporate governance, which gives non-executive directors an important role within the board. See chapter 16 for further details.

A non-executive director's function is to attend Board meetings. Non-executive directors therefore generally work part time for the company and do not have any direct day-to-day involvement in the management of the company.

Independent non-executive directors are useful in that they often have considerable expertise, which often strengthens the Board strategic decision making. They can also use their experience to effectively scrutinise and influence the Board's decisions and independently monitor performance on behalf of the shareholders.

### What is meant by the term 'executive' director?

There is no legal requirement for a company to have executive directors.

An executive director is a company director who also has responsibility for a specific role within the company itself (for example, finance director) as well as the requirement to attend board meetings. He is therefore usually a full time employee receiving a salary.

### What is meant by the term 'managing director'?

The managing director can be known by other titles, such as chief executive.

There is no legal requirement for a company to have an MD but the company articles will usually allow for one to be appointed. The model articles allow the board to appoint the MD if required. The person appointed by the board as MD must already be a director.

The model articles allow the board to delegate to the MD the day-to-day management of the company's business. Thus the board can give the MD actual authority as it sees fit. The MD also has apparent authority to enter into all contracts of a commercial nature (***Freeman & Lockyer v Buckhurst Park Properties*** see below and chapter 7).

# What is meant by the term 'chairman of the board'?

The principal function of the chairman is to chair board meetings (and very likely also meetings of members). The chairman may have additional functions, for example, he commonly acts as spokesman for the company.

There is no legal requirement for a company to have a chairman, although all meetings must have someone as chairman.

# What is meant by the term 'alternate director'?

The company articles may permit an alternate director to be appointed by a director to attend a board meeting on his behalf, if the director cannot attend for some reason. The appointed alternate would be able to vote at the board meeting in place of the director.

# Statutory minimum number of directors – *s154 Companies Act 2006*

Public companies are required to have at least two directors.

Private companies are required to have at least one director.

There is no statutory maximum number of directors for either public or private companies.

# What is meant by the term 'shadow director'? – *s251 Companies Act 2006*

A shadow director is a person who is not a director of the company and therefore if a person has been appointed as a director he cannot be a shadow director even if he does not take part in the management of the company as required.

*s251 Companies Act 2006* states that "a shadow director means a person in accordance with whose directions or instructions the directors of a company are accustomed to act. However, a person is not deemed a shadow director by reason only that the directors act on advice given by him in a professional capacity". Whether or not a person is a shadow director is a question of applying the definition to the facts of the case.

Many statutory provisions regarding directors apply to shadow directors also, for example, the wrongful trading provisions of the *Insolvency Act 1986*, and the *Company Directors Disqualification Act 1986* 'unfitness' provisions.

# APPOINTMENT OF DIRECTORS

# Qualification and Disqualification

### Qualification – *s157 Companies Act 2006*

There is a minimum age requirement for directors of 16 years. There is no maximum age limit.

### Disqualification

Disqualification of a director can arise in a number of ways:

### 1. Disqualification under the provisions of the company Articles of Association

Such provisions will vary from company to company, but it would be common to provide that a director is disqualified from acting if he becomes of unsound mind.

### 2. Disqualification of undischarged bankrupts

Under the provisions of the *Company Directors Disqualification Act 1986* undischarged bankrupts are automatically disqualified from acting as company directors.

### 3. Disqualification by Court disqualification order

The court may make a disqualification order under the *Company Directors Disqualification Act 1986*.

The effect of court disqualification order is that the director subject to the order cannot be concerned, either directly or indirectly, in the management of any company. A disqualified director in addition cannot be a company promoter, insolvency practitioner or member of an LLP.

There are three categories of conduct that can lead to the making of a disqualification order:

### 1. General misconduct

(a) Persistent default in companies' legislation filing requirements.

A director may be disqualified under the provisions of the *Company Directors Disqualification Act 1986* where the director has been persistently in default in complying with particularly the *Companies Act 2006* requiring any return, account or other document to be filed with, delivered or sent, or notice of any matter to be given, to the registrar of companies.

Persistent default in filing is defined in the *Company Directors Disqualification Act 1986* as three or more incidents of default in a period of five years.

The maximum period of disqualification is 5 years.

(b) On conviction of serious offence in connection with management promotion, formation, management or liquidation of a company or with the receivership or management of a company's property.

An example of such a serious offence would be if a director becomes involved in insider dealing. Insider dealing is the acquiring or disposing of securities given access to inside information, whether as a principal or agent, in a regulated market (see later chapter on fraudulent behaviour).

The maximum period of disqualification is 15 years.

(c) In the event that the director is found guilty of the *s993 Companies Act 2006* offence of fraudulent trading (see later chapter on fraudulent behaviour) or been guilty, while an officer or liquidator of the company of any fraud in relation to the company or of any breach of his duty as such officer, liquidator or administrator.

The maximum period of disqualification is 15 years

### 2. Disqualification for unfitness

(a) When a director is or has been a director of a company, which has become insolvent and that his conduct as a director of that company makes him unfit to be concerned in the management of a company.

The minimum period of disqualification is two years and the maximum is 15 years.

(b) A director may be unfit to be concerned in the management of a company as shown after a Government investigation. In addition, an order can be made if it appears to the Secretary of State that it is expedient in the public interest that a disqualification order should be made against the director.

The maximum period of disqualification is 15 years.

In the event that the court is called on to determine whether a director's conduct makes him unfit to be concerned in the management of a company the court should have regard to:

(i) The matters listed in Part I of the First Schedule to the *Company Directors Disqualification Act 1986*.

(ii) In the case of an insolvent company to Part II of the First Schedule to the *Company Directors Disqualification Act 1986*.

Examples of the line taken by the courts in such cases are:

- In **Re Lo-Line Electric Motors Ltd** [1988] Sir Nicholas Browne-Wilkinson VC declared that 'while ordinary commercial misjudgement is not in itself sufficient to establish unfitness, certain conduct would be sufficient to justify disqualification'.

Examples of such conduct include:

- conduct which displays 'a lack of commercial probity';
- conduct which is grossly negligent;
- conduct which displays 'total incompetence'.

The court made clear that the primary purpose of the legislation is to protect the public from directors running companies whose past record in the role of a director has shown that they pose a risk to creditors and other parties, rather than to punish the director for their conduct.

- **Re Sevenoaks Stationers Ltd** [1990] the court held that a director can be unfit to act as a director due to incompetence and negligence despite the fact that there is no evidence of dishonesty on the part of the director.

### 3. Other Cases of Disqualification

Where a director has been found liable for

(a) Fraudulent trading *(s213 Insolvency Act 1986)*

A director will be liable for fraudulent trading if it emerges in the course of winding up a company that a person has knowingly carried on a business with the intent to defraud creditors or for any fraudulent purpose (see later chapter on fraudulent behaviour).

(b) Wrongful trading *(s214 Insolvency Act 1986)*

Liability for wrongful trading occurs where a company is in insolvent liquidation and the director knew or ought to have known that there was no reasonable prospect of avoiding the insolvent liquidation and he failed to take all the steps that he could take in order to minimise the potential loss to creditors. (see later chapter on fraudulent behaviour).

The maximum period for disqualification is 15 years.

### Breach of a disqualification order

In the event that a director breaches a disqualification order:

1. This is a criminal offence and anyone found guilty is liable to a fine or imprisonment or both.

2. The director will have personal liability for any or all of the debts of any company with regard to which he acted whilst subject to a disqualification order.

## Appointment and reappointment procedures

### First directors

The **first** directors are appointed by the company promoters on application for registration of the company. Their details must be on Form IN01.

### Subsequent directors

After incorporation it may be necessary to replace the original directors, particularly in the case of an off the shelf company, or to appoint additional directors.

The appointment procedures will be set out in the company's articles and will therefore vary from company to company.

The statutory model for public companies allows the **initial appointment** to be made by:

- the members by ordinary resolution
- the board of directors either:
    - to fill a casual vacancy;
    - to make an additional appointment.

As regards **retirement and reappointment** the statutory model for public companies provides:

- At the first AGM all directors retire.
- At every subsequent AGM:
  - board appointees retire
  - any director not appointed or reappointed at one of the last two AGMs retire. This provision, commonly called 'retirement by rotation' means that a director's tenure is subject to scrutiny by the members every three years.

All retiring directors may be reappointed by ordinary resolution.

The Combined Code on Corporate Governance makes similar recommendations – see Chapter 16.

## Service contracts of directors

1. Not every director has an expressly agreed service contract. In practice executive directors will have.

2. The *model articles* state that it is for the Board to decide the terms of a director's service contract.

   A director must not vote on his own service contract.

   The Combined Code on Corporate Governance makes further recommendations – see Chapter 16.

3. *s188 Companies Act 2006* states that long term service contracts, which are for a fixed term of two years or more, must be approved by ordinary resolution.

   If the members do not approve the contract the contract is deemed to contain a clause allowing the company to terminate the contract at any time on the giving of reasonable notice.

   Directors' service contracts of long duration is considered an issue. This is due to the fact that it generally increases the possibility that directors do not act in shareholder interests owing to the fact that procedures to remove a director can be complex and their ability to self determine the terms of contract and, in particular, remuneration for a long duration. The issue of the length of the contract also comes to the fore when a director is removed from his office in breach of his contract – the company will be liable in damages for the unexpired term: very long contracts will mean very large damages.

   To counter this, the Combined Code recommends that all directors should be submitted for regular re-election, ideally on an annual basis - see Chapter 16 for further on this aspect.

# TERMINATION OF OFFICE OF DIRECTORS

## Methods of termination of office

A director's period in office can be ended by any of the following methods:

1. **Death.**

2. **Dissolution of company** following liquidation of the company.

3. **Disqualification:**

   (i) By virtue of the company articles

   The company articles may provide grounds under which the director will be unable to continue in the position. Common grounds for disqualification will include bankruptcy and if the director becomes of unsound mind.

(ii) Under the provisions of *Company Directors Disqualification Act 1986.*

A director may be removed from office by reason of disqualification by court order under the provisions of the *Company Directors Disqualification Act 1986.* The court is likely to make a disqualification order under the Act where a director is liable for wrongful or fraudulent trading, has consistently failed to comply with statutory filing requirements or in some way has been found to be unfit to be concerned in the management of a company (see above).

### 4. Retirement:

- On expiry of a fixed term contract (if any).
- By virtue of the company's articles, for example, the rotation procedures (see above).

### 5. Resignation.

### 6. Removal:

- As the individual company's articles may provide. For example, many companies' articles will allow the Board to remove directors who fail to attend board meetings.
- Under the *s168 Companies Act 2006* procedure by ordinary resolution of the members in General Meeting, see below.

## s168 Companies Act 2006

### s168 Companies Act 2006

*s168 Companies Act 2006* provides that a company can remove a director by ordinary resolution at a meeting at any time.

### Procedural steps

1. Whoever is proposing the resolution to remove the director must give special notice to the company of 28 days. The proposers might be the Board or it might be a member or members.

   In general the Board can always set the agenda of a meeting of members and therefore propose resolutions. The ability of members is restricted – this is dealt with in detail in Chapter 14.

2. On receipt of the special notice the company must forthwith send a copy to the director concerned. The director has a right to circulate written representations regarding his removal.

3. At the general meeting the director's written representations must be read out in the event that there was insufficient time to circulate the representations to members prior to the meeting. The director also has the right to address the meeting to make oral representations.

4. The director can then be removed by way of ordinary resolution. This is a simple majority of the votes that are cast.

### Overriding nature of s168 Companies Act 2006

The provisions of *s168 Companies Act 2006* **override** any contrary provisions in the company's constitution and any individual contracts with directors.

Therefore, the *s168 Companies Act 2006* procedure **can always be used to remove a director** despite any contrary provisions either in:

- the company articles, for example if the articles state that a director may only be removed by special resolution; or
- the director's service contract with the company, for example if the contract states that the director cannot be removed before the expiry of a fixed term.

*s168 Companies Act 2006* does not deprive a director of any right to sue for damages for breach of his service contract.

London
School of Business
& Finance

*shaping success in business and finance*

# GENERAL DUTIES OF DIRECTORS – *s171 Companies Act 2006*

*s171 - s177 Companies Act 2006* set out the general duties which company directors owe to the company. Prior to the Companies Act 2006 directors' duties were common law and equitable duties. The Act has codified the duties to provide certainty and clarity. Some of the directors' duties are fiduciary duties, which are higher duties imposed on persons in a position of trust.

The seven duties are cumulative. This means that more than one duty could apply in a given situation. For example, if a director takes a bribe he will be in breach of the duty not to accept benefits from third parties (number 6 below), and in breach of the duty to avoid conflicts of interest (number 5 below), and also possibly in breach of the duty to exercise independent judgment (number 3 below). When the court is deciding whether or not a director has breached his duties, the *Companies Act 2006* requires the court to consider what the director did in the context of each individual duty in turn.

## To whom are the duties owed?

### The general common law rule

The general duties are owed to the company and not individual members of the company. This means that it is for the company to sue directors who are in breach of duty, not shareholders.

Example:

### Percival v Wright [1902]

The directors purchased shares from a member without disclosing to the member that they were in negotiation to sell the company. The sale of the company would inflate the share prices in the company considerably. The court held that the shareholder could not sue to have the sale of his shares set aside because directors owe no duty to individual shareholders.

### The new statutory derivative action

*s260 - s264 Companies Act 2006* provides for a new procedure whereby shareholders can bring actions against a director(s) for negligence, default, breach of duty or breach of trust on behalf of the company. This is a change to the general common law rule that such actions should be brought by the company itself rather than by shareholders.

The derivative action procedure can be used where there is an alleged breach of any of the statutory directors duties contained in the *Companies Act 2006*, considered above.

A filter process has been established by the Act so that claims cannot be brought by shareholders in a situation where this would not be in the interests of the company:

In stage one of the process, the shareholder who wishes to bring a claim must obtain the consent of the court to commence an action against a director. The shareholder will file a claim together with evidence at court. The court will establish whether the shareholder has a prima facie case against the director based on the evidence that has been submitted. The court will either dismiss the claim at this stage or allow it to proceed.

In the second stage of the process, the court will consider evidence from all the parties. The court is required to refuse permission for the claim to continue in the event that:

(a) a person acting in accordance with *s172 Companies Act 2006* duty to promote the success of the company would not seek to continue the claim.

(b) the act of omission complained of has been authorised or ratified by the company.

The court must also consider whether:

- Whether the member bringing the claim is acting in good faith.
- The importance that a person acting in accordance with s172 Companies Act 2006 would attach to continuing the claim.
- Whether the company has decided not to pursue the claim.
- Whether the member has a cause of action they could pursue in their own right.

- In considering whether to give permission to continue the claim the court shall have particular regard to any evidence before it as to the views of members of the company who have no personal interest, direct or indirect, in the matter.

If permission is granted by the court the case against the director will continue as a normal action in the courts.

Note that any damages recovered from a director will be payable to the company, not to the shareholder bringing the action. This is because the shareholder is bringing the action on behalf of the company, not on behalf of himself.

# What are the duties?

## 1. Duty to act within powers – s171 Companies Act 2006

A director must:

### 1. act in accordance with the company's constitution.

If, for example, directors take the company into an ultra vires contract and thereby cause loss to the company, the company can sue the directors for damages. Ultra vires was covered in detail in chapter 9. This means that directors must act in accordance with the company's articles of association, which is the principal source of the directors' powers.

### 2. only exercise powers for the purposes for which they were conferred.

This means that directors must not exercise their powers for an ulterior motive nor for personal gain.

Most of the case law relating to this duty has arisen in relation to the directors' power to allot shares. It is a breach of duty for directors to cause a company to issue shares in order to manipulate control within a company rather than for the proper purpose of raising capital.

Examples:

### Hogg v Cramphorn [1967]

The directors learned of a takeover bid and that should the bid be successful the new controllers would change the board of directors. To defeat the takeover, they caused the company to issue 5,000 new shares to the employees' pension scheme, knowing that the trustees of the pension scheme would vote against the takeover bid. The court held that the share issue was an improper exercise of the directors' powers and was thus invalid.

### Howard Smith v Ampol Petroleum [1974]

The directors supported a takeover bid for the company. They therefore issued shares to the bidder to destroy the voting power of the majority shareholders who the directors knew would vote against the bid. The directors believed they were acting in the best interests of the company. The court held that this was an improper exercise of directors' powers and was therefore invalid. The sole motive for the share issue was to enable a takeover bid to succeed which the majority shareholders were otherwise in a position to block. The court stated: "directors must not use fiduciary powers to manipulate control of a company".

Such transactions, where a director is in breach of the directors' duty to act within their powers, can be set aside by the court. The company can ratify acts in breach of duty by resolution at a meeting. The director involved and any members connected to the director will not be permitted to vote. Any member with shares that have been issued to them in the allotment in question will not be permitted to vote.

## 2. Duty to promote the success of the company – s172 Companies Act 2006

This new statutory duty requires a director

**to act in the way he considers, in good faith, would be most likely to promote the success of the company for the benefit of its members as a whole.**

The duty enshrines into statute the concept commonly referred to as 'Enlightened Shareholder Value'.

'Success' is not specifically defined in the Companies Act 2006.

The *Companies Act 2006* requires directors to consider <u>various stakeholders</u> of the company. The stakeholders are parties who have a direct or indirect interest in the activities of the company, such as employees, consumers or members of the community in which the company conducts its business. The new duty has the aim of requiring directors to consider a more long term view of the company's business and consider wider corporate social responsibility issues.

In performing this duty the *Companies Act 2006* states that directors must have regard to the following list of matters when making business decisions:

- the likely consequences of any decision in the long term,
- the interests of the company's employees,
- the need to foster the company's business relationships with suppliers, customers and others,
- the impact of the company's operations on the community and the environment,
- the desirability of the company maintaining a reputation for high standards of business conduct, and
- the need to act fairly as between members of the company.

The list is not intended to be an exhaustive list of matters to consider. Directors should be able to show that each of the items of the list has been considered, but the Act does not provide for any of the items to have priority over the other matters. This will be a business decision for the directors based on 'good faith judgement' per the Government's explanatory notes to *Companies Act 2006*.

It may prove difficult for directors to successfully deal will all competing interests contained in the list where such matters may be in conflict. For example, if shareholders require payment of a dividend in a situation where the company would benefit from further capital investment or where the use of environmentally friendly products may prove to be more expensive for the business.

Despite the fact that the list deals with the interests of a number of stakeholders, directors will still only be liable to the company for breach of this duty.

## 3. Duty to exercise independent judgment – *s173 Companies Act 2006*

### A director must exercise independent judgment.

The director must therefore avoid situations where his decisions are manipulated by others for example, shareholders, or other directors.

## 4. Duty to exercise reasonable care, skill and diligence – *s174 Companies Act 2006*

### A director must exercise reasonable care, skill and diligence in performing his duties.

Reasonable care, skill and diligence means the care, skill and diligence that would be exercised by a reasonably diligent person with –

(a) the general knowledge, skill and experience that may reasonably be expected of a person carrying out the functions carried out by the director in relation to the company, (the objective test) and

(b) the general knowledge, skill and experience that the director has (the subjective test).

Example:

### Dorchester Finance Company v Stebbing [1989]

The company was a money lending-company and had three directors, Stebbing, Parsons and Hamilton. No board meetings were ever held. Parsons and Hamilton left all the affairs of the company to Stebbing: their only contribution was to sign blank cheques on the company's account and leave them for Stebbing to do what he liked with. Contrary to statute the company had no money-lending licence and therefore all the loans it made were unenforceable.

The court held that all three directors were in breach of a duty of care and skill.

(1) Stebbing was liable because as a chartered accountant he should have known that a money lending licence was necessary.

(2) Parsons and Hamilton were liable because they made no enquiry as to the use of the cheques and therefore this meant they had participated in Stebbing's wrong.

### 5. Duty to avoid conflicts of interest – s175 Companies Act 2006

**A director must avoid a situation in which he has, or can have, a direct or indirect interest that conflicts, or possibly may conflict, with the interests of the company.**

This duty applies in particular to the exploitation of any property, information or opportunity.

This duty does not apply to transactions or arrangements with the company (but such transactions will be caught by s177 *Companies Act 2006* below).

This duty continues to apply to an ex-director as regards any matter he became aware of while he was a director (see *IDC v Cooley* below).

If a director makes a profit from such an interest he is accountable to the company. It is immaterial whether the company could take advantage of the property, information or opportunity.

Examples:

### Regal (Hastings) v Gulliver [1967] HL

The directors of a company pumped capital into a company by buying shares so that the company could run a cinema. The venture was successful and the directors sold their shares at a profit. Control of the company changed hands and the new controllers caused the company to sue the ex-directors for breach of fiduciary duty. The court held that the directors must account to the company for the profit they had made. The directors had made the profit through an opportunity that came to them via their directorships. It was no defence that the company itself was unable to fund the venture.

### IDC v Cooley [1972]

C was the MD of IDC tasked with negotiating consultancy contracts for IDC. In that capacity he met the Gas Board and, using his best endeavours, began negotiations for the award of a contract to IDC. It became apparent that Gas Board would not award the contract to IDC. Being impressed by C's personal qualities the Gas Board indicated he should make a personal pitch for the contract. Over the weekend he prepared his personal presentation. He obtained a release from his service contract with IDC on the ground of mental ill-health. He was then awarded the Gas Board contract. The court ordered C to account to IDC for the profits made under the contract despite the fact that:

(1) IDC itself would not have been awarded the contract in any event;

(2) C gained the contract largely through his personal qualities

(3) C made the profit after he ceased to be a director.

### Provisos:

The duty is not contravened if the matter cannot reasonably be regarded as likely to give rise to a conflict of interest or has been authorised by the directors at a board meeting.

Note the following points regarding board authorisation:

- if the company is public, authorisation by the directors is not allowed unless the company articles specifically provide that authorisation is permitted in the circumstances,
- at the board meeting, the interested director is not counted towards the quorum and, if he votes on the matter, his vote is not counted.

### 6. Duty not to accept benefits from third parties – s176 Companies Act 2006

**A director must not accept a benefit from a third party conferred by reason of his being a director or his doing (or not doing) anything as director.**

For example, a director will contravene this duty if he accepts a payment from a third party to agree to recommend to the board that the company should enter into a contract with a particular company.

There may be some overlap with the duty to avoid conflicts of interest above as with the example given.

This duty is not contravened if the acceptance of the benefit cannot reasonably be regarded as likely to give rise to a conflict of interest.

Note that this duty applies to both current and to ex-directors of the company.

## 7. Duty to declare interest in proposed transaction or arrangement with the company – s177 Companies Act 2006

**If a director is interested, directly or indirectly in a proposed transaction with the company, he must declare the nature and extent of that interest to the other directors before the company enters into the transaction.**

For example, if a director is a member of another company with which the company intends to enter into a contract, the director must declare his interest at the earliest opportunity and this must be prior to the board decision to enter into this contract. Where a director has disclosed an interest he may be excluded from voting in relation to the transaction.

If a declaration of interest proves to be, or becomes, inaccurate or incomplete, a further declaration must be made.

If no declaration is made, the contract is voidable at instance of company and the director must account for any gain whether or not the company may profit from the transaction or arrangement.

Example:

### Aberdeen Railway v Blaikie [1854] HL.

The company bought some goods from a partnership. At the time of the contract one of the company's directors, unknown to the company, was a partner in the firm. The court held that the company could avoid the contract because of this undisclosed conflict of interest on the part of the director. The court rejected the argument of the partnership that this was unjustifiable because the contract was on ordinary commercial terms and the company would not suffer by it. The court stated that the mere fact of non-disclosure renders the contract voidable regardless of whether or not non-disclosure causes any loss to the company.

# Further add-ons

### Declaration of interest in an existing transaction or arrangement with the company – s182 Companies Act 2006

In the same way as s177 Companies Act 2006 (interest in a proposed transaction with the company), a director must declare any interest in a transaction that has already been entered into by the company as soon as is reasonably practicable. Where a declaration has already been made by the director under s177 Companies Act 2006 this section does not apply.

If a declaration of interest proves to be, or becomes, inaccurate or incomplete, a further declaration must be made.

Failure to make the declaration is a criminal offence and any director infringing this section may be fined.

### Substantial property transactions – s190 Companies Act 2006

As a general rule all substantial property transactions must be approved by the members.

A substantial property transaction is a transaction in which a director (or connected person) intends to sell to, or acquire from, the company any one or more non-cash asset which exceeds the lesser of £100,000 or 10% of the company's asset value. (Save that no approval needed where requisite value is less than £5,000).

If there is no such approval:

- the transaction is voidable at instance of company, and
- the director (and connected person, and other directors who authorised transaction) are liable to account to company for any gain and/or indemnify company for any loss.

# AGENCY POSITION OF DIRECTORS

When directors act for the company, they are acting as its agents. The company will be bound by their actions in accordance with the common law principles of agency as applied to company law and as modified by the *Companies Act 2006*.

## Common law rules

Where a director acts outside the scope of his authority, the contract, at common law, is voidable at the company's option. Where the third party has suffered loss as a result, he can sue the director personally for breach of warranty of authority.

Most companies' articles delegate entire running of the business to the board, and further allow the board to sub-delegate to individual directors and others.

The authority of a director may be **express, implied** or **apparent**.

- **Express**

    For example, the board passes a resolution which authorises a director to borrow £50,000 on behalf of the company.

- **Implied**

    If a person occupies a particular office he has implied authority to bind the company to contracts that are usual to that office **(Hely-Hutchinson v Brayhead Ltd)**.

- **Apparent**

    Where a company holds out a person as occupying a particular position it is then stopped from denying that the person has authority usual to that position **(Freeman & Lockyer v Buckhurst Park Properties)**.

### Freeman & Lockyer v Buckhurst Park Properties [1964] CA

Two directors of a company left X, the third director, for some years to run the company's business of property development. X engaged some architects on the company's behalf although he had no express authority to do so. Later the company refused to pay the architects on the ground that X had no authority. It was held:

(1) as director, X's position did not give him usual authority to enter into commercial contracts such as the engaging of architects; but

(2) the position of a managing director does carry such usual authority; and

(3) even though X was not managing director the company had led third parties to believe that he was. Thus the company was stopped from denying that X had authority as if he were managing director. The result, therefore, was that the company had to pay the architects.

A third party cannot rely on apparent authority when he knows of the lack of actual authority.

See chapter 7 for further information on agency.

London
School of Business
& Finance

shaping success in business and finance

# Statutory rules

*s40 Companies Act 2006* provides that where a person deals with a company in good faith, the power of the board of directors to bind the company, or authorise others to do so, shall be deemed to be free of any limitation under the company's constitution.

*s40 Companies Act 2006* further provides that a third party is presumed to be in good faith, unless the contrary is proved; that he is not bound to enquire as to any limitation; and that he is not to be taken to be in bad faith merely because he knows of any lack of authority.

Where a director is the third party *s40 Companies Act 2006* does not apply: instead *s40 Companies Act 2006* applies to provide:

- The transaction is voidable at the instance of the company.
- He is liable to account to the company for any gain.
- He is liable to indemnify the company for any loss.

# 13

## Company Law – other company officers

# Syllabus Content

a) Discuss the appointment procedure relating to, and the duties and powers of, a company secretary.

b) Discuss the appointment procedure relating to, and the duties and powers of company auditors.

# Chapter Contents

COMPANY SECRETARY

    Appointment

    Qualification

    Duties And Functions

    Agency Position

AUDITORS

    Appointment

    Termination Of Office

    Duties And Powers

London
School of Business
& Finance

shaping success in business and finance

# COMPANY SECRETARY

## Appointment

It is a requirement of s271 Companies Act 2006 that every public company must have a company secretary.

A private company is not required to have a Company Secretary. If a private company does appoint a secretary there are no qualification requirements.

The company's articles will give power to the directors to appoint the secretary.

## Qualification *s273*

The company secretary of a **public company** must be a person with sufficient experience and knowledge to perform the role. The company secretary must be **suitably qualified**. It is the responsibility of the board to ensure that the secretary is qualified in one or more of the following ways:

1.  Has been the secretary of a public company for at least three of the preceding five years.

2.  Possesses certain professional qualifications including membership of the major accounting bodies.

3.  Is qualified as a solicitor or barrister.

4.  Is a person who, by virtue of his holding or having held any other position or his being a member of any other body, appears to the directors to be capable of discharging the functions of secretary.

## Duties and functions

It is for the board to decide on the duties of the company secretary as there are no formal statutory duties.

The duties are likely to include:

*   filing various documents with the registrar of companies and ensuring this is done within the correct time limits;

*   maintaining the company's statutory registers;

*   organising board and AGMs and dealing with meeting minutes;

*   ensuring that the company accounts are prepared and filed according to the statutory requirements; and

*   dealing with any other statutory requirements and advising the board on statutory matters.

## Agency position

The company secretary is an agent of the company and can bind the company in contracts with third parties where the secretary has:

*   **Actual authority** given to him explicitly from the board of directors.

*   **Implied authority** by virtue of his office.

The leading case is the 1971 decision of the Court of Appeal in *Panorama Developments v Fidelis Furnishing Fabrics.*

**Panorama Developments v Fidelis Furnishing Fabrics** [1971]

In this case a company secretary hired a car in the name of the company which was actually to be used for his own purposes. He did not have authority from the company to enter into this agreement. The court held that there was a binding agreement between the company and the car hire company as a company secretary would **usually** have the authority of the company to enter into contracts of an administrative nature such as the ordering of cars and the hiring of staff.

In his judgement the judge stated that the company secretary 'is no longer a mere clerk. ... He is entitled to sign contracts connected with the administrative side of a company's affairs, such as employing staff, and ordering cars, and so forth. All such matters now come within the ostensible authority of a company's secretary.'

**Note** it appears from other cases, for example, *Re Maidstone Buildings* [1971] and *Re Cleadon Trust* [1968] that the implied authority of the company secretary will not extend to entering into commercial contracts or entering into loan agreements.

# AUDITORS

The F4 law paper deals with the statutory (or external) auditors that the *Companies Act 2006* requires certain companies to have. Statutory auditors are also called external auditors since they are professional accountants from outside the company. The F4 law paper does not deal with internal auditors that many companies will choose to have.

# Appointment

### Requirement – *s475 Companies Act 2006*

The basic rule is every company must appoint auditors except:

(i)    certain **private** companies with a turnover of less than £5.6m, and

(ii)    any dormant company which has passed a **special** resolution dispensing with the need for auditors.

All non-dormant public companies must appoint auditors regardless of their turnover.

### Qualification

The auditor must be either:

(a)    a member of a recognised supervisory body **and** authorised to audit by that body. The RSBs are:

 • Institute of Chartered Accountants in England & Wales (and Scotland and Northern Ireland);

 • Chartered Association of Certified Accountants; or

(b)    authorised by the Government and having similar overseas qualifications as above.

The auditor must be independent of the company. For example, anyone who is an officer or employee of the company, or is employed by or is a partner of such a person etc is disqualified from being an auditor of the company.

### Procedures

### 1. Appointment by directors

The first auditors of a new company may be appointed by the directors. The first auditors of the company will remain in office until the conclusion of the first general meeting of the company.

Directors may also appoint auditors to fill a casual vacancy. They hold office until the next accounts meeting of the company. The accounts meeting is the meeting at which the accounts are laid before the shareholders.

London
School of Business
& Finance
shaping success in business and finance

## 2. Appointment by members

Public companies must appoint auditors for each financial year – s489 Companies Act 2006.

Subject to the exceptional circumstances given above where the directors may appoint auditors, the general principle is that it is the shareholders who appoint or re-appoint auditors. This will be done by ordinary resolution at the accounts meeting. The auditors will then hold office until the next accounts meeting, unless the auditors resign or are removed part way through office – s489 Companies Act 2006.

Under s485 and s487 Companies Act 2006 private companies required to appoint auditors are not required to be appointed or re-appointed each year. So there is no time limit on the length of their office.

### 3. Appointment by the Secretary of State – *s490 Companies Act 2006*

In the event that the company fails to appoint or reappoint auditors the secretary of State must be informed within one week of the accounts meeting at which the auditor should have been appointed. The Secretary of State can then appoint auditors for the company.

# Termination of office

Apart from not being reappointed at the accounts meeting an auditor can be removed from office in two ways.

### 1. Resignation – *s516 Companies Act 2006*

An auditor may resign at any time by notice in writing to the company. Notice of the resignation must be given to the registrar within 14 days.

Should an auditor resign part way through office, the auditor has the right to convene a General Meeting to explain any circumstances surrounding his departure (s518 Companies Act 2006).

A retiring auditor is required to send a statement of any details that should be brought to the attention of the shareholders and creditors or provide a statement to the effect that there are no details of which they should be made aware (s519 Companies Act 2006).

### 2. Removal – *s510 Companies Act 2006*

Auditors may be removed from office at any time for any reason by the passing of an ordinary resolution by shareholders of which special notice has been given to the company.

A copy of the resolution must be sent to the auditor on receipt by the company.

The auditor may make written representations of a reasonable length, which must be circulated with the notice of the meeting to the members.

If an auditor is removed he must make a statement of any details that should be brought to the attention of the shareholders and creditors or provide a statement to the effect that there are no details of which they should be made aware.

The company must give notice of any resolution passed to remove an auditor within 14 days to the registrar.

# Duties and powers

## DUTIES

The basic statutory duty of an auditor is to report to the shareholders whether or not the accounts give a true and fair view and have been properly prepared in accordance with the *Companies Act 2006*.

In particular the auditor must investigate so far as necessary to form an opinion as to whether:

(i)   Proper accounting records have been kept.

(ii)  Proper returns have been received from branches.

(iii) The accounts are in agreement with the accounting records.

(iv)  The information given in the directors' report is consistent with the accounts.

Where an auditor discovers that any of the above have not been complied with he must state this in his report.

## POWERS

Auditors have the following rights (powers):

1.   Auditors have a statutory right of access at all times to the company's books.

2.   Auditors have a statutory right to obtain from the company's officers and employees or any person holding the company books such information and explanations as the auditors think necessary for the performance of the auditors' duties.

     Where auditors do not receive all the information and explanations they require this should be stated in their report.

     It is a criminal offence to for the company officers or employees to supply false or misleading information to auditors.

3.   Auditors have a right to present their findings to shareholders at meetings and attend meetings.

4.   Auditors have a right to receive appropriate remuneration for carrying out their responsibilities.

5.   Should an auditor resign part way through office, an auditor has the right to convene a General Meeting.

# Company law – company meetings and resolutions

## Syllabus Content

a)      Distinguish between types of meetings: ordinary general meetings and annual general meetings.

b)      Explain the procedure for calling such meetings.

c)      Detail the procedure for conducting company meetings.

d)      Distinguish between types of resolutions: ordinary, special, and written.

## Chapter Content Diagram

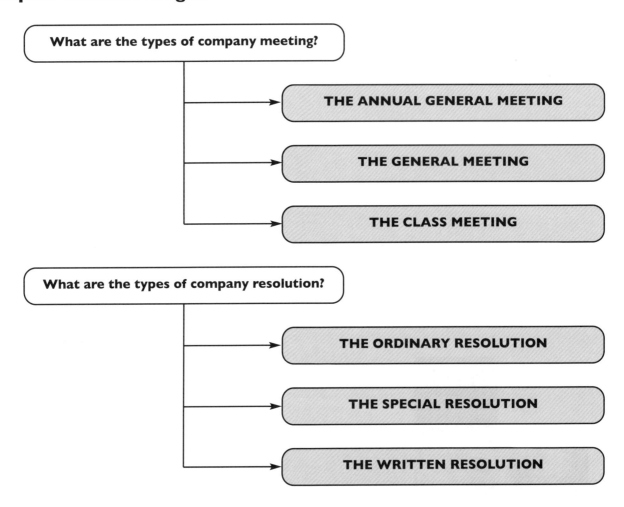

## Chapter Contents

MEETINGS

    Types of Meeting

    The Annual General Meeting

    The General Meeting

RESOLUTIONS

    Resolutions at a Meeting

    Written Resolutions

# MEETINGS

## Types of meeting

There are 3 different types of company meeting.

1.  The **Annual General Meeting**.

2.  The **General Meeting**.

3.  The **Class Meeting** (for example to vary class rights).

Procedures for annual general meetings and for general meetings are a mixture of statute, common law and the company's articles. Procedures for class meetings are largely the same as for general meetings adapted where necessary to cater for the fact that some only of the members will be entitled to attend.

As with the examination, this chapter concentrates on annual general meetings and general meetings.

## The Annual General Meeting

### It is mandatory and must be held at set intervals

All public companies are required to hold an AGM on an annual basis and are required by *s336 Companies Act 2006* to hold the meeting on a date which is not more than six months after the accounting reference date.

If the company fails to hold the meeting as required by *s336 Companies Act 2006*, every officer of the company who is in default commits an offence.

Private companies are not required to hold an AGM.

### Notice of an AGM

By *s377 Companies Act 2006* the members must receive a minimum of 21 days' notice of the meeting and such notice must state that the meeting is to be an AGM.

But:

1.  The notice period given may need to be longer if this is required by the company's articles.

2.  Shorter notice is permitted if every member who is entitled to attend and vote at the meeting agrees to a shorter notice period.

### Business at an AGM

The agenda for the AGM can be dictated by the company as there are no statutory requirements.

The agenda of the AGM would commonly include matters such as:

*   election of directors
*   election of auditors
*   laying of the accounts
*   declaration of a dividend.

By virtue of *s338 Companies Act 2006* members are able to require an item to be included on the agenda if:

*   they hold 5% of the voting rights; or
*   there are 100 members who each hold an average of £100 paid up share capital requesting the item to be put on the agenda.

# The General Meeting

Unlike Annual General Meetings there is no statutory requirement to hold General Meetings. The company will hold such a meeting when it is required.

Public companies can hold a General Meeting in between Annual General Meetings if the need arises for a meeting.

All company meetings of private companies will be General Meetings.

## Who convenes a General Meeting?

General Meetings can either be convened by the board of directors or the Court.

### 1. The Board

The company's articles will give the board power to convene a General Meeting if it is considered necessary.

There are three other instances when the board is required by the provisions of the *Companies Act 2006* to convene a General Meeting:

1. Members holding at least 10% of the paid up voting capital may require the directors to convene a GM (*s303 Companies Act 2006*).

   If the company is private and there has been no general meeting for more than 12 months, members holding at least 5% of the paid up voting capital may require the directors to convene a GM.

2. A resigning auditor may require the directors to convene a GM (*s518 Companies Act 2006*). See chapter 13.

3. If a public company suffers a serious loss of capital the board must convene a GM (*s656 Companies Act 2006*).

   A serious loss is where net assets fall to half or less of its paid up share capital.

### 2. The Court

The court has a default power to convene a General Meeting where it would otherwise be impracticable for the meeting to be called. This may be either on its own motion or if an application is made by a member or director.

The court may make any order it sees fit with regard to the meeting.

## Notice of a General Meeting

By *s307 Companies Act 2006* the members must receive a minimum of 14 days notice of the meeting.

## But:

1. The notice period given may need to be longer if this is required by the company's articles

2. Shorter notice is permitted if a majority of members in number, entitled to attend and vote, holding at least 95% in nominal value of the company's shares so agree.

## Business at a General Meeting

There is no set agenda for a General Meeting, except where a meeting is convened in relation to serious loss of capital by plc where *s656 Companies Act 2006* states that the meeting is convened 'for the purpose of considering whether any, and if so what, steps should be taken to deal with the situation'.

In general, it is for the person who requisitions/convenes the General Meeting to set the agenda.

# The Class Meeting

A class meeting is a meeting for members who hold a particular class of share.

In the event that the company has issued both ordinary and preference shares separate meetings may be required as some company matters may only affect members who hold one of the classes of share. For example, a meeting may be required to vary the rights attached to the preference shares, which would only involve preference shareholders. If preference shareholders have limited voting rights in relation to general company matters, meetings may only be relevant to the ordinary shareholders.

As with the general meetings, class meetings will be called when they are required and the formalities involved in convening such meetings are the same as they are for general meetings.

# RESOLUTIONS

## Resolutions at a meeting

### Types of resolution

1. Ordinary resolution

   An ordinary resolution is a company resolution used where neither the *Companies Act 2006* nor the company's constitution (articles) require a special resolution. It is therefore the default resolution and is used for general company matters, for example, the declaration of a dividend.

   To pass the resolution more than 50% of the votes cast must be in favour (a simple or bare majority).

   There is no general requirement to file ordinary resolutions with the registrar of companies.

2. Special resolution

   Special resolutions are used for matters where either the company's constitution or the *Companies Act 2006* specifies that a special resolution must be used. For example, a special resolution is normally required to amend the company's articles.

   To pass the resolution 75% of the votes cast must be in favour.

   All special resolutions must be filed with the registrar of companies.

### Methods of taking a vote

There are two ways of taking a vote at a meeting:

1. on a show of hands. This means each voting member has one vote (irrespective of how many shares he owns).

2. on a poll. Subject to specific provisions of the company's articles this means one vote per share.

Note that the company articles may contain particular provisions relating to voting at meetings.

### Proxies

Every member has a right to appoint a proxy to attend and vote at the meeting.

A proxy need not be a member of the company.

Every notice of every meeting must state the above two matters.

# Written resolutions

### Introduction

Normally resolutions of shareholders are passed at meetings. But the *Companies Act 2006* provides a procedure whereby private companies (not public companies) can pass resolutions without the need to hold a meeting.

This section of your Manual deals with these special rules for private companies.

### Detail

A written resolution can be used for any company matter except the removal of a director or auditor from office.

- A written resolution can be proposed either by the directors or members. The directors will simply circulate the resolution to all the members who are eligible to vote. Members who hold at least 5% of the voting rights can require directors to circulate a resolution.

- A written resolution is passed when the company receives written agreement from the required majority of members, which will be the same number of votes that would be required to pass that type of resolution at a general meeting. This means that if the written resolution was to be dealt with at a general meeting, if this would be a matter that would require an ordinary resolution the written resolution can be passed by a simple majority of votes by members.

- A proposed written resolution will lapse 28 days after its circulation date. This time period can be amended by the company articles.

- A copy of any proposed written resolution must be sent to auditors. Failure to do so is a criminal offence.

- The company must enter all written resolutions in a Register of Written Resolutions, which must be kept at the registered office.

# Special Notice – *s312 CA 2006*

Special notice must be given to the company in certain cases of the intention to propose a resolution at a meeting. For example, special notice will be required of a resolution to either remove a director or auditor.

Where the *Companies Act 2006* specifies that special notice is to be given, the company must be given 28 days notice of the intention to move the resolution.

On receipt of the special notice the company should send notice of the resolution to members, which must be given at least 14 days before the general meeting.

If the company schedules a meeting to deal with the resolution for a time less than 28 days after receipt of the special notice, satisfactory notice will be deemed to have been given.

# 15

## Company law – insolvency

# Syllabus Content

a) Explain the meaning of and procedure involved in voluntary liquidation.

b) Explain the meaning of and procedure involved in compulsory liquidation.

c) Explain administration as an alternative to winding up.

# Chapter Contents

INTRODUCTION

LIQUIDATION

Compulsory Liquidation Procedures

Members' Voluntary Liquidation Procedures

Creditors' Voluntary Liquidation Procedures

Application Of Assets

ADMINISTRATION

Introduction

Purposes

Appointment of an Administrator

Subsequent Procedures

London
School of Business
& Finance

shaping success in business and finance

# INTRODUCTION

Liquidation or winding up is the process whereby the company's assets are liquidated (the assets are realised and any proceeds are used to pay creditors and any surplus is distributed to the members) and the company itself is dissolved.

A company has a separate legal identity distinct from its members and will continue to exist despite changes in its members until it is formally wound up and removed from the register of companies.

Liquidation will usually take place in the event that the company is experiencing financial difficulties, but may also occur if the company is no longer required.

Compulsory Liquidation occurs where the court orders the winding up of the company. A voluntary liquidation occurs where the members take the decision to wind up the company. There are two methods of voluntary liquidation are a members' voluntary and a creditors' voluntary winding up. The various procedures are governed by the provisions of the *Insolvency Act 1986*.

Administration is an alternative to liquidation for companies with financial difficulties. Administration can have the purpose of saving the business of the company or securing a better result for creditors than would be possible with an insolvency. This is governed by the *Insolvency Act 1986* as amended by the *Enterprise Act 2002*.

# LIQUIDATION

There are two main ways of putting a company into liquidation:

1. by order of the court  – called the compulsory winding up

2. by the company itself – called the voluntary winding up. The voluntary winding up has two sub-types – the members' voluntary winding up and the creditors' voluntary winding up.

## Compulsory liquidation procedures

### Putting the company into liquidation

A compulsory winding up is commenced by presenting a petition to the court for a winding up order. The High Court will deal with the winding up of all companies. The county court has jurisdiction to deal with the winding up of companies with a paid up share capital of less than £120,000. The petition can be either presented by the company, the directors, a member, a creditor or by the Secretary of State.

*s122 IA 1986* states the **grounds** for which a winding up petition can be presented to the court. The principal grounds are:

- ss(a)   the company has passed a special resolution that it be wound up by the court.

- ss(b)   if a plc has failed to obtain a trading certificate (under s761 CA 2006) within a year of the date of incorporation.

- ss(d)   if the company has not started its business within the year of incorporation or has suspended its business for a period of over a year.

- ss(f)   if the company is unable to pay its debts.

  *s123 Insolvency Act 1986* provides that a company is deemed to be unable to pay its debts in the following situations:

  (i)     In the event that a creditor has served a statutory demand on the company, which exceeds £750 and is not settled by the company within three weeks of service.

  (ii)    If the value of the company's assets is less than its liabilities, including the company's contingent and prospective liabilities.

  (iii)   If a creditor can prove to the satisfaction of the court that the company is unable to pay its debts as they fall due. In simple terms this means that the company has cash-flow problems.

- ss(g)  if the court is of the opinion that it is **just and equitable** that the company be wound up.

    Examples of situations in which the just and equitable ground could be used:

    (i)      Where the substratum of the company has gone.

    **Re German Date Coffee** [1882].

    The company's objects clause stated its business to be "the working of a German patent for the manufacture of coffee from dates". The company was unable to obtain a German patent. However, it obtained a Swedish patent from which it successfully made coffee from dates. A minority member petitioned for the winding up of the company on the ground that it would be just and equitable under s122(g) Insolvency Act 1986. The court held that the entire business of the company was ultra vires. Since it was not possible for the company to carry on business within the confines of its objects clause (as a German patent was not forthcoming) it was just and equitable to wind up the company.

    (ii)     Where there is deadlock in management.

    **Re Yenidje Tobacco Company** [1916].

    The company directors (both equal shareholders) were unable to agree on fundamanetal decisions regarding the management of the company and eventually declined to speak to eachother. One of the directors petitioned for just and equitable winding up under s122(g) Insolvency Act 1986. The court held that the company could be wound up using this ground as it was the only solution to the deadlock in the management of the company.

    (iii)    Where there is justifiable lack of confidence in the probity of management.

    **Loch v John Blackwood** [1924].

    The sole director of the company, who was husband of the majority shareholder, refused to hold annual general meetings, refused to produce annual accounts and refused to recommend a dividend. The minority shareholders suspected that this refusal to give them any financial information about the company was in order to conceal the very high profitability of the company so that he and his wife could buy the minority's shares at an undervalue. The minority shareholders petitioned for the just and equitable winding up of the company under s122(g) Insolvency Act 1986. The court held that in the circumstances the minority had justifiably lost confidence in the transparency of management and it was just and equitable to wind up the company.

On hearing the petition the court may grant the order, dismiss the order or adjourn the hearing, stay proceedings or make any other order that it sees fit. The court has complete discretion as to whether to make the order.

If the court makes the order a copy of the order must be sent to the company and the Registrar. The date of the commencement for the winding up is generally deemed to be the date of the winding up petition.

**Effect of the winding up order:**

1. All actions for the recovery of debt against the company cease. The company ceases to carry on business except where necessary for the beneficial winding-up of the company, for example to complete work in progress.

2.  Powers of the directors cease but they still continue in office.

3. Employees are automatically made redundant but the liquidator can re-employ them to help him complete the winding-up.

4. On the making of the winding up order the Official Receiver becomes liquidator. The Official receiver is a court officer who is appointed by the court to deal with the case. The official receiver has a duty to investigate the reasons for failure of the company and the general promotion, formation, business, and affairs of the company and make a report to the court if required.

5. Within 3 months he will normally summon meetings of the creditors and contributories for the purpose of appointing a licensed insolvency practitioner as liquidator to take over the job of winding up the company's affairs and for the purpose of appointing a liquidation committee.

6. Once the winding up is complete the liquidator will summon meetings of the creditors and contributories for the purpose of them approving his final accounts. He will then apply to the Registrar for dissolution of the company.

# Members' voluntary liquidation procedures

A members' voluntary winding up will take place where the members have decided to dissolve the company in a situation where the company is solvent. As the company is solvent there is no need to involve the company creditors.

## Putting the company into liquidation

In order to commence a members' voluntary liquidation the following steps must be followed:

1. A board meeting is held to make a **declaration of solvency.**

   A declaration of solvency is a statutory declaration in which the directors state that the company is able to pay its debts within the next twelve months and is therefore solvent at the time the declaration is made. The declaration must be made within the five weeks immediately preceding the winding up resolution and must be filed with the Registrar within 15 days of the date the resolution is made. The directors must look in detail at the financial state of the company, as it is a criminal offence to make the declaration without having reasonable grounds for making it under the provisions of s89 IA 1986. Those in default are liable to contribute to the assets of the company, imprisonment or a fine or both.

2. A general meeting is held:

   (i) to make either the ordinary or special resolution **to resolve to wind up the company.**

   | Resolution | Ground |
   | --- | --- |
   | **ordinary** | where period fixed for duration of company has expired or an event occurs upon which the Arts state that the company should be wound up |
   | **special** | company is being wound up for any other reason |

   and

   (ii) **to appoint a** named insolvency practitioner as **liquidator**.

## Subsequent procedures

The liquidator will deal with the winding up of the company's affairs and when the formalities are complete will obtain the approval of the members to the final accounts at a final general meeting. The liquidator applies to the registrar of companies for dissolution of the company.

# Creditors' voluntary liquidation procedures

A creditors' voluntary liquidation arises in the event that the members wish to wind up the company but at the time the decision is made to wind up the company the directors cannot make a declaration of solvency. The creditors, therefore must be involved in the dissolution of the company.

## Putting the company into liquidation

In order to commence a members' voluntary liquidation the following steps must be taken:

1. The first step is to hold a general meeting of the members. There are three objectives of this meeting.

   (i.) to resolve to wind up, usually by special resolution,

   (ii.) to appoint a named insolvency practitioner as liquidator, and

   (iii.) to nominate up to five persons, to represent the members, to serve on a liquidation committee.

As from the close of this meeting the company is in liquidation and its assets are under the care and control of the liquidator. But, he may not normally dispose of assets until after the creditors' meeting.

2.  A creditors' meeting must be held within 14 days of the members' meeting *(s98 IA 1986)* and notice of the meeting must be advertised so all creditors have the chance to attend.

    There are three objectives of the creditors' meeting:

    (i.)    to consider a statement of affairs for the company, together with the list of creditors.

    (ii.)   The creditors are invited to appoint a named insolvency practitioner as liquidator (the creditors' choice will prevail over that of the members). Creditors vote by simple majority in value.

    (iii.)  The creditors may appoint up to five persons, to represent the creditors, to serve on a liquidation committee.

            The role of the liquidation committee is to assist the liquidator with the liquidation.

### Subsequent procedures

Once the liquidator has wound up the company's affairs he will summon a meeting of the creditors for their approval of his final accounts and will then apply to the Registrar for dissolution of the company.

# Application of Assets

Once the liquidator has collected in all the assets of the company and sold them, he will then distribute the proceeds in the order required by the *Insolvency Act 1986*.

The order is as follows.

### 1. Fixed chargees

Fixed chargees are creditors who have secured payment of their debt over a specific company asset. On liquidation the charge will provide that the chargee can take control of the asset, sell it and the proceeds will be used to pay the company's debt to the fixed chargee. Any surplus proceeds of sale must be handed to the liquidator. If there is a shortfall, the fixed chargee will rank as an ordinary unsecured creditor in the liquidation for the amount of the shortfall. There may be several fixed charges. The date of the charges and specific provisions within the charges will determine priority.

Fixed charges will be void against the liquidator unless the charge was registered with Companies House within 21 days of creation.

### 2. Preferential creditors

Employees are preferential creditors in respect of:

*   unpaid wages or salaries due during the four months preceding the date of commencement of winding up not exceeding £800 per employee.
*   all accrued holiday pay.

Employees rank equally amongst themselves. This means that if there are insufficient assets to meet the employees claims in full they will all receive the same proportion of the amount they are owed.

### 3. Floating chargees

Floating chargees will crystallise on liquidation of the company. The value of the security is determined by the value of the asset over which the charge has been taken at the date of the liquidation. The outstanding debt to the creditor will be repaid from the value of the charged asset.

The priority of floating charges will be determined by the date of the charges (usually the first charge created will have priority over subsequent charges).

*s245 Insolvency Act 1986* allows the liquidator to invalidate floating charges created within the 12 months before the liquidation by an insolvent company except the extent of new consideration.

Floating charges will be void against the liquidator unless the charge was registered with companies house within 21 days of creation.

### 4. Ordinary unsecured creditors

All other creditors are ordinary unsecured creditors and rank equally amongst themselves.

### 5. Post-liquidation interest

The *Insolvency Act 1986* provides for interest to be paid on the company debts. Such interest runs from the date of winding up until the debt the date is paid in full by the liquidator.

### 6. Surplus to contributories (members) in the following order:

If there are any surplus assets after payment of the above, members may be paid:

- Declared but unpaid dividends (if any).
- The balance of the remaining company assets in accordance with class rights, for example, preferential shareholders may have a prior right to return of their nominal value ahead of the ordinary shareholders.

### Payment of expenses

These are paid out of the fund to which they relate.

# ADMINISTRATION

## Introduction

Administration is a means of dealing with the affairs of a company in financial difficulty as an alternative to liquidation. It may result in the survival of some or all of the company's businesses.

## Purposes of Administration

The *Insolvency Act 1986* as amended by *Enterprise Act 2002* specifies the following three purposes of administration:

1. to rescue the company as a going concern, or

2. to achieve a better result for the company's creditors as a whole than would be likely if the company were to be put into liquidation, (for example, it may be more profitable for the company to have the option to continue trading, whilst some assets are sold offor to complete a profitable contract rather than simply to go into liquidation. This may result in creditors being repaid in full if the company can realise more assets. The administrator must act in the interests of creditors as a whole not one particular creditor.), or if these objectives are not likely to succeed

3. to realise property in order to make a payment to one or more secured or preferential creditors (if neither of the above objectives is possible the administrator may sell the company property to at least repay a secured creditor, for example, a bank with a fixed charge over the company's commercial property or to make a payment to a preferential creditor, for example, to pay employees' unpaid wages).

## Appointment of an administrator

Administration involves the appointment of an administrator to manage the affairs, business and property of the company. The administrator must be a qualified insolvency practitioner.

Once a company has resolved to be voluntarily wound-up or for which a winding-up order has been granted, it will not be possible to appoint an administrator.

An administrator can be appointed by:

### 1. the Court

Either the company, the directors or a creditor(s) can apply to the court for an administration order.

The court is able to make an administration order if it is satisfied:

(a) that the company is or is likely to become unable to pay its debts, and

(b) that the administration order is reasonably likely to achieve the purpose of administration (see above purposes of administration).

Prior to the Enterprise Act coming into force it was only possible for a company to appoint an administrator by way of court order. It is now rare for an administrator to be appointed by court order except if a company is selling its business to a new owner as part of a pre-packaged administration.

### 2. the holder of a 'qualifying' floating charge

A 'qualifying' floating charge enabling the chargee to appoint an administrator is a floating charge which:

(i) Specifically provides that the chargee is able to appoint an administrator.

(ii) relates to the whole or substantially the whole of the company's property.

The floating chargee must give at least two days prior written notice to any other floating chargee which has a prior floating charge or has obtained their consent to the appointment of the administrator.

Notice of the appointment must be filed with the court.

### 3. the company or its directors.

Either the company or the company directors may appoint an administrator provided that:

(i) the company has not been in administration within the preceding twelve months.

(ii) A moratorium or voluntary arrangement has not been in place within the preceding twelve months.

(iii) The company is or is likely to become unable to pay its debts.

Five days written notice must be given to any other parties who have the power to appoint an administrator or receiver.

Notice of the appointment must be filed with the court.

## Subsequent procedures

Following the appointment of an administrator:

1. The company cannot be put into liquidation.

2. There is a moratorium on the rights of creditors. This means that creditors cannot:

    • sue the company for any debts or levy execution on any of the company's assets;
    • take any steps to enforce any security over the company's property;
    • re-possess goods.

3. The administrator is the company's agent and takes control of all company's property. He must act in the best interests of all the company's creditors.

4. He has wide powers to manage the business and property of the company, including the power to bring and defend legal proceedings, sell assets and borrow money.

5. Directors still continue in office but their powers are suspended. The administrator has the power to remove and replace directors.

6. He has 14 days in which to decide which employee contracts to adopt. If an employee's contract is not adopted, the employee will be made redundant.

7. Within eight weeks of commencement of administration, the administrator must draw up a statement of his proposals which must be approved at a creditors meeting. If approval is refused, the court may provide that administrator's appointment shall cease and may make any order it considers to be appropriate.

8. The administrator remains in office for no more than one year. (Although the period can be extended by the court or with the consent of the secured creditors).

# 16

## Corporate governance

London
School of Business
& Finance

shaping success in business and finance

# Syllabus content

a)    Explain the idea of corporate governance.

b)    Recognise the extra-legal codes of corporate governance.

c)    Identify and explain the legal regulation of corporate governance.

# Chapter contents

WHAT IS CORPORATE GOVERNANCE?

LEGAL REGULATION – THE LAW

THE COMBINED CODE ON CORPORATE GOVERNANCE

   Why was the Code introduced?

   How do companies comply with the Combined Code?

   What are the main principles and provisions of the Combined Code?

# WHAT IS CORPORATE GOVERNANCE?

Corporate Governance can be simply described as the way in which a company is run.

Corporate Governance has been defined in two ways:

- As the system by which companies are directed and controlled.

- According to the Organisation for Economic Co-operation and Development, the corporate governance structure specifies the distribution of rights and responsibilities among different participants in the corporation, such as, the board, managers, shareholders and other stakeholders, and spells out the rules and procedures for making decisions on corporate affairs. By doing this, it also provides the structure through which the company objectives are set, and the means of attaining those objectives and monitoring performance.

In the UK corporate governance is regulated by the law and by extra-legal codes. The main one is the Combined Code on Corporate Governance.

# LEGAL REGULATION – THE LAW

The law aspect of corporate governance is covered in other sections of this manual. See:

DIRECTORS

See the chapter on 'Directors' dealing with the provisions of the *Companies Act 2006*.

COMPANY SECRETARY AND AUDITORS

See the chapter on 'Other Officers' for details of the *Companies Act 2006* provisions.

London
School of Business
& Finance

shaping success in business and finance

# THE COMBINED CODE ON CORPORATE GOVERNANCE

## The Development of the Code

The development of corporate governance in the UK has its roots in a series of corporate collapses and scandals in the late 1980s and the Robert Maxwell pension funds scandal in 1991.

The UK business community recognised the need to put its house in order. This led to the setting up in 1991 of the Committee on the Financial Aspects of Corporate Governance, chaired by Sir Adrian Cadbury, which issued a series of recommendations in 1992. The report is known as the Cadbury Report. The Cadbury Report addressed issues such as the relationship between the chairman and chief executive, the role of non-executive directors and reporting on internal control and on the company's position.

The recommendations in the Cadbury Report have been added to at regular intervals since 1992. In 1995 the Greenbury Report set out recommendations on the remuneration of directors. In 1998 the Cadbury and Greenbury reports were brought together and updated in the Combined Code, and in 1999 the Turnbull guidance was issued to provide directors with guidance on how to develop a sound system of internal control.

Following the Enron and WorldCom scandals in the US, the Combined Code was updated in 2003 to incorporate recommendations from reports on the role of non-executive directors (the Higgs Report) and the role of the audit committee (the Smith Report). At this time the UK Government confirmed that the Financial Reporting Council (FRC) was to have the responsibility for publishing and maintaining the Code. The FRC made further, limited, changes to the Code in 2006.

## To What Companies Does the Code Apply?

The Combined Code contains broad principles and more specific provisions to ensure an effective corporate governance framework. All companies that are listed on the London Stock Exchange are required by the listing rules to comply with the code and are required to report in their annual report and accounts:

1.  on how they have applied the principles of the Code; and

2.  either to confirm that they have complied with the Code's specific provisions or, where they have not, to provide an explanation as to the non-compliance. This is referred to as a 'comply or explain' approach.

All other companies are encouraged to follow the Code's recommendations.

## What are the Main Principles and Provisions of the Combined Code?

There are four main sections of the Combined Code. Each section contains several main principals. For each principal there is a specific code provision to which the company must state whether or not it adheres, and if not why not.

The four main sections are:

1.  Directors and Board

2.  Remuneration

3.  Accountability and Audit

4.  Relations with Shareholders

# THE COMBINED CODE IN DETAIL

## 1. Directors and Board

There are seven main principles covered in this section.

(i)   The Board

### Main Principle:

**Every company should be headed by an effective board, which is collectively responsible for the success of the company.**

Summary of major specific provisions:

- The board should meet sufficiently regularly to discharge its duties effectively.

- There should be a formal schedule of matters specifically reserved for its decision

- The annual report should include a statement of how the board operates, including a statement of which types of decision are to be taken by the board and which are to be delegated to management.

(ii)   Board Balance and Independence

### Main Principle:

**The board should include a balance of executive and non-executive directors (and in particular independent non-executive directors) such that no individual or small group of individuals can dominate the board's decision taking.**

Summary of major specific provisions:

- The board should identify in the annual report each non-executive director it considers to be independent. The Code Provisions details what factors determine whether a Director is truly independent, for example, significant shareholding interests.

- Except for smaller companies, at least half the board should comprise non-executive directors determined by the board to be independent.

### Non Executive Directors role and responsibilities

A non-executive director's function is generally to attend Board meetings. Non-executive directors therefore generally work part time for the company and do not have any direct day to day involvement in the management of the company unlike executive Directors. Further they receive a Directors fee not a salary.

However, in terms of their statutory and fiduciary legal position there is no distinction made between executive and non-executive directors.

Independent non-executive directors are helpful in that they often have considerable expertise which often strengthens the Board strategic decision making. They can also use their experience to effectively scrutinise and influence the Board's decisions and independently monitor performance on behalf of the Company's shareholders.

(iii)   Chairman and Chief Executive

### Main Principle:

**There should be a clear division of responsibilities at the head of the company between the running of the board and the executive responsibility for the running of the company's business.**

Summary of major specific provisions:

- The roles of chairman and chief executive should not be exercised by the same individual. The division of responsibilities between the chairman and chief executive should be clearly established, set out in writing and agreed by the board.

- The chairman should be an independent non-executive director.

- A chief executive should not normally go on to be chairman of the same company unless agreed with major shareholders.

(iv)  Appointments to the Board

## Main Principle:

**There should be a formal, rigorous and transparent procedure for the appointment of new directors to the board.**

Summary of major specific provisions:

- There should be a nomination committee which should lead the process for board appointments and make recommendations to the board.

- A majority of members of the nomination committee should be independent non-executive directors.

- For the appointment of a chairman, the nomination committee should prepare a job specification including reviewing the time commitment. The proposed Chairman's existing work commitments should be disclosed to the board before appointment.

(v)  Information and Professional Development

## Main Principle:

**The board should be supplied in a timely manner with information in a form and of a quality appropriate to enable it to discharge its duties.**

Summary of major specific provisions:

- The board should ensure that directors, especially non-executive directors, have access to independent professional advice at the company's expense.

- All directors should have access to the advice and services of the company secretary, who is responsible to the board for ensuring that board procedures are complied with.

- Both the appointment and removal of the company secretary should be a matter for the board as a whole.

(vi)  Performance evaluation

## Main Principle:

**The board should undertake a formal and rigorous annual evaluation of its own performance and that of its committees and individual directors.**

Summary of major specific provisions:

- The annual report should include how performance evaluation of the board, its committees and its individual directors has been conducted. The non-executive directors should be responsible for performance evaluation of the chairman, taking into account the views of executive directors.

(vii)  Re-election

## Main Principle:

**All directors should be submitted for re-election at regular intervals, subject to continued satisfactory performance. The board should ensure planned and progressive refreshing of the board.**

Summary of major specific provisions:

- All directors should be subject to election by shareholders at the first annual general meeting after their appointment, and to re-election thereafter at intervals of no more than three years.

# 2    Remuneration

There are two main principals covered in this section.

### 1.  The Level and Make-up of Remuneration

#### Main Principle:

**Levels of remuneration should be sufficient to attract, retain and motivate directors of the quality required to run the company successfully, but a company should avoid paying more than is necessary for this purpose. A significant proportion of executive directors' remuneration should be structured so as to link rewards to corporate and individual performance.**

Summary of major specific provisions:

*   The performance related elements of executive directors should be designed to align their interests with those of shareholders.

*   Levels of remuneration for non-executive directors should reflect the time commitment and responsibilities of the role. Remuneration for non-executive directors should not include share options.

*   Notice or contract periods should be set at one year or less. If it is necessary to offer longer notice or contract periods to new directors recruited from outside, such periods should reduce to one year or less after the initial period.

### 2.  Procedure

#### Main Principle:

**There should be a formal and transparent procedure for developing policy on executive remuneration and for fixing the remuneration packages of individual directors. No director should be involved in deciding his or her own remuneration.**

Summary of major specific provisions:

*   The board should establish a remuneration committee consisting of at least 3 (2 for small companies) independent non-executive directors.

*   The remuneration committee should have delegated responsibility for setting remuneration for all executive directors and the chairman.

*   The remuneration committee should ensure that all long term incentive schemes are approved by Shareholders

*   The board itself or, where required by the Articles of Association, the shareholders should determine the remuneration of the non-executive directors within the limits set in the Articles of Association

# 3    Accountability and Audit

There are three main principals covered in this section.

### 1.  Financial Reporting

#### Main Principle:

**The board should present a balanced and understandable assessment of the company's position and prospects.**

Summary of major specific provisions:

*   The directors should explain in explain in the annual report their responsibility for preparing the accounts and include a statement that the business is a going concern, with supporting assumptions or qualifications as necessary.

## 2. Internal Control

### Main Principle:

**The board should maintain a sound system of internal control to safeguard shareholders' investment and the company's assets.**

Summary of major specific provisions:

- The board should conduct an annual review of the effectiveness of the Company's system of material internal controls and should report to shareholders that they have done so.

## 3. Audit Committee and Auditors

### Main Principle:

**The board should establish formal and transparent arrangements for considering how they should apply the financial reporting and internal control principles and for maintaining an appropriate relationship with the company's auditors.**

Summary of major specific provisions:

- The board should establish an audit committee consisting of, at least, 3 (2 for small companies) independent non-executive directors.

- The main role and responsibilities of the audit committee should be set out in a written terms of reference to include its role and delegated authority.

- The audit committee should monitor and review the effectiveness of the internal audit activities.

- The audit committee should have primary responsibility for making a recommendation on the appointment, reappointment and removal of the external auditors.

# 4    Relations with Shareholders

There are two main principals covered in this section.

## 1. Dialogue with Institutional Shareholders

### Main Principle:

**There should be a dialogue with shareholders based on the mutual understanding of objectives. The board as a whole has responsibility for ensuring that a satisfactory dialogue with shareholders takes place.**

Summary of major specific provisions:

- The Chairman needs to ensure that the views of shareholders are communicated to the board. The Chairman should discuss governance and strategy with major shareholders at regular meetings. Non executive Directors should also be given the opportunity to attend.

## 2. Constructive Use of the AGM

### Main Principle:

**The board should use the AGM to communicate with investors and to encourage their participation.**

Summary of major specific provisions:

- The company should arrange for the Notice of the AGM and associated papers to be sent to shareholders at least 20 days prior to the AGM.

- The company should ensure that votes cast are properly received and recorded for each resolution and that the results (for, against and abstentions) are published.

- The chairman should arrange for all directors to attend and to be available to answer questions at the AGM.

London
School of Business
& Finance

shaping success in business and finance

# 17

# Fraudulent
# behaviour

London
School of Business
& Finance

shaping success in business and finance

# Syllabus content

a)   Recognise the nature and legal control over insider dealing.

b)   Recognise the nature and legal control over money laundering.

c)   Discuss potential criminal activity in the operation, management and winding up of companies.

d)   Distinguish between fraudulent and wrongful trading.

# Chapter contents

INSIDER DEALING

What are the Punishments?

What are the Offences?

Who can Commit the Offences?

What are the Defences?

MONEY LAUNDERING

What is the Legislation?

What is 'Money Laundering'?

What are the Criminal Offences?

FRAUDULENT TRADING

What is Fraudulent Trading?

What are the Consequences of Liability?

WRONGFUL TRADING

What is Wrongful Trading?

What are the Consequences of Liability?

THE PHOENIX COMPANY

# INTRODUCTION

This chapter deals with the main offences which may occur from the running of businesses. These are a mixture of criminal and civil offences with varying penalties.

The main offences are:

- Insider Dealing

- Money laundering

- Fraudulent trading

- Wrongful trading

- Use of phoenix names

Other offences which may be encountered in the course of running a company, mentioned in previous chapters are:

Breach of *s386 Companies Act 2006*

There is a duty for the company to keep proper accounting records particularly to show at all times the true financial position of the company. If there is a failure to comply with this duty every officer in default may be sentenced to up to 2 years' in prison or a fine or both.

Breach of *s451 Companies Act 2006*

The company has a duty to file accounts and reports within certain time periods allowed under the Act. In default, unless the company officers can prove that they took all reasonable steps to ensure that these requirements would be complied with on time, every director of the company commits an offence.

Breach of *s336 Companies Act 2006*

Public companies are required to hold an AGM in accordance with the provisions of the Act. By s336 CA 2006 if the company does not hold a meeting those company officers in default are liable to a fine.

Breach of *s89 Insolvency Act 1986*

In a members' voluntary winding up by virtue of s89 Insolvency Act 1986 it is a criminal offence for directors to make a declaration of solvency where the directors do not have reasonable grounds for doing so. Those in default are liable to contribute to the assets of the company, imprisonment and or a fine.

# INSIDER DEALING

Insider dealing is defined as the acquiring or disposing of securities given access to inside information, whether as a principal or agent, in a regulated market.

## What are the Punishments?

The offence is governed by **Part V of the Criminal Justice Act** 1993 (CJA) and is punishable by an unlimited fine and/or a maximum of 7 years' imprisonment. Any director found guilty of the offence can be disqualified.

## What are the Offences?

The possible offences of 'insider dealing' are:

1.  Dealing in securities on a regulated market. "Dealing" in securities occurs when a person either acquires or agrees to acquire, disposes or agrees to dispose of securities. (For example, buying or selling shares.) Dealing can occur if the person is also acting through an agent, nominee or any other person acting at his direction.

2.  **Encouraging** another person to deal.

3.  **Disclosing** information to others (otherwise than in the proper performance of his job).

## Who Can Commit the Offences?

The offences can only be committed by an **'insider'** for the purposes of the Act..

An 'insider' is a person who has information if:

1.  The information is, and he **knows** that it is, **inside information**, and

2.  He obtained the information, and he **knows** that he has obtained it, from an **inside source**.

### (a) What is inside information?

To qualify as inside information the following criteria need to be fulfilled:

*   It must relate to particular securities or to a particular company or companies; and

*   It must be specific or precise; and

*   It must not have been made public; and

*   If it were to be made public would it likely to have a significant effect on the price of the securities.

For example, information that a particular company was about to receive a takeover bid, that has not yet been publicly announced, and likely to increase the price of its shares would qualify as inside information.

### (b) When does a person have information from an inside source?

To qualify as information from an **inside source** the person must have obtained the information either:

*   Through being a director, employee or shareholder or through having access by virtue of his job; or

*   Has obtained the information indirectly from a director, employee or shareholder or someone having information by virtue of their job.

### (c) What is a regulated market?

A "regulated market" means any market, which, by an order made by the Treasury, is identified as a regulated market for the purposes of the Act. This would include the London Stock Exchange and the Alternative Investment Market as well as established overseas stock exchanges, for example, the New York Stock Exchange.

# What are the Defences?

1.  There are three general **defences** to insider dealing:

    *   If the defendant can prove that he did not expect the dealing to result in a profit (or the avoidance of a loss)

    *   If the defendant can prove that he believed on reasonable grounds that the information had been widely disclosed

    *   If the defendant can prove that he would taken the same course of action (and dealt, encouraged or disclosed) even if he had not had inside information.

2.  A person prosecuted for the disclosure offence in addition has a defence if he can prove that he reasonably believed that the recipient would not deal etc.

# MONEY LAUNDERING

## What is 'Money Laundering'?

Money Laundering is governed by the Proceeds of Crime Act 2002 (as amended).

Money laundering is the process by which the proceeds of crime, either money or other property, are converted into assets which appear to have a legitimate rather than an illegal origin. The aim of the process is to disguise the source of the property, in order to allow the holder to enjoy it free from suspicion as to its source.

The process generally has 3 stages:

### 1. Placement

This is the initial disposal of the proceeds of criminal activity where the proceeds of crime are used to purchase legitimate assets, for example by buying a business.

### 2. Layering

This involves the transfer of money from, for example, place to place or business to business with the aim of concealing its initial source.

### 3. Integration

This is the end result of placement and integration in that the money now has an appearance of coming from a legitimate source.

## What are the Criminal Offences?

There are three categories of offence.

### 1. Laundering

It is an offence to acquire, possess, or use the proceeds of criminal activity or to assist another to retain the proceeds of criminal activity or to conceal the proceeds of criminal activity.

For example, using money obtained from the sale of illegal drugs to invest in shares.

The penalty for anyone found liable for this offence is a maximum of 14 years' in prison and/or an unlimited fine.

London
School of Business
& Finance

shaping success in business and finance

## 2. Failing to report

Individuals in regulated sectors (for example, accountants in professional practice or solicitors), carrying on a 'relevant business' have a duty to report if they know or suspect, or have reasonable grounds to know or suspect, that another is engaged in money laundering to the Serious and Organised Crime Agency (SOCA).

All relevant businesses should have reporting procedures in place, including the appointment of a money laundering officer who will deal with any suspicions raised in the business and report matters if necessary to SOCA for guidance.

Examples of activities which may raise suspicions maybe a client handling large amounts of cash, buying investments such as shares in small amounts in several different transactions rather than in one investment, buying businesses or property with money coming from a third party.

The penalty for anyone found liable for this offence is a maximum of 5 years' in prison and/or an unlimited fine.

## 3. Tipping off

It is an offence for professionals to disclose to anyone suspected of money laundering any information which is likely to prejudice any investigation under the legislation.

For example, if a solicitor suspects that a client is buying a property with the proceeds of crime she must take advice from SOCA as to how to proceed with the client and the transaction. She will commit an offence if she tells the client that she suspects that he is involved in money laundering and has involved SOCA.

The penalty for anyone found liable for this offence is a maximum of 5 years' in prison and/or an unlimited fine.

# FRAUDULENT TRADING – s213 Insolvency Act 1986

# What is Fraudulent Trading?

Fraudulent Trading is a civil wrong and a criminal offence.

A person will be liable for fraudulent trading if it emerges in the course of winding up a company that a person has knowingly carried on a business with the intent to defraud creditors or for any fraudulent purpose.

For example, in the case of R v Grantham [1985] the court decided that ordering goods on credit where it was known that the goods would not be paid for amounted to fraudulent trading.

### R v Grantham [1985]

The two directors ordered a consignment of potatoes on a month's credit at a time when they knew that the potatoes would not be paid for at the end of the month. **Held.** They had committed to crime of fraudulent trading.

To establish liability for fraudulent it is necessary to establish the person involved was acting **dishonestly**. Where there is an honest belief that the creditors will not be adversely affected by the action the person involved will not be liable.

In the case of **Re William C Leitch Bros.** [1932] the company steadily lost money, which eventually resulted in the company becoming insolvent. The director of the company, with full knowledge of the company's financial position, ordered goods far in excess of the company's actual requirements. A winding up order was subsequently made. The court held that the carrying on of the business and incurring of debts for which there was no honest prospect of paying meant that the business was being carried on with intent to defraud creditors. The defendant was held personally liable for a proportion of the company's debts.

It is also only possible for those directly involved in the active management of the company making decisions to be liable. Therefore, directors who do not take part in the active management of the company or shadow directors will not be liable for this wrong, but may be liable for wrongful trading.

# What are the Consequences of Liability?

1. If a liquidator believes that those controlling the company have engaged in fraudulent trading he can apply to court for an order compelling those responsible to made a contribution to the company's assets.

2. Under the CDDA 1986 a director can be disqualified for up to 15 years.

3. S993 Companies Act 2006 has created a separate criminal offence of fraudulent trading which is not restricted to companies that are being wound up. Anyone found guilty of this offence can be sentenced to a maximum 10 years in prison and/or an unlimited fine.

# WRONGFUL TRADING – *s214 Insolvency Act 1986*

# What is Wrongful Trading?

Wrongful trading is a civl wrong, not a criminal offence.

A director or shadow director will be liable for wrongful trading where a company is in insolvent liquidation and if it can be established that:

- he knew or ought to have known that there was no reasonable prospect of avoiding the insolvent liquidation; and

- the director or shadow director did not take all the steps that he could take in order to minimise the potential loss to creditors.

The wrong includes objective and subjective tests:

- What the director himself knew taking account of his own skills and qualifications. For example, if a director is a professional accountant he would be expected to have greater knowledge of the company's financial position than an unqualified director; and

- What a reasonably skilled person in his position ought to have known. This means the standard expected of a reasonably competent director of the company.

  It is not possible for the defendant director to argue that he lacked information or knowledge particularly where this is due to his own default, as in the case of **Re Produce Marketing Consortium Ltd (No.2)** [1989]. In this case the directors were not aware of the full extent of the company's financial difficulties at a crucial point as they had failed to produce the accounts required by the provisions of the *Companies Act 1986*. When they became aware of the problems they began to dispose of assets only and did not minimise losses to the creditors. They had therefore failed to take every step they could have taken to minimise losses to creditors and were liable.

# Defence

The defendant has a defence if he can prove "he took every step he ought to have taken with a view to minimising the potential loss to creditors".

The facts which a director of a company ought to know or ascertain, the conclusions which he ought to reach and the steps which he ought to take in order to minimise potential losses to creditors are those which would be known or ascertained, or reached or taken, by a reasonably diligent person having both:

(a) The general knowledge, skill and experience that may reasonably be expected of a director carrying out the same functions, as are carried out by that director in relation to the company; and

(b) The general knowledge, skill and experience that that director has.

See **Re Produce Marketing Consortium Ltd (No.2)** above. In this case the defendants were unable to rely on the defence as they had not taken every step they should have taken to minimise potential losses to creditors. Merely disposing of assets was not sufficient to avoid liability.

London
School of Business
& Finance
shaping success in business and finance

## What are the Consequences of Liability?

1.  A director who is found liable for this wrong can be ordered by the court to contribute to the assets of the company on the application of the liquidator.

2.  Under the the Company Directors Disqualification Act 1986 a director can be disqualified for up to 15 years.

## THE PHOENIX COMPANY (RESTRICTION ON RE-USE OF NAME OF IN-SOLVENT COMPANY) – *s216 Insolvency Act 1986*

The name of an insolvent company can on occasions be re-used to create a phoenix company by directors of the insolvent company this is a criminal offence.

The *Insolvency Act 1986* prohibits:

*   a person from being involved in the running of a company (directly or indirectly) with a similar or the same name as a company that went into insolvent liquidation (in order to suggest a connection between the two companies); and

*   where the person was a director of the insolvent company at any time in the 12 months leading up to the liquidation, for a period of five years following the liquidation.

## What are the Consequences of Liability?

*   The director involved has criminal liability and will be liable to imprisonment and or a fine.

*   the director involved will have personal liability for the debts of the phoenix company.

# F4
## (ENG)

Appendix –
Model Articles
for Public
Companies

# Schedule 3    REGULATION 4

MODEL ARTICLES FOR PUBLIC COMPANIES

## Index To The Articles

## Part I

## Interpretation And Limitation Of Liability

## Part 2

## Directors

### DIRECTORS' POWERS AND RESPONSIBILITIES

### DECISION-MAKING BY DIRECTORS

### APPOINTMENT OF DIRECTORS

London
School of Business
& Finance

shaping success in business and finance

# Part I

# Interpretation And Limitation Of Liability

## Defined terms

1.    In the articles , unless the context requires otherwise—

"alternate" or "alternate director" has the meaning given in article 25;

"appointor" has the meaning given in article 25;

"articles" means the company's articles of association;

"bankruptcy" includes individual insolvency proceedings in a jurisdiction other than England and Wales or Northern Ireland which have an effect similar to that of bankruptcy;

"call" has the meaning given in article 54;

"call notice" has the meaning given in article 54;

"certificate" means a paper certificate (other than a share warrant) evidencing a person's title to specified shares or other securities;

"certificated" in relation to a share, means that it is not an uncertificated share or a share in respect of which a share warrant has been issued and is current;

"chairman" has the meaning given in article 12;

"chairman of the meeting" has the meaning given in article 31;

"Companies Acts" means the Companies Acts (as defined in section 2 of the Companies Act 2006), in so far as they apply to the company;

"company's lien" has the meaning given in article 52;

"director" means a director of the company, and includes any person occupying the position of director, by whatever name called;

"distribution recipient" has the meaning given in article 72;

"document" includes, unless otherwise specified, any document sent or supplied in electronic form;

"electronic form" has the meaning given in section 1168 of the Companies Act 2006;

"fully paid" in relation to a share, means that the nominal value and any premium to be paid to the company in respect of that share have been paid to the company;

London
School of Business
& Finance
shaping success in business and finance

"hard copy form" has the meaning given in section 1168 of the Companies Act 2006;

"holder" in relation to shares means the person whose name is entered in the register of members as the holder of the shares, or, in the case of a share in respect of which a share warrant has been issued (and not cancelled), the person in possession of that warrant;

"instrument" means a document in hard copy form;

"lien enforcement notice" has the meaning given in article 53;

"member" has the meaning given in section 112 of the Companies Act 2006;

"ordinary resolution" has the meaning given in section 282 of the Companies Act 2006;

"paid" means paid or credited as paid;

"participate", in relation to a directors' meeting, has the meaning given in article 9;

"partly paid" in relation to a share means that part of that share's nominal value or any

premium at which it was issued has not been paid to the company;

"proxy notice" has the meaning given in article 38;

"securities seal" has the meaning given in article 47;

"shares" means shares in the company;

"special resolution" has the meaning given in section 283 of the Companies Act 2006;

"subsidiary" has the meaning given in section 1159 of the Companies Act 2006;

"transmittee" means a person entitled to a share by reason of the death or bankruptcy of a shareholder or otherwise by operation of law;

"uncertificated" in relation to a share means that, by virtue of legislation (other than section 778 of the Companies Act 2006) permitting title to shares to be evidenced and transferred without a certificatee, title to that share is evidenced and may be transferred without a certificate; and

"writing" means the representation or reproduction of words, symbols or other information in a visible form by any method or combination of methods, whether sent or supplied in electronic form or otherwise.

Unless the context otherwise requires, other words or expressions contained in these articles bear the same meaning as in the Companies Act 2006 as in force on the date when these articles become binding on the company.

## Liability of members

**2.**    The liability of the members is limited to the amount, if any, unpaid on the shares held by them.

# Part 2

# Directors

## DIRECTORS' POWERS AND RESPONSIBILITIES

### Directors' general authority

**3.** Subject to the articles, the directors are responsible for the management of the company's business, for which purpose they may exercise all the powers of the company.

### Members' reserve power

**4.** (1) The members may, by special resolution, direct the directors to take, or refrain from taking, specified action.

(2) No such special resolution invalidates anything which the directors have done before the passing of the resolution.

### Directors may delegate

**5.** (1) Subject to the articles, the directors may delegate any of the powers which are conferred on them under the articles:

(a) to such person or committee;

(b) by such means (including by power of attorney);

(c) to such an extent;

(d) in relation to such matters or territories; and

(e) on such terms and conditions;

as they think fit.

(2) If the directors so specify, any such delegation may authorise further delegation of the directors' powers by any person to whom they are delegated.

(3) The directors may revoke any delegation in whole or part, or alter its terms and conditions.

### Committees

**6.** (1) Committees to which the directors delegate any of their powers must follow procedures which are based as far as they are applicable on those provisions of the articles which govern the taking of decisions by directors.

(2) The directors may make rules of procedure for all or any committees, which prevail over rules derived from the articles if they are not consistent with them.

## DECISION-MAKING BY DIRECTORS

### Directors to take decisions collectively

**7.** Decisions of the directors may be taken:

(a) at a directors' meeting, or

(b) in the form of a directors' written resolution.

London
School of Business
& Finance

shaping success in business and finance

## Calling a directors' meeting

**8.** (1)     Any director may call a directors' meeting.

(2)     The company secretary must call a directors' meeting if a director so requests.

(3)     A directors' meeting is called by giving notice of the meeting to the directors.

(4)     Notice of any directors' meeting must indicate:

    (a)    its proposed date and time;

    (b)    where it is to take place; and

    (c)    if it is anticipated that directors participating in the meeting will not be in the same place, how it is proposed that they should communicate with each other during the meeting.

(5)     Notice of a directors' meeting must be given to each director, but need not be in writing.

(6)     Notice of a directors' meeting need not be given to directors who waive their entitlement to notice of that meeting, by giving notice to that effect to the company not more than 7 days after the date on which the meeting is held. Where such notice is given after the meeting has been held, that does not affect the validity of the meeting, or of any business conducted at it.

## Participation in directors' meetings

**9.** (1)     Subject to the articles, directors participate in a directors' meeting, or part of a directors' meeting, when:

    (a)    the meeting has been called and takes place in accordance with the articles, and

    (b)    they can each communicate to the others any information or opinions they have on any particular item of the business of the meeting.

(2)     In determining whether directors are participating in a directors' meeting, it is irrelevant where any director is or how they communicate with each other.

(3)     If all the directors participating in a meeting are not in the same place, they may decide that the meeting is to be treated as taking place wherever any of them is.

## Quorum for directors' meetings

**10.** (1)     At a directors' meeting, unless a quorum is participating, no proposal is to be voted on, except a proposal to call another meeting.

(2)     The quorum for directors' meetings may be fixed from time to time by a decision of the directors, but it must never be less than two, and unless otherwise fixed it is two.

Meetings where total number of directors less than quorum

**11.** (1)     This article applies where the total number of directors for the time being is less than the quorum for directors' meetings.

(2)     If there is only one director, that director may appoint sufficient directors to make up a quorum or call a general meeting to do so.

(3)     If there is more than one director:

    (a)    a directors' meeting may take place, if it is called in accordance with the articles and at least two directors participate in it, with a view to appointing sufficient directors to make up a quorum or calling a general meeting to do so, and

    (b)    if a directors' meeting is called but only one director attends at the appointed date and time to participate in it, that director may appoint sufficient directors to make up a quorum or call a general meeting to do so.

## Chairing directors' meetings

**12.** (1) The directors may appoint a director to chair their meetings.

(2) The person so appointed for the time being is known as the chairman.

(3) The directors may appoint other directors as deputy or assistant chairmen to chair directors' meetings in the chairman's absence.

(4) The directors may terminate the appointment of the chairman, deputy or assistant chairman at any time.

(5) If neither the chairman nor any director appointed generally to chair directors' meetings in the chairman's absence is participating in a meeting within ten minutes of the time at which it was to start, the participating directors must appoint one of themselves to chair it.

## Voting at directors' meetings: general rules

**13.** (1) Subject to the articles, a decision is taken at a directors' meeting by a majority of the votes of the participating directors.

(2) Subject to the articles, each director participating in a directors' meeting has one vote.

(3) Subject to the articles, if a director has an interest in an actual or proposed transaction or arrangement with the company:

(a) that director and that director's alternate may not vote on any proposal relating to it, but

(b) this does not preclude the alternate from voting in relation to that transaction or arrangement on behalf of another appointor who does not have such an interest.

## Chairman's casting vote at directors' meetings

**14.** (1) If the numbers of votes for and against a proposal are equal, the chairman or other director chairing the meeting has a casting vote.

(2) But this does not apply if, in accordance with the articles, the chairman or other director is not to be counted as participating in the decision-making process for quorum or voting purposes.

## Alternates voting at directors' meetings

**15.** A director who is also an alternate director has an additional vote on behalf of each appointor who is:

(a) not participating in a directors' meeting, and

(b) would have been entitled to vote if they were participating in it.

## Conflicts of interest

**16.** (1) If a directors' meeting, or part of a directors' meeting, is concerned with an actual or proposed transaction or arrangement with the company in which a director is interested, that director is not to be counted as participating in that meeting, or part of a meeting, for quorum or voting purposes.

(2) But if paragraph (3) applies, a director who is interested in an actual or proposed transaction or arrangement with the company is to be counted as participating in a decision at a directors' meeting, or part of a directors' meeting, relating to it for quorum and voting purposes.

(3) This paragraph applies when:

(a) the company by ordinary resolution disapplies the provision of the articles which would otherwise prevent a director from being counted as participating in, or voting at, a directors' meeting;

(b) the director's interest cannot reasonably be regarded as likely to give rise to a conflict of interest; or

(c) the director's conflict of interest arises from a permitted cause.

(4) For the purposes of this article, the following are permitted causes:

    (a) a guarantee given, or to be given, by or to a director in respect of an obligation incurred by or on behalf of the company or any of its subsidiaries;

    (b) subscription, or an agreement to subscribe, for shares or other securities of the company or any of its subsidiaries, or to underwrite, sub-underwrite, or guarantee subscription for any such shares or securities; and

    (c) arrangements pursuant to which benefits are made available to employees and directors or former employees and directors of the company or any of its subsidiaries which do not provide special benefits for directors or former directors.

(5) Subject to paragraph (6), if a question arises at a meeting of directors or of a committee of directors as to the right of a director to participate in the meeting (or part of the meeting) for voting or quorum purposes, the question may, before the conclusion of the meeting, be referred to the chairman whose ruling in relation to any director other than the chairman is to be final and conclusive.

(6) If any question as to the right to participate in the meeting (or part of the meeting) should arise in respect of the chairman, the question is to be decided by a decision of the directors at that meeting, for which purpose the chairman is not to be counted as participating in the meeting (or that part of the meeting) for voting or quorum purposes.

## Proposing directors' written resolutions

**17.**   (1) Any director may propose a directors' written resolution.

    (2) The company secretary must propose a directors' written resolution if a director so requests.

    (3) A directors' written resolution is proposed by giving notice of the proposed resolution to the directors.

    (4) Notice of a proposed directors' written resolution must indicate:

        (a) the proposed resolution, and

        (b) the time by which it is proposed that the directors should adopt it.

    (5) Notice of a proposed directors' written resolution must be given in writing to each director.

    (6) Any decision which a person giving notice of a proposed directors' written resolution takes regarding the process of adopting that resolution must be taken reasonably in good faith.

## Adoption of directors' written resolutions

**18.**   (1) A proposed directors' written resolution is adopted when all the directors who would have been entitled to vote on the resolution at a directors' meeting have signed one or more copies of it, provided that those directors would have formed a quorum at such a meeting.

    (2) It is immaterial whether any director signs the resolution before or after the time by which the notice proposed that it should be adopted.

    (3) Once a directors' written resolution has been adopted, it must be treated as if it had been a decision taken at a directors' meeting in accordance with the articles.

    (4) The company secretary must ensure that the company keeps a record, in writing, of all directors' written resolutions for at least ten years from the date of their adoption.

## Directors' discretion to make further rules

**19.**   Subject to the articles, the directors may make any rule which they think fit about how they take decisions, and about how such rules are to be recorded or communicated to directors.

APPOINTMENT OF DIRECTORS

## Methods of appointing directors

**20.** Any person who is willing to act as a director, and is permitted by law to do so, may be appointed to be a director:

(a) by ordinary resolution, or

(b) by a decision of the directors.

## Retirement of directors by rotation

**21.** (1) At the first annual general meeting all the directors must retire from office.

(2) At every subsequent annual general meeting any directors:

(a) who have been appointed by the directors since the last annual general meeting, or

(b) who were not appointed or reappointed at one of the preceding two annual general meetings, must retire from office and may offer themselves for reappointment by the members.

## Termination of director's appointment

**22.** A person ceases to be a director as soon as:

(a) that person ceases to be a director by virtue of any provision of the Companies Act 2006 or is prohibited from being a director by law;

(b) a bankruptcy order is made against that person;

(c) a composition is made with that person's creditors generally in satisfaction of that person's debts;

(d) a registered medical practitioner who is treating that person gives a written opinion to the company stating that that person has become physically or mentally incapable of acting as a director and may remain so for more than three months;

(e) by reason of that person's mental health, a court makes an order which wholly or partly prevents that person from personally exercising any powers or rights which that person would otherwise have;

(f) notification is received by the company from the director that the director is resigning from office as director, and such resignation has taken effect in accordance with its terms.

## Directors' remuneration

**23.** (1) Directors may undertake any services for the company that the directors decide.

(2) Directors are entitled to such remuneration as the directors determine:

(a) for their services to the company as directors, and

(b) for any other service which they undertake for the company.

(3) Subject to the articles, a director's remuneration may:

(a) take any form, and

(b) include any arrangements in connection with the payment of a pension, allowance or gratuity, or any death, sickness or disability benefits, to or in respect of that director.

(4) Unless the directors decide otherwise, directors' remuneration accrues from day to day.

(5) Unless the directors decide otherwise, directors are not accountable to the company for any remuneration which they receive as directors or other officers or employees of the company's subsidiaries or of any other body corporate in which the company is interested.

## Directors' expenses

**24.** The company may pay any reasonable expenses which the directors properly incur in connection with their attendance at:

(a) meetings of directors or committees of directors,

(b) general meetings, or

(c) separate meetings of the holders of any class of shares or of debentures of the company, or otherwise in connection with the exercise of their powers and the discharge of their responsibilities in relation to the company.

London
School of Business
& Finance
shaping success in business and finance

## ALTERNATE DIRECTORS

### Appointment and removal of alternates

**25.** (1) Any director (the "appointor") may appoint as an alternate any other director, or any other person approved by resolution of the directors, to:

    (a) exercise that director's powers, and

    (b) carry out that director's responsibilities,

    in relation to the taking of decisions by the directors in the absence of the alternate's appointor.

    (2) Any appointment or removal of an alternate must be effected by notice in writing to the company signed by the appointor, or in any other manner approved by the directors.

    (3) The notice must:

    (a) identify the proposed alternate, and

    (b) in the case of a notice of appointment, contain a statement signed by the proposed alternate that the proposed alternate is willing to act as the alternate of the director giving the notice.

### Rights and responsibilities of alternate directors

**26.** (1) An alternate director has the same rights, in relation to any directors' meeting or directors' written resolution, as the alternate's appointor.

    (2) Except as the articles specify otherwise, alternate directors:

    (a) are deemed for all purposes to be directors;

    (b) are liable for their own acts and omissions;

    (c) are subject to the same restrictions as their appointors; and

    (d) are not deemed to be agents of or for their appointors.

    (3) A person who is an alternate director but not a director:

    (a) may be counted as participating for the purposes of determining whether a quorum is participating (but only if that person's appointor is not participating), and

    (b) may sign a written resolution (but only if it is not signed or to be signed by that person's appointor).

    No alternate may be counted as more than one director for such purposes.

    (4) An alternate director is not entitled to receive any remuneration from the company for serving as an alternate director except such part of the alternate's appointor's remuneration as the appointor may direct by notice in writing made to the company.

### Termination of alternate directorship

**27.** An alternate director's appointment as an alternate terminates:

    (a) when the alternate's appointor revokes the appointment by notice to the company in writing specifying when it is to terminate;

    (b) on the occurrence in relation to the alternate of any event which, if it occurred in relation to the alternate's appointor, would result in the termination of the appointor's appointment as a director;

    (c) on the death of the alternate's appointor; or

    (d) when the alternate's appointor's appointment as a director terminates, except that an alternate's appointment as an alternate does not terminate when the appointor retires by rotation at a general meeting and is then re-appointed as a director at the same general meeting.

# Part 3

# Decision-Making By Members

ORGANISATION OF GENERAL MEETINGS

### Members can call general meeting if not enough directors

**28.**   If:

(a)   the company has fewer than two directors, and

(b)   the director (if any) is unable or unwilling to appoint sufficient directors to make up a quorum or to call a general meeting to do so, then two or more members may call a general meeting (or instruct the company secretary to do so) for the purpose of appointing one or more directors.

### Attendance and speaking at general meetings

**29.**   (1)   A person is able to exercise the right to speak at a general meeting when that person is in a position to communicate to all those attending the meeting, during the meeting, any information or opinions which that person has on the business of the meeting.

(2)   A person is able to exercise the right to vote at a general meeting when:

(a)   that person is able to vote, during the meeting, on resolutions put to the vote at the meeting, and

(b)   that person's vote can be taken into account in determining whether or not such resolutions are passed at the same time as the votes of all the other persons attending the meeting.

(3)   The directors may make whatever arrangements they consider appropriate to enable those attending a general meeting to exercise their rights to speak or vote at it.

(4)   In determining attendance at a general meeting, it is immaterial whether any two or more members attending it are in the same place as each other.

(5)   Two or more persons who are not in the same place as each other attend a general meeting if their circumstances are such that if they have (or were to have) rights to speak and vote at that meeting, they are (or would be) able to exercise them.

### Quorum for general meetings

**30.**   No business other than the appointment of the chairman of the meeting is to be transacted at a general meeting if the persons attending it do not constitute a quorum.

### Chairing general meetings

**31.**   (1)   If the directors have appointed a chairman, the chairman shall chair general meetings if present and willing to do so.

(2)   If the directors have not appointed a chairman, or if the chairman is unwilling to chair the meeting or is not present within ten minutes of the time at which a meeting was due to start:

(a)   the directors present, or

(b)   (if no directors are present), the meeting,

must appoint a director or member to chair the meeting, and the appointment of the chairman of the meeting must be the first business of the meeting.

(3)   The person chairing a meeting in accordance with this article is referred to as "the chairman of the meeting".

London
School of Business
& Finance

shaping success in business and finance

## Attendance and speaking by directors and non-members

**32.**    (1)    Directors may attend and speak at general meetings, whether or not they are members.

(2)    The chairman of the meeting may permit other persons who are not:

(a)    members of the company, or

(b)    otherwise entitled to exercise the rights of members in relation to general meetings,

to attend and speak at a general meeting.

## Adjournment

**33.**    (1)    If the persons attending a general meeting within half an hour of the time at which the meeting was due to start do not constitute a quorum, or if during a meeting a quorum ceases to be present, the chairman of the meeting must adjourn it.

(2)    The chairman of the meeting may adjourn a general meeting at which a quorum is present if:

(a)    the meeting consents to an adjournment, or

(b)    it appears to the chairman of the meeting that an adjournment is necessary to protect the safety of any person attending the meeting or ensure that the business of the meeting is conducted in an orderly manner.

(3)    The chairman of the meeting must adjourn a general meeting if directed to do so by the meeting.

(4)    When adjourning a general meeting, the chairman of the meeting must:

(a)    either specify the time and place to which it is adjourned or state that it is to continue at a time and place to be fixed by the directors, and

(b)    have regard to any directions as to the time and place of any adjournment which have been given by the meeting.

(5)    If the continuation of an adjourned meeting is to take place more than 14 days after it was adjourned, the company must give at least 7 clear days' notice of it (that is, excluding the day of the adjourned meeting and the day on which the notice is given):

(a)    to the same persons to whom notice of the company's general meetings is required to be given, and

(b)    containing the same information which such notice is required to contain.

(6)    No business may be transacted at an adjourned general meeting which could not properly have been transacted at the meeting if the adjournment had not taken place.

## VOTING AT GENERAL MEETINGS

## Voting: general

**34.**    A resolution put to the vote of a general meeting must be decided on a show of hands unless a poll is duly demanded in accordance with the articles.

## Errors and disputes

**35.**    (1)    No objection may be raised to the qualification of any person voting at a general meeting except at the meeting or adjourned meeting at which the vote objected to is tendered, and every vote not disallowed at the meeting is valid.

(2)    Any such objection must be referred to the chairman of the meeting whose decision is final.

## Demanding a poll

**36.**   (1)   A poll on a resolution may be demanded:

   (a)   in advance of the general meeting where it is to be put to the vote, or

   (b)   at a general meeting, either before a show of hands on that resolution or immediately after the result of a show of hands on that resolution is declared.

(2)   A poll may be demanded by:

   (a)   the chairman of the meeting;

   (b)   the directors;

   (c)   two or more persons having the right to vote on the resolution; or

   (d)   a person or persons representing not less than one tenth of the total voting rights of all the members having the right to vote on the resolution.

(3)   A demand for a poll may be withdrawn if:

   (a)   the poll has not yet been taken, and

   (b)   the chairman of the meeting consents to the withdrawal.

## Procedure on a poll

**37.**   (1)   Subject to the articles, polls at general meetings must be taken when, where and in such manner as the chairman of the meeting directs.

(2)   The chairman of the meeting may appoint scrutineers (who need not be members) and decide how and when the result of the poll is to be declared.

(3)   The result of a poll shall be the decision of the meeting in respect of the resolution on which the poll was demanded.

(4)   A poll on:

   (a)   the election of the chairman of the meeting, or

   (b)   a question of adjournment,

   must be taken immediately.

(5)   Other polls must be taken within 30 days of their being demanded.

(6)   A demand for a poll does not prevent a general meeting from continuing, except as regards the question on which the poll was demanded.

(7)   No notice need be given of a poll not taken immediately if the time and place at which it is to be taken are announced at the meeting at which it is demanded.

(8)   In any other case, at least 7 days' notice must be given specifying the time and place at which the poll is to be taken.

## Content of proxy notices

**38.** (1) Proxies may only validly be appointed by a notice in writing (a "proxy notice") which:

    (a) states the name and address of the member appointing the proxy;

    (b) identifies the person appointed to be that member's proxy and the general meeting in relation to which that person is appointed;

    (c) is signed by or on behalf of the member appointing the proxy, or is authenticated in suchmanner as the directors may determine; and

    (d) is delivered to the company in accordance with the articles and any instructions contained in the notice of the general meeting to which they relate.

(2) The company may require proxy notices to be delivered in a particular form, and may specify different forms for different purposes.

(3) Proxy notices may specify how the proxy appointed under them is to vote (or that the proxy is to abstain from voting) on one or more resolutions.

(4) Unless a proxy notice indicates otherwise, it must be treated as:

    (a) allowing the person appointed under it as a proxy discretion as to how to vote on any ancillary or procedural resolutions put to the meeting, and

    (b) appointing that person as a proxy in relation to any adjournment of the general meeting to which it relates as well as the meeting itself.

## Delivery of proxy notices

**39.** (1) Any notice of a general meeting must specify the address or addresses ("proxy notification address") at which the company or its agents will receive proxy notices relating to that meeting, or any adjournment of it, delivered in hard copy or electronic form.

(2) A person who is entitled to attend, speak or vote (either on a show of hands or on a poll) at a general meeting remains so entitled in respect of that meeting or any adjournment of it, even though a valid proxy notice has been delivered to the company by or on behalf of that person.

(3) Subject to paragraphs (4) and (5), a proxy notice must be delivered to a proxy notification address not less than 48 hours before the general meeting or adjourned meeting to which it relates.

(4) In the case of a poll taken more than 48 hours after it is demanded, the notice must be delivered to a proxy notification address not less than 24 hours before the time appointed for the taking of the poll.

(5) In the case of a poll not taken during the meeting but taken not more than 48 hours after it was demanded, the proxy notice must be delivered:

    (a) in accordance with paragraph (3), or

    (b) at the meeting at which the poll was demanded to the chairman, secretary or any director.

(6) An appointment under a proxy notice may be revoked by delivering a notice in writing given by or on behalf of the person by whom or on whose behalf the proxy notice was given to a proxy notification address.

(7) A notice revoking a proxy appointment only takes effect if it is delivered before:

    (a) the start of the meeting or adjourned meeting to which it relates, or

    (b) (in the case of a poll not taken on the same day as the meeting or adjourned meeting) the time appointed for taking the poll to which it relates.

(8) If a proxy notice is not signed by the person appointing the proxy, it must be accompanied by written evidence of the authority of the person who executed it to execute it on the appointor's behalf.

**Amendments to resolutions**

40. (1) An ordinary resolution to be proposed at a general meeting may be amended by ordinary resolution if:

   (a) notice of the proposed amendment is given to the company secretary in writing by a person entitled to vote at the general meeting at which it is to be proposed not less than hours before the meeting is to take place (or such later time as the chairman of the meeting may determine), and

   (b) the proposed amendment does not, in the reasonable opinion of the chairman of the meeting, materially alter the scope of the resolution.

   (2) A special resolution to be proposed at a general meeting may be amended by ordinary resolution, if:

   (a) the chairman of the meeting proposes the amendment at the general meeting at which the resolution is to be proposed, and

   (b) the amendment does not go beyond what is necessary to correct a grammatical or other non-substantive error in the resolution.

   (3) If the chairman of the meeting, acting in good faith, wrongly decides that an amendment to a resolution is out of order, the chairman's error does not invalidate the vote on that resolution.

## RESTRICTIONS ON MEMBERS' RIGHTS

**No voting of shares on which money owed to company**

41. No voting rights attached to a share may be exercised at any general meeting, at any adjournment of it, or on any poll called at or in relation to it, unless all amounts payable to the company in respect of that share have been paid.

## APPLICATION OF RULES TO CLASS MEETINGS

**Class meetings**

42. The provisions of the articles relating to general meetings apply, with any necessary modifications, to meetings of the holders of any class of shares.

London
School of Business
& Finance

shaping success in business and finance

# Part 4

# Shares And Distributions

ISSUE OF SHARES

## Powers to issue different classes of share

**43.** (1) Subject to the articles, but without prejudice to the rights attached to any existing share, the company may issue shares with such rights or restrictions as may be determined by ordinary resolution.

(2) The company may issue shares which are to be redeemed, or are liable to be redeemed at the option of the company or the holder, and the directors may determine the terms, conditions and manner of redemption of any such shares.

## Payment of commissions on subscription for shares

**44.** (1) The company may pay any person a commission in consideration for that person:

(a) subscribing, or agreeing to subscribe, for shares, or

(b) procuring, or agreeing to procure, subscriptions for shares.

(2) Any such commission may be paid:

(a) in cash, or in fully paid or partly paid shares or other securities, or partly in one way and partly in the other, and

(b) in respect of a conditional or an absolute subscription.

INTERESTS IN SHARES

## Company not bound by less than absolute interests

**45.** Except as required by law, no person is to be recognised by the company as holding any share upon any trust, and except as otherwise required by law or the articles, the company is not in any way to be bound by or recognise any interest in a share other than the holder's absolute ownership of it and all the rights attaching to it.

SHARE CERTIFICATES

## Certificates to be issued except in certain cases

**46.** (1) The company must issue each member with one or more certificates in respect of the shares which that member holds.

(2) This article does not apply to:

(a) uncertificated shares;

(b) shares in respect of which a share warrant has been issued; or

(c) shares in respect of which the Companies Acts permit the company not to issue a certificate.

(3) Except as otherwise specified in the articles, all certificates must be issued free of charge.

(4) No certificate may be issued in respect of shares of more than one class.

(5) If more than one person holds a share, only one certificate may be issued in respect of it.

## Contents and execution of share certificates

**47.** (1) Every certificate must specify:

    (a) in respect of how many shares, of what class, it is issued;

    (b) the nominal value of those shares;

        (c) the amount paid up on them; and

        (d) any distinguishing numbers assigned to them.

(2) Certificates must:

    (a) have affixed to them the company's common seal or an official seal which is a facsimile of the company's common seal with the addition on its face of the word "Securities" (a "securities seal"), or

    (b) be otherwise executed in accordance with the Companies Acts.

## Consolidated share certificates

**48.** (1) When a member's holding of shares of a particular class increases, the company may issue that member with:

    (a) a single, consolidated certificate in respect of all the shares of a particular class which that member holds, or

    (b) a separate certificate in respect of only those shares by which that member's holding has increased.

(2) When a member's holding of shares of a particular class is reduced, the company must ensure that the member is issued with one or more certificates in respect of the number of shares held by the member after that reduction. But the company need not (in the absence of a request from the member) issue any new certificate if:

    (a) all the shares which the member no longer holds as a result of the reduction, and

    (b) none of the shares which the member retains following the reduction,

were, immediately before the reduction, represented by the same certificate.

(3) A member may request the company, in writing, to replace:

    (a) the member's separate certificates with a consolidated certificate, or

    (b) the member's consolidated certificate with two or more separate certificates representing such proportion of the shares as the member may specify.

(4) When the company complies with such a request it may charge such reasonable fee as the directors may decide for doing so.

(5) A consolidated certificate must not be issued unless any certificates which it is to replace have first been returned to the company for cancellation.

## Replacement share certificates

**49.** (1) If a certificate issued in respect of a member's shares is:

    (a) damaged or defaced, or

    (b) said to be lost, stolen or destroyed,

that member is entitled to be issued with a replacement certificate in respect of the same shares.

(2) A member exercising the right to be issued with such a replacement certificate:

    (a) may at the same time exercise the right to be issued with a single certificate or separate certificates;

    (b) must return the certificate which is to be replaced to the company if it is damaged or defaced; and

    (c) must comply with such conditions as to evidence, indemnity and the payment of a reasonable fee as the directors decide.

## SHARES NOT HELD IN CERTIFICATED FORM

### Uncertificated shares

**50.** (1) In this article, "the relevant rules" means:

    (a) any applicable provision of the Companies Acts about the holding, evidencing of title to, or transfer of shares other than in certificated form, and

    (b) any applicable legislation, rules or other arrangements made under or by virtue of such provision.

  (2) The provisions of this article have effect subject to the relevant rules.

  (3) Any provision of the articles which is inconsistent with the relevant rules must be disregarded, to the extent that it is inconsistent, whenever the relevant rules apply.

  (4) Any share or class of shares of the company may be issued or held on such terms, or in such a way, that:

    (a) title to it or them is not, or must not be, evidenced by a certificate, or

    (b) it or they may or must be transferred wholly or partly without a certificate.

  (5) The directors have power to take such steps as they think fit in relation to:

    (a) the evidencing of and transfer of title to uncertificated shares (including in connection with the issue of such shares);

    (b) any records relating to the holding of uncertificated shares;

        (c) the conversion of certificated shares into uncertificated shares; or

        (d) the conversion of uncertificated shares into certificated shares.

  (6) The company may by notice to the holder of a share require that share:

    (a) if it is uncertificated, to be converted into certificated form, and

    (b) if it is certificated, to be converted into uncertificated form,

  to enable it to be dealt with in accordance with the articles.

  (7) If:

    (a) the articles give the directors power to take action, or require other persons to take action, in order to sell, transfer or otherwise dispose of shares, and

    (b) uncertificated shares are subject to that power, but the power is expressed in terms which assume the use of a certificate or other written instrument,

  the directors may take such action as is necessary or expedient to achieve the same results when exercising that power in relation to uncertificated shares.

  (8) In particular, the directors may take such action as they consider appropriate to achieve the sale, transfer, disposal, forfeiture, re-allotment or surrender of an uncertificated share or otherwise to enforce a lien in respect of it.

  (9) Unless the directors otherwise determine, shares which a member holds in uncertificated form must be treated as separate holdings from any shares which that member holds in certificated form.

(10) A class of shares must not be treated as two classes simply because some shares of that class are held in certificated form and others are held in uncertificated form.

## Share warrants

**51.** (1) The directors may issue a share warrant in respect of any fully paid share.

(2) Share warrants must be:

   (a) issued in such form, and

   (b) executed in such manner,

   as the directors decide.

(3) A share represented by a share warrant may be transferred by delivery of the warrant representing it.

(4) The directors may make provision for the payment of dividends in respect of any share represented by a share warrant.

(5) Subject to the articles, the directors may decide the conditions on which any share warrant is issued. In particular, they may:

   (a) decide the conditions on which new warrants are to be issued in place of warrants which are damaged or defaced, or said to have been lost, stolen or destroyed;

   (b) decide the conditions on which bearers of warrants are entitled to attend and vote at general meetings;

   (c) decide the conditions subject to which bearers of warrants may surrender their warrant so as to hold their shares in certificated or uncertificated form instead; and

   (d) vary the conditions of issue of any warrant from time to time, and the bearer of a warrant is subject to the conditions and procedures in force in relation to it, whether or not they were decided or specified before the warrant was issued.

(6) Subject to the conditions on which the warrants are issued from time to time, bearers of share warrants have the same rights and privileges as they would if their names had been included in the register as holders of the shares represented by their warrants.

(7) The company must not in any way be bound by or recognise any interest in a share represented by a share warrant other than the absolute right of the bearer of that warrant to that warrant.

PARTLY PAID SHARES

## Company's lien over partly paid shares

**52.** (1) The company has a lien ("the company's lien") over every share which is partly paid for any part of:

   (a) that share's nominal value, and

   (b) any premium at which it was issued,

   which has not been paid to the company, and which is payable immediately or at some time in the future, whether or not a call notice has been sent in respect of it.

(2) The company's lien over a share:

   (a) takes priority over any third party's interest in that share, and

   (b) extends to any dividend or other money payable by the company in respect of that share and (if the lien is enforced and the share is sold by the company) the proceeds of sale of that share.

(3) The directors may at any time decide that a share which is or would otherwise be subject to the company's lien shall not be subject to it, either wholly or in part.

London
School of Business
& Finance
shaping success in business and finance

## Enforcement of the company's lien

**53.** (1) Subject to the provisions of this article, if:

    (a) a lien enforcement notice has been given in respect of a share, and

    (b) the person to whom the notice was given has failed to comply with it,

the company may sell that share in such manner as the directors decide.

(2) A lien enforcement notice:

    (a) may only be given in respect of a share which is subject to the company's lien, in respect of which a sum is payable and the due date for payment of that sum has passed;

    (b) must specify the share concerned;

    (c) must require payment of the sum payable within 14 days of the notice;

    (d) must be addressed either to the holder of the share or to a person entitled to it by reason of the holder's death, bankruptcy or otherwise; and

    (e) must state the company's intention to sell the share if the notice is not complied with.

(3) Where shares are sold under this article:

    (a) the directors may authorise any person to execute an instrument of transfer of the shares to the purchaser or a person nominated by the purchaser, and

    (b) the transferee is not bound to see to the application of the consideration, and the transferee's title is not affected by any irregularity in or invalidity of the process leading to the sale.

(4) The net proceeds of any such sale (after payment of the costs of sale and any other costs of enforcing the lien) must be applied:

    (a) first, in payment of so much of the sum for which the lien exists as was payable at the date of the lien enforcement notice,

    (b) second, to the person entitled to the shares at the date of the sale, but only after the certificate for the shares sold has been surrendered to the company for cancellation or a suitable indemnity has been given for any lost certificates, and subject to a lien equivalent to the company's lien over the shares before the sale for any money payable in respect of the shares after the date of the lien enforcement notice.

(5) A statutory declaration by a director or the company secretary that the declarant is a director or the company secretary and that a share has been sold to satisfy the company's lien on a specified date:

    (a) is conclusive evidence of the facts stated in it as against all persons claiming to be entitled to the share, and

    (b) subject to compliance with any other formalities of transfer required by the articles or by law, constitutes a good title to the share.

## Call notices

**54.** (1) Subject to the articles and the terms on which shares are allotted, the directors may send a notice (a "call notice") to a member requiring the member to pay the company a specified sum of money (a "call") which is payable in respect of shares which that member holds at the date when the directors decide to send the call notice.

(2) A call notice:

    (a) may not require a member to pay a call which exceeds the total sum unpaid on that member's shares (whether as to the share's nominal value or any amount payable to the company by way of premium);

    (b) must state when and how any call to which it relates it is to be paid; and

    (c) may permit or require the call to be paid by instalments.

(3) A member must comply with the requirements of a call notice, but no member is obliged to pay any call before 14 days have passed since the notice was sent.

(4)  Before the company has received any call due under a call notice the directors may:

    (a)  revoke it wholly or in part, or

    (b)  specify a later time for payment than is specified in the notice,

by a further notice in writing to the member in respect of whose shares the call is made.

### Liability to pay calls

**55.**   (1)  Liability to pay a call is not extinguished or transferred by transferring the shares in respect of which it is required to be paid.

    (2)  Joint holders of a share are jointly and severally liable to pay all calls in respect of that share.

    (3)  Subject to the terms on which shares are allotted, the directors may, when issuing shares, provide that call notices sent to the holders of those shares may require them:

      (a)  to pay calls which are not the same, or

      (b)  to pay calls at different times.

### When call notice need not be issued

**56.**   (1)  A call notice need not be issued in respect of sums which are specified, in the terms on which a share is issued, as being payable to the company in respect of that share (whether in respect of nominal value or premium):

    (a)  on allotment;

    (b)  on the occurrence of a particular event; or

    (c)  on a date fixed by or in accordance with the terms of issue.

    (2)  But if the due date for payment of such a sum has passed and it has not been paid, the holder of the share concerned is treated in all respects as having failed to comply with a call notice in respect of that sum, and is liable to the same consequences as regards the payment of interest and forfeiture.

Failure to comply with call notice: automatic consequences

**57.**   (1)  If a person is liable to pay a call and fails to do so by the call payment date:

    (a)  the directors may issue a notice of intended forfeiture to that person, and

    (b)  until the call is paid, that person must pay the company interest on the call from the call payment date at the relevant rate.

    (2)  For the purposes of this article:

      (a)  the "call payment date" is the time when the call notice states that a call is payable, unless the directors give a notice specifying a later date, in which case the "call payment date" is that later date;

      (b)  the "relevant rate" is:

        (i)  the rate fixed by the terms on which the share in respect of which the call is due was allotted;

        (ii)  such other rate as was fixed in the call notice which required payment of the call, or has otherwise been determined by the directors; or

        (iii)  if no rate is fixed in either of these ways, 5 per cent per annum.

    (3)  The relevant rate must not exceed by more than 5 percentage points the base lending rate most recently set by the Monetary Policy Committee of the Bank of England in connection with its responsibilities under Part 2 of the Bank of England Act 1998[*].

    (4)  The directors may waive any obligation to pay interest on a call wholly or in part.

[*]1998 c.11.

## Notice of intended forfeiture

**58.** A notice of intended forfeiture:

(a) may be sent in respect of any share in respect of which a call has not been paid as required by a call notice;

(b) must be sent to the holder of that share or to a person entitled to it by reason of the holder's death, bankruptcy or otherwise;

(c) must require payment of the call and any accrued interest by a date which is not less than 14 days after the date of the notice;

(d) must state how the payment is to be made; and

(e) must state that if the notice is not complied with, the shares in respect of which the call is payable will be liable to be forfeited.

## Directors' power to forfeit shares

**59.** If a notice of intended forfeiture is not complied with before the date by which payment of the call is required in the notice of intended forfeiture, the directors may decide that any share in respect of which it was given is forfeited, and the forfeiture is to include all dividends or other moneys payable in respect of the forfeited shares and not paid before the forfeiture.

## Effect of forfeiture

**60.** (1) Subject to the articles, the forfeiture of a share extinguishes:

(a) all interests in that share, and all claims and demands against the company in respect of it, and

(b) all other rights and liabilities incidental to the share as between the person whose share it was prior to the forfeiture and the company.

(2) Any share which is forfeited in accordance with the articles:

(a) is deemed to have been forfeited when the directors decide that it is forfeited;

(b) is deemed to be the property of the company; and

(c) may be sold, re-allotted or otherwise disposed of as the directors think fit.

(3) If a person's shares have been forfeited:

(a) the company must send that person notice that forfeiture has occurred and record it in theregister of members;

(b) that person ceases to be a member in respect of those shares;

(c) that person must surrender the certificate for the shares forfeited to the company for cancellation;

(d) that person remains liable to the company for all sums payable by that person under the articles at the date of forfeiture in respect of those shares, including any interest (whether accrued before or after the date of forfeiture); and

(e) the directors may waive payment of such sums wholly or in part or enforce payment without any allowance for the value of the shares at the time of forfeiture or for any consideration received on their disposal.

(4) At any time before the company disposes of a forfeited share, the directors may decide to cancel the forfeiture on payment of all calls and interest due in respect of it and on such other terms as they think fit.

## Procedure following forfeiture

**61.** (1) If a forfeited share is to be disposed of by being transferred, the company may receive the consideration for the transfer and the directors may authorise any person to execute the instrument of transfer.

(2) A statutory declaration by a director or the company secretary that the declarant is a director or the company secretary and that a share has been forfeited on a specified date:

   (a) is conclusive evidence of the facts stated in it as against all persons claiming to be entitled to the share, and

   (b) subject to compliance with any other formalities of transfer required by the articles or by law, constitutes a good title to the share.

(3) A person to whom a forfeited share is transferred is not bound to see to the application of the consideration (if any) nor is that person's title to the share affected by any irregularity in or invalidity of the process leading to the forfeiture or transfer of the share.

(4) If the company sells a forfeited share, the person who held it prior to its forfeiture is entitled to receive from the company the proceeds of such sale, net of any commission, and excluding any amount which:

   (a) was, or would have become, payable, and

   (b) had not, when that share was forfeited, been paid by that person in respect of that share,

   but no interest is payable to such a person in respect of such proceeds and the company is not required to account for any money earned on them.

## Surrender of shares

**62.** (1) A member may surrender any share:

   (a) in respect of which the directors may issue a notice of intended forfeiture;

   (b) which the directors may forfeit; or

   (c) which has been forfeited.

(2) The directors may accept the surrender of any such share.

(3) The effect of surrender on a share is the same as the effect of forfeiture on that share.

(4) A share which has been surrendered may be dealt with in the same way as a share which has been forfeited.

## TRANSFER AND TRANSMISSION OF SHARES

## Transfers of certificated shares

**63.** (1) Certificated shares may be transferred by means of an instrument of transfer in any usual form or any other form approved by the directors, which is executed by or on behalf of:

   (a) the transferor, and

   (b)     (if any of the shares is partly paid) the transferee.

(2) No fee may be charged for registering any instrument of transfer or other document relating to or affecting the title to any share.

(3) The company may retain any instrument of transfer which is registered.

(4) The transferor remains the holder of a certificated share until the transferee's name is entered in the register of members as holder of it.

(5) The directors may refuse to register the transfer of a certificated share if:

   (a) the share is not fully paid;

   (b) the transfer is not lodged at the company's registered office or such other place as the directors have appointed;

    (c)    the transfer is not accompanied by the certificate for the shares to which it relates, or such other evidence as the directors may reasonably require to show the transferor's right to make the transfer, or evidence of the right of someone other than the transferor to make the transfer on the transferor's behalf;

    (d)    the transfer is in respect of more than one class of share; or

    (e)    the transfer is in favour of more than four transferees.

(6)    If the directors refuse to register the transfer of a share, the instrument of transfer must be returned to the transferee with the notice of refusal unless they suspect that the proposed transfer may be fraudulent.

## Transfer of uncertificated shares

**64.**    A transfer of an uncertificated share must not be registered if it is in favour of more than four transferees.

## Transmission of shares

**65.**    (1)    If title to a share passes to a transmittee, the company may only recognise the transmittee as having any title to that share.

    (2)    Nothing in these articles releases the estate of a deceased member from any liability in respect of a share solely or jointly held by that member.

## Transmittees' rights

**66.**    (1)    A transmittee who produces such evidence of entitlement to shares as the directors may properly require:

    (a)    may, subject to the articles, choose either to become the holder of those shares or to have them transferred to another person, and

    (b)    subject to the articles, and pending any transfer of the shares to another person, has the same rights as the holder had.

    (2)    But transmittees do not have the right to attend or vote at a general meeting in respect of shares to which they are entitled, by reason of the holder's death or bankruptcy or otherwise, unless they become the holders of those shares

## Exercise of transmittees' rights

**67.**    (1)    Transmittees who wish to become the holders of shares to which they have become entitled must notify the company in writing of that wish.

    (2)    If the share is a certificated share and a transmittee wishes to have it transferred to another person, the transmittee must execute an instrument of transfer in respect of it.

    (3)    If the share is an uncertificated share and the transmittee wishes to have it transferred to another person, the transmittee must:

    (a)    procure that all appropriate instructions are given to effect the transfer, or

    (b)    procure that the uncertificated share is changed into certificated form and then execute an instrument of transfer in respect of it.

    (4)    Any transfer made or executed under this article is to be treated as if it were made or executed by the person from whom the transmittee has derived rights in respect of the share, and as if the event which gave rise to the transmission had not occurred.

## Transmittees bound by prior notices

**68.**    If a notice is given to a member in respect of shares and a transmittee is entitled to those shares, the transmittee is bound by the notice if it was given to the member before the transmittee's name has been entered in the register of members.

## CONSOLIDATION OF SHARES

### Procedure for disposing of fractions of shares

**69.** (1) This article applies where:

    (a) there has been a consolidation or division of shares, and

    (b) as a result, members are entitled to fractions of shares.

(2) The directors may:

    (a) sell the shares representing the fractions to any person including the company for the best price reasonably obtainable;

    (b) in the case of a certificated share, authorise any person to execute an instrument of transfer of the shares to the purchaser or a person nominated by the purchaser; and

    (c) distribute the net proceeds of sale in due proportion among the holders of the shares.

(3) Where any holder's entitlement to a portion of the proceeds of sale amounts to less than a minimum figure determined by the directors, that member's portion may be distributed to an organisation which is a charity for the purposes of the law of England and Wales, Scotland or Northern Ireland.

(4) The person to whom the shares are transferred is not obliged to ensure that any purchase money is received by the person entitled to the relevant fractions.

(5) The transferee's title to the shares is not affected by any irregularity in or invalidity of the process leading to their sale.

## DISTRIBUTIONS

### Procedure for declaring dividends

**70.** (1) The company may by ordinary resolution declare dividends, and the directors may decide to pay interim dividends.

(2) A dividend must not be declared unless the directors have made a recommendation as to its amount. Such a dividend must not exceed the amount recommended by the directors.

(3) No dividend may be declared or paid unless it is in accordance with members' respective rights.

(4) Unless the members' resolution to declare or directors' decision to pay a dividend, or the terms on which shares are issued, specify otherwise, it must be paid by reference to each member's holding of shares on the date of the resolution or decision to declare or pay it.

(5) If the company's share capital is divided into different classes, no interim dividend may be paid on shares carrying deferred or non-preferred rights if, at the time of payment, any preferential dividend is in arrear.

(6) The directors may pay at intervals any dividend payable at a fixed rate if it appears to them that the profits available for distribution justify the payment.

(7) If the directors act in good faith, they do not incur any liability to the holders of shares conferring preferred rights for any loss they may suffer by the lawful payment of an interim dividend on shares with deferred or non-preferred rights.

### Calculation of dividends

**71.** (1) Except as otherwise provided by the articles or the rights attached to shares, all dividends must be:

    (a) declared and paid according to the amounts paid up on the shares on which the dividend is paid, and

    (b) apportioned and paid proportionately to the amounts paid up on the shares during any portion or portions of the period in respect of which the dividend is paid.

(2) If any share is issued on terms providing that it ranks for dividend as from a particular date, that share ranks for dividend accordingly.

(3) For the purposes of calculating dividends, no account is to be taken of any amount which has been paid up on a share in advance of the due date for payment of that amount.

## Payment of dividends and other distributions

**72.** (1) Where a dividend or other sum which is a distribution is payable in respect of a share, it must be paid by one or more of the following means:

    (a) transfer to a bank or building society account specified by the distribution recipient either in writing or as the directors may otherwise decide;

    (b) sending a cheque made payable to the distribution recipient by post to the distribution recipient at the distribution recipient's registered address (if the distribution recipient is a holder of the share), or (in any other case) to an address specified by the distribution recipient either in writing or as the directors may otherwise decide;

    (c) sending a cheque made payable to such person by post to such person at such address as the distribution recipient has specified either in writing or as the directors may otherwise decide; or

    (d) any other means of payment as the directors agree with the distribution recipient either in writing or by such other means as the directors decide.

  (2) In the articles, "the distribution recipient" means, in respect of a share in respect of which a dividend or other sum is payable:

    (a) the holder of the share; or

    (b) if the share has two or more joint holders, whichever of them is named first in the register of members; or

    (c) if the holder is no longer entitled to the share by reason of death or bankruptcy, or otherwise by operation of law, the transmittee.

## Deductions from distributions in respect of sums owed to the company

**73.** (1) If:

    (a) a share is subject to the company's lien, and

    (b) the directors are entitled to issue a lien enforcement notice in respect of it,

  they may, instead of issuing a lien enforcement notice, deduct from any dividend or other sum payable in respect of the share any sum of money which is payable to the company in respect of that share to the extent that they are entitled to require payment under a lien enforcement notice.

  (2) Money so deducted must be used to pay any of the sums payable in respect of that share.

  (3) The company must notify the distribution recipient in writing of:

    (a) the fact and amount of any such deduction;

    (b) any non-payment of a dividend or other sum payable in respect of a share resulting from any such deduction; and

    (c) how the money deducted has been applied.

## No interest on distributions

**74.** The company may not pay interest on any dividend or other sum payable in respect of a share unless otherwise provided by:

(a) the terms on which the share was issued, or

(b) the provisions of another agreement between the holder of that share and the company.

## Unclaimed distributions

**75.**     (1)     All dividends or other sums which are:

(a)     payable in respect of shares, and

(b)     unclaimed after having been declared or become payable,

may be invested or otherwise made use of by the directors for the benefit of the company until claimed.

(2)     The payment of any such dividend or other sum into a separate account does not make the company a trustee in respect of it.

(3)     If:

(a)     twelve years have passed from the date on which a dividend or other sum became due for payment; and

(b)     the distribution recipient has not claimed it,

the distribution recipient is no longer entitled to that dividend or other sum and it ceases to remain owing by the company.

## Non-cash distributions

**76.**     (1)     Subject to the terms of issue of the share in question, the company may, by ordinary resolution on the recommendation of the directors, decide to pay all or part of a dividend or other distribution payable in respect of a share by transferring non-cash assets of equivalent value (including, without limitation, shares or other securities in any company).

(2)     If the shares in respect of which such a non-cash distribution is paid are uncertificated, any shares in the company which are issued as a non-cash distribution in respect of them must be uncertificated.

(3)     For the purposes of paying a non-cash distribution, the directors may make whatever arrangements they think fit, including, where any difficulty arises regarding the distribution:

(a)     fixing the value of any assets;

(b)     paying cash to any distribution recipient on the basis of that value in order to adjust the rights of recipients; and

(c)     vesting any assets in trustees.

## Waiver of distributions

**77.**     Distribution recipients may waive their entitlement to a dividend or other distribution payable in respect of a share by giving the company notice in writing to that effect, but if:

(a)     the share has more than one holder, or

(b)     more than one person is entitled to the share, whether by reason of the death or bankruptcy of one or more joint holders, or otherwise,

the notice is not effective unless it is expressed to be given, and signed, by all the holders or persons otherwise entitled to the share.

CAPITALISATION OF PROFITS

**Authority to capitalise and appropriation of capitalised sums**

**78.** (1) Subject to the articles, the directors may, if they are so authorised by an ordinary resolution:

(a) decide to capitalise any profits of the company (whether or not they are available for distribution) which are not required for paying a preferential dividend, or any sum standing to the credit of the company's share premium account or capital redemption reserve; and

(b) appropriate any sum which they so decide to capitalise (a "capitalised sum") to the persons who would have been entitled to it if it were distributed by way of dividend (the "persons entitled") and in the same proportions.

(2) Capitalised sums must be applied:

(a) on behalf of the persons entitled, and

(b) in the same proportions as a dividend would have been distributed to them.

(3) Any capitalised sum may be applied in paying up new shares of a nominal amount equal to the capitalised sum which are then allotted credited as fully paid to the persons entitled or as they may direct.

(4) A capitalised sum which was appropriated from profits available for distribution may be applied:

(a) in or towards paying up any amounts unpaid on existing shares held by the persons entitled, or

(b) in paying up new debentures of the company which are then allotted credited as fully paid to the persons entitled or as they may direct.

(5) Subject to the articles the directors may:

(a) apply capitalised sums in accordance with paragraphs (3) and (4) partly in one way and partly in another;

(b) make such arrangements as they think fit to deal with shares or debentures becoming distributable in fractions under this article (including the issuing of fractional certificates or the making of cash payments); and

(c) authorise any person to enter into an agreement with the company on behalf of all the persons entitled which is binding on them in respect of the allotment of shares and debentures to them under this article.

# Part 5

# Miscellaneous Provisions

## COMMUNICATIONS

### Means of communication to be used

**79.** (1) Subject to the articles, anything sent or supplied by or to the company under the articles may be sent or supplied in any way in which the Companies Act 2006 provides for documents or information which are authorised or required by any provision of that Act to be sent or supplied by or to the company.

(2) Subject to the articles, any notice or document to be sent or supplied to a director in connection with the taking of decisions by directors may also be sent or supplied by the means by which that director has asked to be sent or supplied with such notices or documents for the time being.

(3) A director may agree with the company that notices or documents sent to that director in a particular way are to be deemed to have been received within a specified time of their being sent, and for the specified time to be less than 48 hours.

### Failure to notify contact details

**80.** (1) If:

   (a) the company sends two consecutive documents to a member over a period of at least 12 months, and

   (b) each of those documents is returned undelivered, or the company receives notification that it has not been delivered,

   that member ceases to be entitled to receive notices from the company.

(2) A member who has ceased to be entitled to receive notices from the company becomes entitled to receive such notices again by sending the company:

   (a) a new address to be recorded in the register of members, or

   (b) if the member has agreed that the company should use a means of communication other than sending things to such an address, the information that the company needs to use that means of communication effectively.

## ADMINISTRATIVE ARRANGEMENTS

### Company seals

**81.** (1) Any common seal may only be used by the authority of the directors.

(2) The directors may decide by what means and in what form any common seal or securities seal is to be used.

(3) Unless otherwise decided by the directors, if the company has a common seal and it is affixed to a document, the document must also be signed by at least one authorised person in the presence of a witness who attests the signature.

(4) For the purposes of this article, an authorised person is:

   (a) any director of the company;

   (b) the company secretary; or

   (c) any person authorised by the directors for the purpose of signing documents to which the common seal is applied.

(5) If the company has an official seal for use abroad, it may only be affixed to a document if its use on that document, or documents of a class to which it belongs, has been authorised by a decision of the directors.

(6) If the company has a securities seal, it may only be affixed to securities by the company secretary or a person authorised to apply it to securities by the company secretary.

(7) For the purposes of the articles, references to the securities seal being affixed to any document include the reproduction of the image of that seal on or in a document by any mechanical or electronic means which has been approved by the directors in relation to that document or documents of a class to which it belongs.

## Destruction of documents

**82.** (1) The company is entitled to destroy:

(a) all instruments of transfer of shares which have been registered, and all other documents on the basis of which any entries are made in the register of members, from six years after the date of registration;

(b) all dividend mandates, variations or cancellations of dividend mandates, and notifications of change of address, from two years after they have been recorded;

(c) all share certificates which have been cancelled from one year after the date of the cancellation;

(d) all paid dividend warrants and cheques from one year after the date of actual payment; and

(e) all proxy notices from one year after the end of the meeting to which the proxy notice relates.

(2) If the company destroys a document in good faith, in accordance with the articles, and without notice of any claim to which that document may be relevant, it is conclusively presumed in favour of the company that:

(a) entries in the register purporting to have been made on the basis of an instrument of transfer or other document so destroyed were duly and properly made;

(b) any instrument of transfer so destroyed was a valid and effective instrument duly and properly registered;

(c) any share certificate so destroyed was a valid and effective certificate duly and properly cancelled; and

(d) any other document so destroyed was a valid and effective document in accordance with its recorded particulars in the books or records of the company.

(3) This article does not impose on the company any liability which it would not otherwise have if it destroys any document before the time at which this article permits it to do so.

(4) In this article, references to the destruction of any document include a reference to its being disposed of in any manner.

## No right to inspect accounts and other records

**83.** Except as provided by law or authorised by the directors or an ordinary resolution of the company, no person is entitled to inspect any of the company's accounting or other records or documents merely by virtue of being a member.

## Provision for employees on cessation of business

**84.** The directors may decide to make provision for the benefit of persons employed or formerly employed by the company or any of its subsidiaries (other than a director or former director or shadow director) in connection with the cessation or transfer to any person of the whole or part of the undertaking of the company or that subsidiary.

## DIRECTORS' INDEMNITY AND INSURANCE

### Indemnity

**85.** (1) Subject to paragraph (2), a relevant director of the company or an associated company may be indemnified out of the company's assets against:

    (a) any liability incurred by that director in connection with any negligence, default, breach of duty or breach of trust in relation to the company or an associated company,

    (b) any liability incurred by that director in connection with the activities of the company or an associated company in its capacity as a trustee of an occupational pension scheme (as defined in section 235(6) of the Companies Act 2006),

    (c) any other liability incurred by that director as an officer of the company or an associated company.

(2) This article does not authorise any indemnity which would be prohibited or rendered void by any provision of the Companies Acts or by any other provision of law.

(3) In this article:

    (a) companies are associated if one is a subsidiary of the other or both are subsidiaries of the same body corporate, and

    (b) a "relevant director" means any director or former director of the company or an associated company.

### Insurance

**86.** (1) The directors may decide to purchase and maintain insurance, at the expense of the company, for the benefit of any relevant director in respect of any relevant loss.

(2) In this article:

    (a) a "relevant director" means any director or former director of the company or an associated company,

    (b) a "relevant loss" means any loss or liability which has been or may be incurred by a relevant director in connection with that director's duties or powers in relation to the company, any associated company or any pension fund or employees' share scheme of the company or associated company, and

    (c) companies are associated if one is a subsidiary of the other or both are subsidiaries of the same body corporate.

London
School of Business
& Finance

shaping success in business and finance

# F4

## Index

# Index

## A

## B

# C

# D

# E

# F

# G

# H

# I

# J

# L

# M

# N

# O

# P

# Q

# R

# S

# T

# U

# V

# W

London
School of Business
& Finance

shaping success in business and finance

# F4

## Feedback and Review Form

Please take the time to complete this feedback and review form about the study materials that you have used for your ACCA exams.  We really appreciate your comments.

## YOUR DETAILS

Name :

Address :

How did you use this material?

☐    Home study (only using books)

☐    Home study (books and InterActive videos)

☐    Classroom course

What made you buy this material?

☐    Saw information on LSBF website

☐    Saw information on InterActive website

☐    Saw advertisement

☐    Recommendation from friend/colleague

☐    Recommended by lecturer at college

☐    Used LSBF/InterActive materials before

☐    Other

## INTERACTIVE VIDEOS

Please make an assessment about the quality of the videos in the following areas:

|                                 | Very useful | Useful | Not useful |
| ------------------------------- | ----------- | ------ | ---------- |
| Clarity of tutor explanations   | ☐           | ☐      | ☐          |
| Engaging and interesting tutor  | ☐           | ☐      | ☐          |
| Exam focus, hints and tips      | ☐           | ☐      | ☐          |
| Examples and exercises          | ☐           | ☐      | ☐          |
| Overall opinion                 | ☐           | ☐      | ☐          |

## STUDY MANUALS

Please make an assessment about the quality of the manuals in the following areas:

|                                 | Very useful | Useful | Not useful |
| ------------------------------- | ----------- | ------ | ---------- |
| Clarity of tutor explanations   | ☐           | ☐      | ☐          |
| Engaging and interesting tutor  | ☐           | ☐      | ☐          |
| Exam focus, hints and tips      | ☐           | ☐      | ☐          |
| Examples and exercises          | ☐           | ☐      | ☐          |

Would you use our materials again?

☐    Yes          ☐    No

Please return this form to: Paul Merison, Publications Manager, London School of Business and Finance, 8-9 Holborn, London ECIN 2LL.

London
School of Business
& Finance

shaping success in business and finance

Please use this space to make any additional comments that you have about either the study videos, manuals or any other aspect of our service.

Thank you for taking your time to complete this form. Good luck in your forthcoming exams.

If you would like to make any other general comments about this manual, please forward them to **feedback@studyinteractive.org** or complete our electronic feedback on **www.lsbf.org.uk/pbfeedback**

London
School of Business
& Finance

shaping success in business and finance